D1452883

MAN OF FIRE

MAN
OF FIRE

FIRE

SELECTED WRITINGS

ERNESTO GALARZA

EDITED BY ARMANDO IBARRA
AND RODOLFO D. TORRES

UNIVERSITY OF ILLINOIS PRESS
Urbana, Chicago, and Springfield

Frontispiece: Ernesto Galarza, man of fire. Courtesy of the Seaver Center for Western History Research, Los Angeles County Museum of Natural History.

Introduction, commentary, and compilation © 2013
by the Board of Trustees of the University of Illinois
All rights reserved
Manufactured in the United States of America
C 5 4 3 2 1
♾ This book is printed on acid-free paper.

Library of Congress Control Number: 2013937514

Among the extraordinary persons who have made the farm workers' cause their own, one of the most exceptional is Ernesto Galarza, a wiry man with a shock of graying hair and penetrating eyes under full black eyebrows, a brilliant speaker and writer, a doctor of philosophy from Columbia University.

Galarza fought, at times simultaneously and almost single-handedly, the power of agribusiness, federal and state governments, and Big Labor. In the uneven contest, he may seem to have lost, as the world usually reckons winning and losing. But social movements have their own secret reckonings. Galarza kept alive the embers of the farm labor movement in California during a long night in which they came close to being extinguished altogether.

SO YE SHALL REAP, 1970
by Henry P. Anderson, activist scholar, public intellectual,
and lifelong friend and confidant of Ernesto Galarza

CONTENTS

ILLUSTRATIONS

ACKNOWLEDGMENTS

We have many people to thank, and we want to acknowledge them and hope that those we have overlooked will forgive us.

First and foremost, we would like to thank our families for all their sacrifices, inspiration, support, and wisdom that set the foundation for the accomplishment of this labor. *Muchísimas gracias.* Each of you has had a fundamental role in shaping our thoughts and scholarship.

Several of our colleagues deserve particular mention. We have learned much from our never-ending conversation on Mexican American labor and the work of Ernesto Galarza from Professor Gilbert G. González—thanks, Gil. From the beginning, Manuel Gómez believed in this project and provided financial support—a very special thank-you.

We owe special thanks to Victor Becerra, director of the Community Outreach Partnership Center at the University of California, Irvine; Richard A. Matthew, director of the Center for Unconventional Security; Frank Bean, director of the Center for Research on Immigration, Population and Public Policy; Caesar D. Sereseres, associate dean of undergraduate studies in the School of Social Sciences and Professor of Political Science at the University of California, Irvine; and the University of Wisconsin's School for Workers for making research and travel funds available. We owe a special debt to our students at UC Irvine, Alfredo Carlos, Luis Fonseca, and Carla Rodriguez Gonzalez, for their assistance and hard work.

A number of librarians and archivists have been very helpful. Special thanks to the library staff at the Department of Special Collections and University Archives at Stanford University, the Bancroft Library at the University of California Berkeley, and the Butler Library at Columbia University. A very special thank-you to Christina Woo at UCI's Langson Library. We also received enthusiastic support from the University of Wisconsin's School for Workers.

Our gratitude to Henry P. Anderson for providing selected letters for the volume and for sharing his memories of Ernesto Galarza. The title of our book comes from a chapter title that appears in Joan London and Henry Anderson's book *So Shall Ye Reap.* We are grateful to William Estrada for his assistance in acquiring photographs used in this volume.

We would like to thank the office staff of the Department of Planning, Policy, and Design (PPD) at UCI. In particular, many thanks to Kate Hartshorn for research support and to Mervyn Vaz, PPD department manager, for being so patient. *Mil gracias* to David L. Feldman, chair of the Department of Planning, Policy, and Design, for his support in this endeavor. We are very grateful to Laurie Matheson, senior acquisitions editor at UIP, for her patience and support.

We offer our deepest respect to all the people laboring in the orchards and fields of the United States. Your pride, sincerity, hard work, and perseverance in the face of adversity are exemplary and are an inspiration to all Americans.

We have made every effort to trace copyright holders and to obtain permission to print selected archival material. We apologize for any omissions and would be grateful to be notified of any corrections that should be made in future editions of this book.

This was a collaborative effort to get selected works of Ernesto Galarza to a wider audience and a new generation of scholars.

To my son, Jacob, for his warmth and honesty, and for my wife, Patricia, for her love and comradeship.

Rodolfo D. Torres

Finalmente, para mi querida esposa y compañera, Veronica D. Ibarra, y para mis padres, Maria de los Angeles y Jose Armando Ibarra Salazar, que con cariño y ejemplo me enseñaron las virtudes que forman mi persona: Trabajo, Amor, Dignidad, Respeto, Derecho, Vergüenza y Valor Civil.

Armando Ibarra Salazar

INTRODUCTION

Galarza is a man of courage, integrity, scholarship and compassion,
an idealist who remains quite unapologetic about his special brand
of social idealism, which today is all too rare.

—Carey McWilliams, 1970,
    from foreword to *Spiders in the House*
    and Workers in the Field, by Ernesto Galarza

Ernesto Galarza (1905–1984) was the most significant and prolific Mexican American social critic and public intellectual of the twentieth century. He eludes classification: his passion, integrity, dignity, and grit as a labor organizer, a researcher, an expert witness, an educator, and the voice of the farm worker labor movement earned him the well-suited name of "man of fire" by admirers as well as critics.

From his initial writings on the church in Mexico in 1928 to his later publications on Mexican labor in the United States, the Bracero Program, Mexican migration, urban politics, planning, and education, social and economic justice remained central to his endeavors. Dr. Galarza rigorously engaged in critical scholarship committed to social change. During his life, Galarza confronted and analyzed some of the most momentous socioeconomic transformations of the twentieth century. His conceptual clarity remains an essential guidepost for research and political activism in the twenty-first century.

This book in many ways offers the reader a counternarrative to past interrogations of Galarza's scholarship and to the failure to recognize and build on his critical insights about the dynamics of capitalism and the so-called Mexican problem. Galarza's anti-imperialist stance in his writings and his political activism on immigration politics, his intervention on behalf of farm workers, his engaged community organizing, and his democratic community development are evident in this volume. Galarza's observation that the logic of capitalist accumulation was the root cause of Mexican migration to the United States is especially insightful and relevant. It is a contribution of originality and analytical specificity. Moreover, seen against the current backdrop of intense sociopolitical and policy debates about Mexican migration and the changing nature of the Mexican American presence in the United States, Galarza's critique of American imperialism and corporate capitalism continues to resonate, as does his deep identification with those who suffer the most under the domination of global capital.

Although his works are clearly relevant to an understanding of contemporary immigration, organized labor, education, and policy and how these topics relate to the position of Mexicans and Mexican Americans within the United States, they continue to largely be unread. His titles are conspicuously absent in today's syllabi at colleges and universities in the United States, even though during the height of the Chicano movement his work was regularly assigned in Chicano Studies classes, in the social sciences curriculum, and in some courses in literature and education because of his very popular autobiography, *Barrio Boy*, published by the University of Notre Dame Press in 1971. Galarza achieved critical acclaim and international prominence as a writer in the 1970s and 1980s.

But what has not received attention has been his more critical scholarship on political economy, especially his scholarly and political assault on the Bracero Program (1942–1964), which authorized the recruitment of millions of Mexican male nationals for temporary agricultural work in the United States. Galarza understood that the only way farm workers could successfully organize and form unions that could bargain collectively with growers was to defeat this program. At its peak, the Bracero Program supplied over 500,000 braceros per year to the agricultural industry; this effectively crippled the farm worker labor movement. Braceros were explicitly barred from having any labor rights and were often used as strikebreakers by growers. Consequently, there was no successful farm worker organizing effort during the life of the program. In no other instance during the twentieth century was a group of people permanently excluded from the political, social, and civic realms of American life even though this group was integral to its economic mainstream. The defeat of this program is one of the most uncelebrated labor victories of the twentieth century.

In light of the current period of growing anti-immigrant sentiment and discussions of a renewed guest worker program in the second decade of the twenty-first century, Galarza's critique of capital and labor and the questions he raised about democratic alternatives make this book a timely intervention.

The readings in the volume reveal that Galarza believed that one cannot separate one's scholarship from political activism. Ernesto Galarza was a quintessential American intellectual of his generation: informed by radical pragmatism, eclectic in his disciplinary approaches to social and economic problems, and driven by sociological imagination and social justice. Thus, a major strand in this collection looks at Galarza's use of action research coupled with economic organization as a method for achieving sustainable and equitable social and political change.

Dr. Galarza was doing action-oriented social science research long before it became widespread in academia. His specialized and robust approach sought to link academia and working communities for the purpose of causing policy change and ultimately social change. He often drew from sources commonly used by most scholars, including government reports, U.S. census data, newspaper articles, scholarly journals, and books. In other cases, he was a participant observer and an insider in the communities he studied. Almost all of his path-breaking research that linked immigration, community development, and labor and management relations was informed by his early life experiences and his work as an official, researcher, and organizer in the labor movement.

Galarza's writings can be interpreted in many ways. His engaged scholarship is an affirmation of a critique of political economy and the analytical utility of that critique. He believed it was wrong to treat people who performed similar work tasks differently because of their gender, race, ethnicity, or immigrant status. In his view, a worker was a worker regardless of identity markers and all workers should be treated with dignity, respect, and equality.

This book should not be seen as an alternative to a systematic study of Galarza's writings of nearly five decades. It is a modest attempt to anthologize selected materials. It is our hope that the selections we have made will resonate with new readers and open new opportunities for young scholars to engage with this important writer and public intellectual. Even though Galarza was a prolific writer and the most important Mexican American scholar of his generation, we have no biography of him and his work has not been collected. This book attempts to correct this situation by offering readers an introduction to selected published and unpublished articles, popular essays, speeches, interviews, letters, and book excerpts. The entries document his personal trajectory and some of the most important issues he faced as a public intellectual. These selections also reflect Galarza's respect for ideas; in his writings, he combined intellectual rigor with concern for the laboring classes.

Ernesto Galarza's aptitude is exemplified through his educational journey, which began when he was an orphaned farm worker in California's Central Valley and culminated in his status as one the first Mexican immigrants to receive a Ph.D. in U.S. history. After high school, he attended Occidental College in Los Angeles, then he earned a master's degree in Latin American Studies at Stanford University and a Ph.D. at Columbia University.[1]

Galarza was a passionate public intellectual. His work is not the work of an academic writing for a narrow readership; it is not meant to be quickly shelved in an academic library. He wrote to be read by a wider audience and to advance social justice beyond the academy. More importantly, we hope that readers will see how his work was a political intervention during an era when power was concentrated on the side of global capital. The selections in this book will help readers understand how and why that was the case.

Some readers may be disappointed to find that their favorite Galarza essay or book chapter is not included. We have selected entries for this book, including the material in the appendix, based on several interconnected themes that emerged in Galarza's published and unpublished works. (We chose to present the unpublished essays, speeches, and letters in full in order to preserve their authenticity and Galarza's voice.)² The material we chose highlights much of his analysis of the power relations in politics, in class hierarchies, and between labor and management and the impacts these relations had on organizing in the fields and in Mexican American urban and rural neighborhoods. The material collected here reveals a writer who produced intensely personal accounts informed by first-rate research. Of course, including material over such a span of years will unavoidably lead to some redundancy in the volume. Those whose appetites are whetted by reading this volume are urged to go to the original texts; a bibliography of Galarza's published work is provided in the appendix.

An example of one of the editorial decisions is our selection of an excerpt from *Barrio Boy*, Galarza's most celebrated and circulated book. We frame the two entries from this memoir as an insightful account of the development of Galarza's class consciousness, unlike past treatments by most writers, who have simply read it as a coming-of-age story. (This is regrettably the case with the new introduction to *Barrio Boy* for the fortieth anniversary edition that was published in 2011.)

In addition, Galarza's scholarship and activism in urban studies and democratic community development must not be overlooked, especially his role as an activist human geographer and planner in the Mexican community of Alviso (located at the southern part of the Bay Area in San Francisco), where Galarza, as a member of the Alviso Study Team, devoted considerable time to addressing the critical problems of community redevelopment and urban inequality. This volume includes several entries on this important part of Galarza's critical scholarship as a planner and spatial theorist.

The changing political context of Galarza's life should be understood when considering the evolution of his scholarship and political activism. We can enrich our understanding of Galarza and the wider radical currents of the period by examining his work alongside the work of intellectuals and union activists H. L. Mitchell and A. Philip Randolph. In the 1930s, H. L. Mitchell was a campaigner for the Socialist Party and a labor organizer for the Southern Tenant Farmers' Union. In the 1950s, he helped organize the National Agriculture Workers' Union. Mitchell recruited Galarza to help reach out to and continue to build the farm labor movement in California. Many do not know that Galarza was a labor organizer for the Amalgamated Meat Cutters Union in 1960 and worked with A. Philip Randolph, the founder of the Brotherhood of Sleeping Car Porters and the organizer of the first March on Washington in the summer of 1941 to demand the desegregation of war industries. These labor and civil rights actions became part of broader pattern of collective actions against the state being undertaken by multiple communities that cumulatively became the foundations for the civil rights movement of the 1950s and 1960s.

Galarza embraced the trade union labor movement for the greater part of his adult life. In 1947, he resigned as head of the Division of Labor and Social Information of the Pan-American Union, where he had been working since 1940, and became the director of research and education in California for the Southern Tenant Farmers Union (STFU).[3] This professional move placed him at the center of the battle to organize farm workers. Immediately, he joined the organizing campaign that targeted the DiGiorgio Fruit Corporation. This agribusiness giant owned much of the farmland in California's Central Valley and had the largest fruit-packing plant in the nation. The organized workers sustained a thirty-month strike and boycott in an attempt to pressure the company to recognize their labor union. This transition from public servant to labor organizer is indicative of Galarza's character. He was a relentless and vigorous worker who was unafraid to fight for a just cause.

In 1959, AFL-CIO president George Meany and other national labor leaders decided the fate of the National Agricultural Workers Union (NAWU) by defunding and ultimately pulling its charter. Through a series of jurisdictional battles and a forced merger with the United Packinghouse Workers of America (later absorbed by Amalgamated Meat Cutters and Butcher Workmen of North America union [AMCBW]) and the creation of the Agricultural Workers Organizing Committee (AWOC), the AFL-CIO effectively dissolved the NAWU. When the leaders of "big labor" decided who would lead AWOC, the new farm worker union, they passed up Galarza and instead chose Norman Smith, a former organizer of auto workers. Galarza was appointed as the assistant director of AWOC. By that point, many labor leaders felt that Galarza was too divisive a figure. His public fights with the agribusiness owners and public officials who had suppressed the farm worker movement by supporting the Bracero Program and his solidarity with the NAWU and H. L Mitchell eventually led to his decision to resign from organized labor.

But his work with organized labor was not insignificant. With patient work over several decades, Galarza had built a union and a national network that connected labor and scholar activists with farm workers and other allies. If not for these organizing efforts, the United Farm Workers of America and its leader, Cesar E. Chavez, would have encountered an even more difficult organizing environment in the 1960s and 1970s.[4]

Galarza's departure from organized labor allowed him to enter a new phase of activism and research. He began to engage with larger conceptual and substantive issues, such as community development and educational reform.[5] He also began teaching elementary school in San Jose, California, and accepted short-term visiting appointments at colleges. In addition, he lectured at campuses across the United States and Latin America. Throughout this phase, he rejected the comforts of a full-time academic position so he could do the much harder work of community organizing and engaging in political scholarship. This volume includes several essays that touch on how Galarza worked outside the mainstream throughout his career so that he could continue to speak truth to power and to the working class.

Much of his work and political action critiqued the political economy of Mexican migration and the established political and economic order. The reader will find in his writings a bold critique of imperialism, especially his work on Mexican migration, agribusiness, geospatial studies of the Mexican American community, and the Bracero Program.

Galarza comprehended early in his career that labor migration from Mexico could not be understood without first understanding the principle role U.S. capital played. He asserted that Mexican citizens were displaced and then integrated into U.S. systems of production through the calculated efforts of U.S. industrial leaders that were supported by the state. This is the kind of domination Gilbert G. Gonzalez, a noted labor historian, refers to as a "peaceful conquest."[6] Galarza publicly criticized U.S. foreign policy and posited that from the start of the nineteenth century, the American empire actively worked to secure its dominance over the Western Hemisphere. He explicitly blamed the economic machine of the United States for the socioeconomic position of workers in both the United States and Mexico. This insight and research are Galarza's most important contributions to a growing literature on the political economy of international labor migration.

Galarza firmly believed that the negative position of the Mexican American within the United States was caused by the erosion of labor rights and the increased criminalization of Mexican immigrants. He argued that capital had thoroughly corrupted the institutions that were created to protect working people. Galarza's solution was to conduct research with a clear purpose, organize labor and communities, and mobilize these groups when a collective pushback was needed. Galarza's personal manifesto was that action research could be used as an agent for change.

The anti-immigrant and labor context Galarza experienced are not so different from what immigrants and working communities face today. Individual states have begun to recreate the unreceptive environments Galarza observed, but now the contexts of reception are not merely semi-inclusive, as they were in Galarza's day. Today they are openly hostile. Right-to-work and anti-immigrant laws have been created specifically to target immigrants from Latin America in the states of Arizona, Alabama, Indiana, Georgia, and Mississippi.[7]

Current intellectual fashions in Chicano studies (and among the academic left in general) that emphasize identity politics and "postmodern" fragmentation can barely accommodate the ideas that underpinned many of Galarza's implicit and at times more explicit critiques of American imperialism and how it influences Mexican migration, exploitation, and inequality. Galarza was once asked if he considered himself a "Chicano." He replied that ethnic labels were analytically insufficient to describe his position as a member of society. He believed that social class was a much more useful way to assess a person's position in the wider political economy.

> I don't think [ethnic labels] lead very far, because if you look at these terms— currently, what do they mean—you'll find people who are called Chicanos in San Jose; they're called Chicanos in Imperial Valley; they're called Chicanos in San Francisco. But if you know those people, the occupational differences are more important. To me, anyway. It may be because I have a certain bias against ethnic identity. I don't think people should be handled that way, or should be identified, or should be catalogued, or described—because it's not a permanent characteristic other than to those who believe in very strong racial, ethnic characteristics—and I don't.[8]

Galarza's stance that U.S. corporate interests were the driving forces that led to mass labor migration from Mexico is well documented. Nonetheless, his critical publications are rarely acknowledged, much less critically interrogated today by immigration scholars (Mexican and non-Mexican) as relevant in framing current scholarly and policy debates on Mexican migration to the United States and the state of Mexican Americans in the United States. The discourse of the American dream, incorporation, assimilation, social capital, and social networks are the new orthodoxies in immigration research.

Galarza was also involved in the civil rights movement and focused much of his research and activism on exposing the structural barriers workers faced to their participation in formal politics. His skepticism about traditional party politics stemmed from his experiences as an immigrant and worker. Galarza had come to the conclusion that neither the Democratic nor the Republican Party adequately represented Mexican and Mexican American interests. This is why he boycotted President Johnson's Inter-Agency Committee on Mexican American Affairs conference in San Antonio, Texas, in 1967. Instead, Galarza joined other activist scholars, students, and community members at the inaugural meeting of La Raza Unida, where he was elected chair of the organization. La Raza Unida believed that only a party that understood the unique history of Mexican and Mexican Americans and had made their concerns part of its platform could represent the interests of this working community.

If Galarza were alive today, he would be asking probing questions about the market-driven North American Free Trade Agreement (NAFTA) of 1994 and doing research about the massive disruptions of rural economies in Mexico that have led to the increasing rate of migration to the United States. One of the goals of this volume is to show how relevant Dr. Galarza's work is to critiques of today's political economy. His insights are relevant to the current social order and its growing class inequalities.

It is our contention that Galarza would not have been caught off guard, as so many contemporary immigration scholars and pundits were, by the momentous social actions for worker and immigrant justice that culminated in the largest protests in U.S. history. The collective pushback in 2006 by millions of immigrants, workers, and labor and community activists and their supporters around the United States against H.R. 4437, also known as the Border Protection, Anti-Terrorism, and Illegal Immigration Control Act, was not a spontaneous or an isolated incident. This pro-immigrant-rights movement had been escalating, fueled by anti-immigration policies based on the militarization of the border, surveillance of workplaces and homes, and further criminalization of the labor migrant. It was further intensified by international trade agreements that, in Mexico, continued to displace an estimated 600 people a day who would have otherwise not migrated and by a booming U.S. economy that thrived on what seemed to be an endless supply of foreign workers. This combination of factors is similar to those that international migrant laborers encountered during Galarza's lifetime; he would have identified them in their early onset and actively organized and published research to combat them as he did with his book *Merchants of Labor* (1964), which helped document the abuses of the bracero guest worker program and led to the rescinding of Public Law 78 and the end of the Bracero Program.

The contemporary movement based on mass protests politicized millions of immigrants and citizens, and within this contingency of newly active Americans were thousands of farm workers from food-producing areas in the Southwest. History has shown that when the Latino community perceives that it is being attacked, naturalization rates increase, as do the levels of participation of its members in protests and formal electoral politics. Although H.R. 4437 passed the House of Representatives, it failed in the Senate. Many immigrant rights leaders, activists, and leftists framed the defeat of this legislation as a victory. However, the immigrant community was left waiting for comprehensive immigration reform that did not come.

Not much has changed for the community Galarza organized and advocated for during his lifetime. For example, the agriculture industry continues to thrive on pooled labor and employs hundreds of thousands of migrant and seasonal farm workers each year. In California, it is estimated that there are currently more than 730,000 migrant and seasonal farm workers (predominantly Mexican foreign-born), which makes it the largest industry of employment in the Central Valley. The agriculture industry's economic position, both locally and in the state of California; the number of workers it employs; and its power in local, state, and national politics continue to be just as strong as they were during Galarza's days as a labor organizer, a researcher, and a community organizer. These are the reasons why the organizing of agriculture workers has been an area of interest for the labor movement for at least seventy years.

No other agricultural region in the United States compares to the Central Valley in terms of scope and production. It stretches from Kern County to the Oregon border and is connected by a series of interstate highways that run side by side, splitting the valley into multiple growing regions. A number of rivers and state-funded, manmade lakes and aqueducts supply water to the region, making the valley the most fertile and productive area in the world. More than 250 agricultural crops are grown and harvested in the Central Valley for export, and the region supplies more than 25 percent of all the food consumed in the United States. This production requires vast amounts of physical labor that is exploitable and replaceable. This is the primary reason why the political economy of international labor migration has not changed much since Galarza attempted to organize agricultural workers in the 1940s and 50s.

This anthology looks at three distinct but interrelated epochs in Galarza's career as a scholar-activist. During the first stage, Galarza worked to organize agricultural laborers. In the 1940s and 50s, Galarza believed that America could be radically transformed into a more just society if workers organized and demanded such justice from employers and the state. Galarza's experiences during these decades help us understand why he chose to conduct action research, publish in progressive left and pro-labor journals and media outlets, and partake in direct labor actions against certain employers. To this day, the strike he led against the DiGiorgio Corporation, which lasted for thirty months (1947–1950), and his book *Strangers in Our Fields* continue to be hallmarks of the farm worker labor movement.

The second epoch of his career was devoted to the Mexican American civil rights movement. Galarza was in his mid-fifties when he decided to use his research and organizing skills to help reform the political structures that affected Mexican Americans in the Southwest. During this period Galarza was instrumental in helping establish two institutions that continue to be at the forefront of Latino civil and political rights: the Mexican American Legal Defense Fund and the Southwest Council of La Raza (later the National Council of La Raza).

Galarza devoted his final years as a scholar-activist to community organizing and advocating for bilingual education curricula in public school systems. During this era he wrote *Barrio Boy* and was a celebrated figure among certain elements in academia and progressive organizations. This respect and admiration led to his formal nomination for the Nobel Prize in Literature; he was the first Mexican American in history to receive this honor. This book focuses primarily on Galarza's work and scholarship during his days in the labor movement and as a political and community activist.

Ernesto Galarza exposed a paradox that continues to this day for most Mexican and Mexican American members of working communities in the United States. No matter how hard they work, most will never achieve the American dream because they are bound to a system of capitalist production that thrives on exploitation. They will continue to work in some of the most difficult industries until their bodies no longer allow them to do so. Workers know this. Bosses, politicians, pundits, academics, and many progressive thinkers know it too. But few are willing to engage in the kind of sustained action Galarza modeled for us to change these political and economic dynamics.

NOTES

1. Previously published biographical information has been inconsistent about which discipline Galarza earned his doctoral degree in and what year it was granted. A recent example of this inconsistency includes Ilan Stavans's introduction in the 40th anniversary edition of *Barrio Boy*. Stavans states that Galarza earned his degree in economics, while the back cover of the book says that Galarza earned his degree in history. According to biographical documents held in the Department of Special Collections at Stanford University, the repository of the Ernesto Galarza Papers, 1936–1984, Galarza obtained his Ph.D. in history and public law from Columbia University in 1946. The ProQuest Digital

Dissertations database records a degree in economics granted in 1947. In January 2010, with the assistance of the public services archivist at Columbia University, we confirmed that Dr. Galarza earned his Ph.D. in history and public law in 1946. To add to the confusion, El Fondo Cultural de Mexico published a version of his "dissertation" in book form in 1941, five years before the degree was conferred.

2. Selections based on archival research in San Jose, California; the University of California, Berkeley; Stanford University; and The National Steinbeck Center in Salinas, California; interviews with migrant farm workers throughout California's Central Valley; consultations with Columbia University librarians; interviews with Galarza's personal friend, confidant, and comrade Henry Anderson; and very useful and informed suggestions from external reviewers.

3. The Southern Tenant Farmers' Union, the National Farm Labor Union, and the National Agricultural Workers Union represent an evolution of the same labor union.

4. This assessment is based on a series of interviews conducted with historian Henry Pope Anderson, author of *The Bracero Program in California* and Galarza's longtime friend.

5. However, in his later years, he devoted considerable attention to Mexican American education and multiculturalism. His works on education offered a less strident critique of socioeconomic and class relations; the paradigm of the anti-corporate critique of capitalism and imperialism that Galarza had spent so much time advancing earlier had been hollowed out to the point that his writings on education offered little more than a liberal critique of Mexican American schooling in the United States that emphasized best teaching and classroom practices.

6. Gilbert G. Gonzalez, "The Ideology and Practice of Empire: The U.S., Mexico, and the Education of Mexican Immigrants," *Cultural Logic* 4, no. 1 (2000).

7. Right-to-work laws weaken the influence of labor unions by allowing individuals to opt out of paying union membership dues. These workers, also known as "free-riders," still receive all the benefits of union representation even though they do not contribute financially to the union.

8. Ernesto Galarza, *The Burning Light: Action and Organizing in the Mexican Community in California*, interviews conducted by Gabrielle Morris and Timothy Beard in 1977, 1978, and 1981 (Regional Oral History Office, The Bancroft Libraries, University of California, 1982), 50.

ORGANIZATION OF THE BOOK

We have included excerpts from significant publications as well as un-published work, interviews, speeches, and letters. The selected entries acquaint the reader with the breadth of Dr. Galarza's work in political economy, labor studies, Mexican labor migration, organizing, and education reform. They point to the urgent need to develop new ways of excavating Galarza's work and new ways of critique and political action. Each entry is preceded by a headnote that provides an introduction to and brief summary of the selected entry. Also, following most headnotes are selected notable life events that correspond to the time the entry was written. These and life events appear in the Selected Chronology located in the appendix. We purposely chose to place the entries in thematic sections and not in a strict chronological order based on our understanding of Galarza's stance about the impacts that the political economy of production had on the social, political, and economic position of working communities. Galarza wrote about the challenges working communities endured across generations that were context specific and not necessarily bound by time.

Part 1, "Coming of Age in a Class Society," is composed of excerpts from the 40th anniversary edition of *Barrio Boy* (University of Notre Dame Press, 2011). We selected two entries that demonstrate Galarza's keen awareness of the social, economic, and political position of Mexican and Mexican Americans in larger historical transnational contexts. We would like to briefly point to three themes that we feel became central in Galarza's development of class consciousness. The first is learning to stand up for what is just. Galarza writes about one of his earliest childhood memories and its impact on him. As an adolescent he saw his family's rooster, Coronel, fight off the *zopilote* that was threating the flock. Coronel proved to everyone that he was *muy gallo* and was not afraid. The second is the search for work. Work and looking for the next better *chanza* dictated the majority of the family's decisions. The search for work was one of the main reasons the family migrated north and was central to their lives in Sacramento and the Central Valley. The final theme is one of organizing. A life lesson came when he was chosen as the advocate for a group of farm workers who lived at a grower's seasonal labor camp simply because he knew a few words of English. This experience is the first time he learned of the "organizing model" and its utility for resolving issues through collective and deliberate worker actions, a skill he would master in later life.

Part 2, "Mexican Labor, Migration, and the American Empire," highlights three works that lay out the historical foundations that, Galarza argued, led to the structural inequalities that Mexican and Mexican American communities faced in the United States. In his estimation, the unequal treatment of these communities and their placement in the lower ranks of society were direct consequences of the coordinated efforts of industries and the state to ensure a continual source of cheap, exploitable, and expendable labor. We also include a document in which Galarza offers a plan of action for the Mexican community rooted in organizing and democratic action.

Part 3, "Action Research in Defense of the Barrio," offers some of Galarza's most mature work. By his mid-fifties, he had moved away from the traditional trade unionist model of organizing and had begun to push for social and economic justice with the use of action research—research with a purpose. We include two case studies that Galarza actively participated in and documented, in Alviso and Oakland, California. By no means are these two studies the only ones that demonstrate Galarza's impact on society, but they are well-articulated examples of Galarza's action research. These entries also demonstrate his ability to incorporate the analytical tools of human geography with rigor and clarity in order to advance a critical informed spatial justice.

Part 4, "Power, Culture, and History," offers Galarza's writings on the political and economic processes, including power and class relations, that led to the development of a Mexican culture in the Southwest. This section also provides excerpts of testimony he gave before the Subcommittee on Migratory Labor of the Senate Committee on Labor and Public Welfare in July 1969. Central to the "culture" question is the fact that it was necessary for the state to treat Mexicans unequally in order to incorporate their labor in a position in the capitalist system that suited growers.

Part 5, "Organizing against Capital," is an assortment of writings that deal with the history, strategies, and challenges of organizing farm workers. Galarza provides a level of detail and insight into labor and social movements that rarely reached progressives and activists outside inner circles, let alone the general public. Galarza purposely pursued this strategy because he believed that words could be used to expose exploitation and could ultimately be part of a coordinated effort to liberate workers. Scholars and activists alike agree that one of his greatest contributions to the labor movement was his advancement of an action-oriented research agenda that brought down the Bracero Program.

Part 6, "Letters from an Activist," includes nine letters Galarza wrote that offer insights into Galarza's struggles with elected officials, bureaucrats, organized labor, Eastern liberals, and, the agro-industrial complex. Each letter is contextualized with personal reflections gathered from one of Galarza's closest friends, activist and self-proclaimed radical social democrat Henry Pope Anderson.

We organized the entries in this section in chronological order to highlight a major transition in Galarza's personal, professional, and political life. This correspondence took place during 1957 to 1959, toward the end of Galarza's eleven-year career as a trade unionist. The American Federation of Labor and Congress of Industrial Organizations (AFL-CIO) decided to take a different approach to organizing agriculture workers in California, and throughout 1959 their activities undermined the efforts and gains of the National Agricultural Workers' Union. This compelled Galarza to resign from organized labor and participate in economic justice and other social movements.

Part 7 is an appendix that consists of a speech given at Stanford University by his widow, Mae Galarza, his lifetime partner in activism. A select bibliography and an abridged chronology of Galarza's life follow.

PART 1

COMING OF AGE
IN A CLASS SOCIETY

IN A MOUNTAIN VILLAGE

Excerpt from Ernesto Galarza, *Barrio Boy* (1971; repr., Notre Dame, Ind.: University of Notre Dame Press, 1977), 17–51.

This is the introductory chapter to *Barrio Boy* and offers Galarza's early childhood memories of growing up in a Mexican mountain village. The lessons he learned in Jalcocotán, Nayarit, about family and community, culture, nature, and standing up for oneself are not so different than those he practiced and taught later in life. Note that the starting point to his story is at the onset of the Mexican Revolution (1910–1921).

Later publications and interviews reveal that Galarza did not solely blame the revolution for his family's forced migration from Mexico. Rather, he pointed to a more complex set of factors that highlighted how foreign capital controlled Mexico's democratic and economic structures.

Notable life events during this era:

- 1971: Honorary Doctorate of Humane Letters is conferred on Galarza by Occidental College.
- 1971: Establishes the Studio Laboratory for Bilingual Education, a resource center used by San Jose Unified School District teachers, staff, students, and families. The Studio Laboratory emphasized immersion in one's first language and the teaching of cultural values as vehicles for acquisition of and fluency in English.

Aunt Esther had married Don Catarino López, one of a numerous family of Jalco. Don Catarino, his father, and brothers worked the corn patches and the *milpas* on the mountain, tilled and harvested bananas deep in the forest and earned a living in other ways from the countryside. Don Catarino had brought his bride, Esther, to the pueblo where they were living with their two boys—Jesús, a year older than myself, and Catarino junior, a year younger. The four of them hardly filled the one big room of the cottage. The extra beds behind the curtain and the *tapanco* [sleeping loft] could accommodate us all, cramped or cozy, depending on how you looked at it. . . .

Breakfast was before daybreak and regularly announced by our rooster, Coronel. He was always a half hour ahead of the dawn, crowing lustily in our back yard. It was the signal to get up. Up in the *tapanco* we stirred on our mattress of cornhusks and mats, sitting up hunched in our *sarapes*, listening. In the *corrals* of the village the other roosters picked up the reveille, trumpeting as if this was the first dawn of time and a marvelous sight to see. Up and down the mountain the cocks of the *ranchos* and the other *pueblos* took up the fanfare, their calls fading with distance.

One by one we came down the notched pole, still snug in our *sarapes*.

"*Buenos días, muchachos.*"

"*Buenos días, Don Catarino.*"

"*Buenos días, Tía.*"

"*Buenos días, Tío.*"

"*Buenos días, mamá.*"

We huddled around the fire in the *pretil* [fire pit] as close as we could without getting in the way of the business of preparing breakfast. Over our heads the oil lamp sputtered, giving off more smoke than light. My mother stirred the coals she had bedded down the night before under a thick bank of ashes. On top of them she dropped small splinters of pine heavy with resin, the pungent *ocote* [pine wood]. With a small mat she fanned the splinters into a flame, feeding it with larger pieces of *ocote* to set the fresh charcoal on fire. From the center pit coals were scooped and transferred to the side burners. On the three fires now going the pots were arranged, their black bottoms sitting on the ruby coals. The *tortillas* were already warming on the *comal* [flat griddle], the beans coming to a boil in one pot, the coffee in another. . . .

We ate breakfast in silence. The men, sitting on the edge of the beds, were served first—a plate with beans and red pepper rolled in *tortillas*, a large bowl of coffee, still boiling, to warm their hands and burn their stomachs on account of the early morning chill. The *tacos* for their lunch were already rolled in cornhusks and a napkin, tucked into the haversacks of woven hemp. My aunt took down the crossbar from the front door and the men stepped out into the dark, wrapped in *sarapes*. Their *huaraches* sandpapered the hard surface of the street, the white stuff of their clothes disappearing like dim blobs into the night. They would be in the fields by daybreak.

My aunt closed the door and served breakfast to the three boys, huddled around the *pretil*. It was a bowl of coffee, a *tortilla* with beans and pepper, and a few sucks on a chunk of brown sugar, the *panocha* [brown sugar] that was kept in a clay pot on a shelf out of our reach. The women always ate last.

"Now, up the *tapanco* and raise your bed." I could never understand why Aunt Esther always said "raise your bed." *Al tapanco y alzar la cama* was what she called this part of the morning routine. We climbed up the notched pole again, to spread the cornhusks evenly, lining up the woven mats on top, like a bed cover. We did this crawling on all fours, butting one another like goats. By the time we came down it was time to round up Coronel and his hens in the corral for their daily ration of maize. When the chickens were fed we called Nerón, our dog, to the kitchen door for a *tortilla* dipped in bean juice. In one swallow Nerón finished his breakfast and he chased us to the edge of the woods back of the *corral*. While Nerón stood by, as if he understood what was going on, we lined up along the wall for a minute or two. Whoever won the race back to the kitchen when my mother called would get the first licks on the *panocha*.

Doing chores and chasing one another we warmed ourselves during the morning chill, playing as much as possible between the routine jobs we were assigned. Most of these jobs were as agreeable as the games we made up. When it was full daylight, both doors of the cottage were opened. Jesús and I walked Nerón up and down the street so he could explore the fresh garbage in the gutter. He was then left on his own, except when he got into a fight and barked for help. Coronel and his hens were ushered through the kitchen into the street to scratch in the litter. . . .

The protection of Coronel and his hens and the supervision of Nerón were two of the important tasks assigned to us. There was one other—to look after Relámpago, the *burro* that didn't belong to anyone in particular. . . .

He was a small, brownish-grey donkey. His left ear always drooped and he didn't swish his tail like other *burros*. Nothing in Jalco moved as slowly and deliberately as Relámpago, for which reason he was called "Lightning." He didn't belong to anyone and no one knew where he had come from. But his way of gazing at people, of stopping in front of doors to stare, and his willingness to give the children rides, made him at least a cousin to every family in the village. José hoisted me on Relámpago's back now and then, walking us from one end of the street to the other. No reins, no saddle, no stirrups, almost no hands, except that José would be alongside to steady me on top of the *burro*. Whenever Relámpago cared to do so, he was welcome to walk through our cottage and into the *corral* to spend the night. . . .

Whether we were playing in a neighbor's *corral*, or on the street, or down by the pond, we knew the afternoon was about over by the voices. "Juan." "Neto." "Chuy." "Melesio." They were calling our names, the voices of mothers and aunts poking their heads out of doorways or over the walls of the *corrals*. The voices were not shouts. They were tunes. And we knew when we heard them—being only five or six years old—that we had to dance to them, at once. "*Si, señora.*" "*Ya vengo*" [on my way]. "*Voy*" [coming]. When we answered we were already on the trot. We obeyed by trotting. We showed respect by answering. Failure to do either could mean that you would have your ear pinched at the doorway or

Young Ernesto Galarza. Courtesy of the Seaver Center
for Western History Research, Los Angeles County
Museum of Natural History.

be asked that ominous question that nobody knew how to answer and had better
not try to: "*¿Qué pasó?*"—how come?

The voices always called about the time the shadows began stretching from
the forest side of the pueblo over the cottages. After reporting in, Jesús and Catarino and I looked after Coronel and the hens. Usually they were on their way
home, dawdling as they scratched. If Nerón wasn't around he had to be caught
and turned home by the scruff of his furry neck. We herded all of them—usually Nerón first, the hens next and Coronel last—through the doors and into the
corral. From then until supper we hopped to chores and errands—some charcoal
for the *pretil,* bringing in the straw *petates* [mats] that had hung freshening in the

sun on the walls of the *corral*, stopping a ruckus between Nerón and Coronel, or propping the rickety ladder the hens climbed to roost in the willow tree.

While supper was being prepared, a quietness settled on the family waiting for the men to return from work. On one corner of the *pretil* there were the freshly baked tortillas, wrapped in a double jacket of napkins and stacked in the cream-colored basket with the musical name, the *chiquihuite*.

Don Catarino was always the first to walk in out of the dusk, if he and Gustavo and José had been working the same field. Gustavo was second and José last. They unfastened the *machetes* and hung them in their sheaths on pegs by the back door. They dropped the *sarapes*, folded, on the beds. Without a word they stepped into the darkening corral to wash from clay bowls. We stood by, a boy to each man, holding the chips of soap and the mended towels.

In the same order as at breakfast, the men were served first. The food was laid out on a side table not much wider than a shelf. As the men ate they tore the fresh, warm corncakes into halves and quarters and eighths, making tiny spoons with which they scooped the food, eating the spoon along with it.

When they finished, the men rose from the table. Don Catarino rumbled "*Buen provecho*" [bon appetite], which was a Jalcocotán way of wishing the diners a comfortable digestion of the meal.

Jesús, Catarino, and I took the places of the men. The beans came steaming out of the tall pot, red-brown, frijoles de la olla, sprinkled with browned rice and washed down with coffee, but no pepper. With the last tortilla spoon we sopped up the bean juice and nitpicked the last grain of rice on our plates. When my aunt Esther said "*Buen provecho,*" the meal was over. While the women ate, we loitered, any place where the men were not.

In the corral, by the bright orange light of a long stick of flaming *ocote*, they sharpened the *machetes*, or secured a hoe handle that had come loose. We could watch, careful not to get under foot, for we knew the men were irritable at the end of a bone-tiring day in the *milpa* [corn field]. Don Catarino looked menacing with the shadows the dancing *ocote* flame made on his dark face. Gustavo hummed as he whetted his *machete*. José tested the edge of his blade, feeling it gently with his thumb crosswise, licking it before testing—one of the tricks of a good *machetero*. . . .

At a signal from Doña Esther we turned in, climbing the notched pole to the *tapanco*. Wrapped in our *sarapes* we settled quickly into the cornhusk mattress and the mats and stopped squirming the better to hear the low-keyed talk that continued below us. It was easier to hear up there. The words climbed up the wall and in through the space between the thatch and the top of the adobe wall.

What we heard were bits of village gossip, the names of people we didn't know, talk of things that had happened somewhere else a long time past, or things that might happen in a day or a year or two. Even though we understood little we knew we were listening secretly. The grown-ups were in no hurry to talk. They, too, seemed to be listening to the sounds of the night—the rumble of the *arroyo* [stream], and the stirrings of the forest. . . .

The morning of one memorable day Jesús, Catarino and I climbed down from the *tapanco* as usual. Bundled in our blankets, we scrunched ourselves against the wall as close as we could to the warmth of the fire without getting in the way. . . .

Breakfast over, the men left, and pink shafts began to show through the gray sky over the *corral*. Nerón was standing at the back door, observing the food on the *pretil* and waiting for his tortilla dipped in bean juice. That day it was my turn to run with it to the back wall of the *corral*, tantalizing Nerón until he managed to grab it from me.

Coronel and the hens were already scratching in the patio. They were used to the daily commotion of Nerón's *tortilla*, but they always made one of their own, cackling and flapping their wings as they scattered.

Coronel himself was always cool and dignified. He circled around the hens, highstepping carefully between them and me and Nerón, his body stretched tall. Wobbling his comb from side to side like a red pennant he turned his head to watch us now with one yellow, beady eye, now with the other. It was a mean look.

More than the *jefe de familia* [head of family] among his hens, Coronel was part of the security system of the family. With Nerón he patrolled the *corral* when he was not on the street, as puffy and important as an officer of the watch. In Jalco any boy or man who was not afraid of anything was known as *muy gallo* [very rooster]. Coronel was the most rooster of them all.

After Jesús and Catarino and I had done our morning chores that day, I went to the *corral* to escort Coronel and his household through the cottage and into the street. He was circling one of the hens, making passes at her, his neck feathers ruffled. She ducked and swiveled away from him, but Coronel drew nearer and nearer. Suddenly Coronel was on top of her, his yellow beak clamped on the hen's crest, his talons and spurs on her back.

I ran to the back door, excited and angry. My aunt was tidying up the kitchen. "*Tía, tía,*" I yelled. "Coronel is squashing the hen. Shall I hit him?" My aunt stepped to the door and looked at the scene. She didn't seem worried. She turned to me and said matter-of-factly: "Leave Coronel alone. He knows what he is doing. The hen will be all right."

The hen, after her horrifying experience, had straightened up and gone about her pecking and scratching as usual. Coronel renewed his strutting. He did, indeed, seem to know what he was doing, but what was it? It was one of those things that adults were always leaving half explained. I would have to think about it in the *tapanco*.

My mother called out, "Take the hens out." I rounded up Coronel and his flock and shooed them through the cottage into the street. Nerón followed us.

Up and down the street the chickens of the pueblo had begun their daily search along the gutter. The pigs and dogs had spotted themselves where the garbage looked most promising. Halfway up the street, a *zopilote* [turkey vulture] was already pecking at something. . . .

Coronel and his hens were making their way up the street between scratches. The hens kept their beaks down, pecking; and he paced this way and that, flaunting his comb, his feathers glistening in the sunlight.

When they were a few steps from the *zopilote*, the hens became alert. They stood still, some on both legs, some on one, looking intently at something that lay between the talons of the buzzard, which held his attention completely. He lowered his bald white head and tore at the garbage with his hooked beak. Among the pigs and dogs and chickens there seemed to be an understanding not to bother the *zopilotes* that came down to scavenge. To all the residents of Jalcocotán, including the domestic animals, the vulture's looks, not to mention his smell, were enough to discourage sociability.

Nerón and I were watching when one of the hens left the flock and went in for a peck at the *zopilote*'s breakfast. She moved head low, neck forward, more greedy than afraid.

The buzzard struck. With a squawk the hen flipped over and scratched the air madly, as if she were pedaling a bicycle.

Coronel sailed in. His wings spread, his beak half open and his legs churning over the hard earth, he struck the *zopilote* full front, doubled forward so that his beak and his spurs were at the *zopilote*'s breast feathers. The buzzard flapped one great wing over Coronel and bowled him over. The rooster twisted to his feet and began making short passes in cock-fighting style, leaping into the air and snapping his outstretched legs, trying to reach his antagonist with his spurs.

Up and down the street the alarm spread. "Coronel is fighting the *zopilote*."

"He is killing Coronel."

"Get him, Coronel. *Éntrale, éntrale.*"

A ring of small children, women, pigs and dogs had formed around the fighters. Nerón and I had run to the battleground, Nerón snapping at the big bird while I tried to catch Coronel.

As suddenly as it had started, the fight was over. The *zopilote*, snatching at the heap of chicken guts that had tempted the hen, wheeled and spread his great wings, lifting himself over the crowd. He headed for a nearby tree, where he perched and finished his spoils.

Coronel, standing erect among the litter, gave his wings a powerful stretch, flapped them and crowed like a winning champ. His foe, five times larger, had fled, and all the *pueblo* could see that he was indeed *muy gallo* [fighting rooster].

Seeing that Coronel was out of danger, Nerón and I dashed back to the cottage to tell the epic story. We reported how our rooster had dashed a hundred times against the vulture, how he had driven his spurs into the huge bird inflicting fatal wounds. Nerón, my dumb witness, wagged his tail and barked.

My mother had stepped to the door when she heard the tumult. She had seen it all and heard me through my tale solemnly. Coronel himself was strutting home prodding his flock and followed by the children who had seen the fight.

That night, after Jesús and Catarino and I were in bed in the *tapanco*, we heard Doña Esther give the men an account of the battle. Coming through to me in the dark, the story seemed tame, nothing more exciting than throwing the dishwater into the street.

"The boys think Coronel was magnificent," my mother commented.

Gustavo chuckled. Don Catarino drew on his cigarette and said: "Coronel is smart. *Zopilotes* are very chicken. They will fight among themselves, but if it's alive they won't even fight a fly."

The next day I asked my mother what it meant that somebody was chicken if he was not a chicken.

"It means he is not very brave," she explained.

"Is Coronel chicken?"

She guessed what was troubling me. "In no way. He is not chicken. He is the most rooster in Jalco. And I think he is the most rooster from here to Tepic."

I looked out into the corral. Coronel was standing on one foot, erect and watchful, under the willow. I knew something that he didn't—that people were talking about him as the only *gallo* that had ever beaten up a *zopilote*—something to be proud of even if a *zopilote* was, in some fashion, chicken. . . .

Like many other mountain pueblos, Jalcocotán has no school. Once, the village had sent a committee to Tepic to petition the government for a teacher. The committee assured the government that the neighbors would be willing to build the school themselves and to provide the teacher with a place to live. Once in a great while, when the *jefe político*, who represented the government, visited Jalco he would be asked very discreetly and courteously about the petition. The answer was always the same: "It is under consideration." Many years had passed—how many no one really knew—and Jalco still had neither teacher nor school when we went to live there.

Reading, writing, and arithmetic were held in great esteem by the *jalcocoteca-nos*. A few adults in the town had finished the third or fourth grade somewhere else. They taught their own children the a, b, c's and simple arithmetic with the abacus. For writing they had the *pizarra* [chalkboard] and the *pizarrín*—a small square of slate with a decorated wooden frame and a slate pencil.

Books were rare. My mother had one, which she kept in the cedar box. It had a faded polychrome drawing on the cover with the title *La Cocinera Poblana*, a cookbook which had belonged to Grandmother Isabel. We did not need it for cooking the simple, never-changing meals of the family. It was the first book from which Doña Henriqueta ever read to me.

. . .

In Jalco it was easy to think about what you would be when you grew up. On the street, in the *corrales*, and in the family workshops people who had decided what they would be and had become what they had wanted to be, showed you how, if you watched. . . .

Up and down the street, there was somebody who could weave the shoulder bags in which the men carried their lunch to the fields; or cut, trim, and fit a pair of *huaraches*. We saw the butcher kill a steer, rip open its belly, yank out the guts, hang the carcass on a crossbar, peel off the hides with a knife, and cut up the raw red meat into strips for drying in the sun.

The girls of Jalco learned from the women of the *pueblo* how to sew and embroider. But my cousins and I, like the rest of the boys, paid no attention to such matters. An exception to this was my mother's letter writing. When she wrote one for a neighbor, she explained to us that in the large cities there were *escribanos* in the public squares who wrote letters for people who didn't know how. Since the *escribanos* were men, I thought that letter writing might also be a worthy profession for me.

. . .

If you were past six and going on seven, life in Jalco could be made disagreeable by neighbors who seemed to think that they could scold you and tell you how to behave. You never knew when a *compadre* or *comadre* of your aunt, or uncle, or your father, or your mother was watching. For that matter, even people who were not *compadres* to your family thought they had some sort of rights over you. If you did or said something slightly irregular at the farthest end of the street from your cottage, where your legitimate bosses lived, somebody would be watching and ready to call out: "*Mira, qué muchachito tan malcriado*" [Look at this badly brought-up boy]. And if the offense was considered serious, the voice would say,

"You will see, I am going to tell your mother." In a village so full of snitchers and busybodies you could get an extra ear-pull for any trivial breach of good manners—the *buena educación* which the adults prized so highly.

As a result you paid attention to what was expected of *a muchachito muy bien educado* [very well-educated boy]. You never broke into an adult conversation. This was called putting your spoon in, or the way I remember the rule: "*Los muchachitos bien educados no meten su cuchara*" [Well educated young boys don't meddle in adult conversations]. No one ever entered a house, or left the room without saying "*Con su permiso.*" It was "with your permission this" and "your permission that" practically all day long, unless you were playing with your friends. Whoever called you, for whatever reason, if you answered "what do you want?" you were in trouble. You had to answer by asking for a command: "*¿Mande Usted?*" People talked to one another on the street in low tones; only drunks and *muchachitos mal educados* [poorly educated children] raised their voices, or the *arrieros* [mule drivers] when they shouted to their donkeys.

Every mother in the village could ask you to do an errand. If I was in the middle of a game, or just sitting in the street watching the *zopilotes*, some neighbor would call me: "Ernesto, come here and take this to Doña Eduvijes." What right she had to order me around no one ever explained, but I was taught to move right up, answer "*Sí, señora,*" and do the errand.

In fact, running errands was the special business of any boy or girl between the ages of four and six. When you delivered something you always began by saying: "My mother sends greetings and says may God give you a good day, and here is an egg." When you reported the accomplishment of your mission, you repeated the other half of the ceremony by heart: "She says that she sends greetings, how is the family, and many thanks for the egg." Any neighborhood courtesy—an exchange of a banana for a red pepper, or the return of a borrowed utensil—was sure to pass through our messenger system.

Some errands were special. Going for milk was one. There was one cow in the village. She was stabled in a corral on the *arroyo* side of the town, where she could be walked across the stream and tethered in the pasture beyond. No family drank milk every day, only when there was pudding or chocolate to make on feast days. It seemed to work out smoothly, with just enough milk whenever it was wanted, because nobody wanted much. I went to the one-cow dairy with a small pitcher about quart size. The cow was milked straight into it, nobody minding the flies or manure among the cornhusks that littered the corral. On the walk home the important thing was to avoid the pigs and dogs and hens with strict attention to getting the milk home unspilled. . . .

The priest came to visit Jalco . . . once or twice a year. Instead of drinking songs, we heard the chants and the litanies that he sang with the chapel choir.

José, besides serving as an altar boy, sang in the choir, and for a time his future as a chorister looked promising. But he composed comical Spanish versions of Dominus vobiscum and other Latin bits of the ritual. The priest heard about this and expelled him because his translations were disrespectful. One of them was to the effect that "if you are an awful sinner, just invite the priest to dinner." José was scolded (but not very severely) for entertaining us with his sing-song imitations of religious rites.

The expulsion of José made it much less likely that we would be sent to mass or that the priest would receive from us gifts that the *jalcocotecanos* usually presented him on his visits—a roasted chicken, a pot of *tamales*, a comb of honey, and other savory foods that kept him overweight. He never visited a cottage without sending advance notice, so that when he knocked on the door there would be a milk pudding or a whole barbecued banana dripping with syrup ready to serve. Jose's humiliation put a stop to these visits to our family. After that we heard more and more family criticisms of the religious man. He charged too much for funerals. He collected fees for baptizing children as well as for blessing pigs and goats and other domestic animals. He sold scapularies, which, my mother said darkly, a seamstress in San Blas made from his underwear. My cousins and I vowed that if José was not reinstated in the chapel none of us would ever become a priest.

For nearly everyone else in town the infrequent visits of the priest, his sermons and incantations, and his sprinkling of holy water in places where a ghost had appeared were serious matters. People spoke of El Diablo [The Devil] and of La Muerte [Death] as if they were persons you might run into any moment. The Devil could descend on you from a tree in the shape of a monstrous lizard or block you on the trail dressed in flames and aiming a spear at you. Death was a gangling skeleton who perched her rattling bones (Death was always a She) on the roof ridge of your cottage, or signaled you with a bony finger to follow her into the forest. Against the powerful black magic of El Diablo and La Muerte, the *jalcocotecanos* needed the equally powerful protection of their scapularies, the sign of the cross, and Our Lady of Talpa and the Holy Child of Atocha, the most revered saints among or neighbors.

Pictures in polychrome colors of the holy ones of Talpa and Atocha were carried at the head of funeral processions that went by the front of our house. When a playmate died down the street, I saw the small coffin wrapped in a white sheet carried by a man on his shoulder. People stood in their doorways and made the sign of the cross and prayed silently as the procession passed. I didn't know the prayers exactly, which sounded to me between a whisper and a mumble, so I bowed my head and whispered and mumbled. The next day we made a bouquet of geraniums and carnations from the pots in our corral. We took it to the mother when we went to offer our *pésame* [condolences], the mourning visit to the family of my dead friend. My mother spoke, and I repeated the traditional words: "I come to keep you company in your grief. May he rest in peace." My mother was dressed in black and there was a narrow black ribbon around my arm. When she walked me home I complained that she was holding my hand too tightly. I looked at her face. She was weeping. The dead boy had been about my own age. . . .

ON THE EDGE OF THE BARRIO

Excerpt from Ernesto Galarza, *Barrio Boy* (1971; repr., Notre Dame, Ind.:
University of Notre Dame Press, 1977), 247–266.

The final chapter of *Barrio Boy* leaves us with Galarza looking into the horizon over the Sacramento Valley contemplating his future. The journey from
Jalcocotán to Sacramento has been difficult and has been dictated by work
and the search for the next best *chanza* (job). By the time he had finished
middle school, he had worked as a paper boy, a messenger, a store clerk, a
musician, and a field hand. The rich descriptions he provides of his working-
class neighborhood in downtown Sacramento are indicative of descriptions of
industries and other neighborhoods his family had encountered while migrating north to the United States. These final pages provide a conceptual map
that reveals the awakening of Galarza's class consciousness and the laying of
a foundation for a lifetime of activism.

To make room for a growing family it was decided that we should
move, and a house was found in Oak Park, on the far side of town where the
open country began. The men raised the first installment for the bungalow on
Seventh Avenue even after Mrs. Dodson explained that if we did not keep up the
monthly payments we would lose the deposit as well as the house.

The real estate broker brought the sale contract to the apartment one evening.
Myself included, we sat around the table in the living room, the *gringo* explaining
at great length the small print of the document in a torrent of words none of us
could make out. Now and then he would pause and throw in the only word he
knew in Spanish: "*Sabee*?" The men nodded slightly as if they had understood.
Doña Henriqueta was holding firmly to the purse which contained the down
payment, watching the broker's face, not listening to his words. She had only
one question. Turning to me she said: "Ask him how long it will take to pay all of
it." I translated, shocked by the answer: "Twenty years." There was a long pause
around the table, broken by my stepfather:

"What do you say?" Around the table the heads nodded agreement. The broker
passed his fountain pen to him. He signed the contract and after him Gustavo
and Jose. Doña Henriqueta opened the purse and counted out the greenbacks.
The broker pocketed the money, gave us a copy of the document, and left.

The last thing I did when we moved out of 418 L was to dig a hole in the corner of the backyard for a tall carton of Quaker Oats cereal, full to the brim with the marbles I had won playing for keeps around the *barrio*. I tamped the earth over my buried treasure and laid a curse on whoever removed it without my permission. . . .

We could not have moved to a neighborhood less like the *barrio*. All the families around us were Americans. The grumpy retired farmer next door viewed us with alarm and never gave us the time of day, but the Harrisons across the street were cordial. Mr. Harrison loaned us his tools, and Roy, just my age but twice my weight, teamed up with me at once for an exchange of visits to his mother's kitchen and ours. I astounded him with my Mexican rice, and Mrs. Harrison baked my first waffle. Roy and I also found a common bond in the matter of sisters. He had an older one and by now I had two younger ones. It was a question between us whether they were worse as little nuisances or as big bosses. The answer didn't make much difference but it was a relief to have another man to talk with. . . .

With a bike I was able to sign on as a carrier of the Sacramento Bee, learning in due course the art of slapping folded newspapers against people's porches instead of into the bushes or on their roofs. Roy and I also became assistants to a neighbor who operated a bakery in his basement, taking our pay partly in dimes and partly in broken cookies for our families.

For the three men of the household as well as for me the bicycle became the most important means for earning a living. Oak Park was miles away from the usual places where they worked and they pedaled off, in good weather and bad, in the early morning. It was a case of saving carfare.

I transferred to the Bret Harte School, a gingerbread two story building in which there was a notable absence of Japanese, Filipinos, Koreans, Italians, and the other nationalities of the Lincoln School. It was at Bret Harte that I learned how an English sentence could be cut up on the blackboard and the pieces placed on different lines connected by what the teacher called a diagram. The idea of operating on a sentence and rearranging its members as a skeleton of verbs, modifiers, subject, and prepositions set me off diagraming whatever I read, in Spanish and English. Spiderwebs, my mother called them, when I tried to teach her the art. . . .

It was Gustavo, in fact, who began to give my books a vague significance. He pointed out to me that with diagrams and dictionaries I could have a choice of becoming a lawyer or a doctor or an engineer or a professor. These, he said, were far better careers than growing up to be a *camello* [camel], as he and Jose always would be. *Camellos*, I knew well enough, was what the chicanos called themselves as the workers on every job who did the dirtiest work. And to give our home the professional touch he felt I should be acquiring, he had a telephone installed. . . .

It was clearly explained by Gustavo that the instrument was to provide me with a quick means of reaching the important people I knew at the Y.M.C.A., the boy's band, or the various public offices where I interpreted for chicanos in distress. Sooner or later some of our friends in the barrio would also have telephones and we could talk with them. . . .

Every member of the family, in his own way, missed the *barrio.* Jose and Gustavo could no longer join the talk of the poolrooms and the street corners by walking two blocks down the street. The sign language and simple words my mother had devised to communicate with the Americans at 418 L didn't work with the housewives on 7th Avenue. The families we had known were now too far away to exchange visits. We knew no one in Oak Park who spoke Spanish. Our street was always quiet and often lonely with little to watch from our front porch other than boys riding bicycles or Mrs. Harrison hanging out her wash. Pork Chops and the Salvation Army never played there.

I, too, knew that things were different. There was no corner where I could sell the Union, and my income from running errands and doing chores around the rooming house stopped. There were no alleys I could comb for beer bottles or docks where I could gather saleable or edible things. . . .

We now had an infant boy in the family who with my two sisters made four of us. The baby was himself no inconvenience to me, but it meant that I had to mind the girls more, mostly chasing them home from the neighbors. If I had been the eldest girl in the family I would have stepped into my mother's place and taken over the management of all but the youngest. But being a boy, the female chores seemed outrageous and un-Mexican. Doña Henriqueta tried telling me that I was now the *jefe de familia* [head] of all the juniors. But she was a gentle mother and the freedom of the house, the yard, and my personal property that she gave the two girls did nothing to make them understand that I was their *jefe* [boss]. When Nora, the oldest of the two, demolished my concertina with a hammer (no doubt to see where the notes came from) I asked for permission to strangle her. Permission was denied.

During the first year we lived at Oak Park we began to floor and partition the basement. Some day, we knew, the Lopez's would come through and we would have a temporary home ready for them. With three-and-a-half men in the house earning wages, if work was steady, we were keeping up with the installments and saving for the reunion.

An epidemic erased the quiet life on 7th Avenue and the hopes we had brought with us.

I had been reading to the family stories in the Bee of the Spanish influenza. At first it was far off, like the war, in places such as New York and Texas. Then the stories told of people dying in California towns we knew, and finally the Bee began reporting the spread of the "flu" in our city.

One Sunday morning we saw Gustavo coming down the street with a suitcase in his hand, walking slowly. I ran out to meet him. By the front gate, he dropped the suitcase, leaned on the fence, and fainted. He had been working as a sandhog on the American River, and had come home weak from fever.

Gustavo was put to bed in one of the front rooms. Jose set out to look for a doctor, who came the next day, weary and nearly sick himself. He ordered Gustavo to the hospital. Three days later I answered the telephone call from the hospital telling us he was dead. Only Jose went to Gustavo's funeral. The rest of us, except my stepfather, were sick in bed with the fever.

In the dining room, near the windows where the sunlight would warm her, my mother lay on a cot, a kerosene stove at her feet. The day Gustavo died she was delirious. Jose bicycled all over the city, looking for oranges, which the doctor said were the best medicine we could give her. I sweated out the fever, nursed by Jose, who brought me glasses of steaming lemonade and told me my mother was getting better. The children were quarantined in another room, lightly touched by the fever, more restless than sick.

Late one afternoon Jose came into my room, wrapped me in blankets, pulled a cap over my ears, and carried me to my mother's bedside. My stepfather was holding a hand mirror to her lips. It didn't fog. She had stopped breathing. In the next room my sister was singing to the other children, "A birdie with a yellow bill / hopped upon my windowsill / cocked a shiny eye and said / Shame on you you sleepy head."

The day we buried Doña Henriqueta, Mrs. Dodson took the oldest sister home with her. The younger children were sent to a neighbor. That night Jose went to the *barrio*, got drunk, borrowed a pistol, and was arrested for shooting up Second Street. . . .

A month later I made a bundle of the family keepsakes my stepfather allowed me to have, including the butterfly *sarape*, my books, and some family pictures. With the bundle tied to the bars of my bicycle, I pedaled to the basement room Jose had rented for the two of us on O Street near the corner of Fifth, on the edge of the barrio.

Jose was now working the riverboats and, in the slack season, following the round of odd jobs about the city. In our basement room, with a kitchen closet, bathroom, and laundry tub on the back porch and a woodshed for storage, I kept house. We bought two cots, one for me and the other for Jose when he was home.

Our landlords lived upstairs, a middle-aged brother and sister who worked and rented rooms. As part payment on our rent I kept the yard trim. They were friends of Doña Transito, the grandmother of a Mexican family that lived in a weather-beaten cottage on the corner. Doña Transito was in her sixties, round as a barrel, and she wore her gray hair in braids and smoked hand-rolled cigarettes on her rickety front porch. To her tiny parlor chicanos in trouble came for advice, and the firm old lady with the rasping voice and commanding ways often asked me to interpret or translate for them in their encounters with the *autoridades* [authorities]. Since her services were free, so were mine. . . .

When troubles made it necessary for the *barrio* people to deal with the Americans uptown, the *autoridades*, I went with them to the police court, the industrial accident office, the county hospital, the draft board, the county clerk. We got lost together in the rigamarole of functionaries who sat, like *patrónes* [bosses], behind desks and who demanded licenses, certificates, documents, affidavits, signatures, and witnesses. And we celebrated our successes, as when the worker for whom I interpreted in interviews that lasted many months, was awarded a thousand dollars for a disabled arm. Don Crescendo congratulated me, saying that in Mexico for a thousand American dollars you could buy the lives of many peons.

Jose had chosen our new home in the basement on O Street because it was close to the Hearkness Junior High School, to which I transferred from Bret Harte. As the *jefe de familia* he explained that I could help earn our living but that I was to study for a high school diploma. That being settled, my routine was clearly divided into school-time and worktime, the second depending on when I was free from the first.

Few Mexicans of my age from the *barrio* were enrolled at the junior high school when I went there. At least, there were no other Mexican boys or girls in Mr. Everett's class in civics, or Miss Crowley's English composition, or Mrs. Stevenson's Spanish course. Mrs. Stevenson assigned me to read to the class and to recite poems by Amado Nervo, because the poet was from Tepic and I was, too. Miss Crowley accepted my compositions about Jalcocotan and the buried treasure of Acaponeta while the others in the class were writing about Sir Patrick Spence and the Beautiful Lady without Mercy, whom they had never met. For Mr. Everett's class, the last of the day, I clipped pieces from the Sacramento Bee about important events in Sacramento.

From him I learned to use the ring binder in which I kept clippings to prepare oral reports. Occasionally he kept me after school to talk. He sat on his desk, one leg dangling over a corner, behind him the frame of a large window and the arching elms of the school yard, telling me he thought I could easily make the debating team at the high school next year, that Stanford University might be the place to go after graduation, and making other by-the-way comments that began to shape themselves into my future.

Afternoons, Saturdays, and summers allowed me many hours of worktime I did not need for study. Jose explained how things now stood. There were two funerals to pay for. More urgently than ever, Doña Esther and her family must be brought to live with us. He would pay the rent and buy the food. My clothes, books, and school expenses would be up to me.

On my vacations, and when he was not on the riverboats, he found me a job as water boy on a track gang. We chopped wood together near Woodland and stacked empty lug boxes in a cannery yard. Cleaning vacant houses and chopping weeds were jobs we could do as a team when better ones were not to be had. As the apprentice, I learned from him how to brace myself for a heavy lift, to lock my knee under a loaded handtruck, to dance rather than lift a ladder, and to find the weakest grain in a log. Like him I spit into my palms to get the feel of the axe handle and grunted as the blade bit into the wood. Imitating him I circled a tree several times, sizing it up, *tanteando*, as he said, before pruning or felling it.

Part of one summer my uncle worked on the river while I hired out as a farmhand on a small ranch south of Sacramento. My senior on the place was Roy, a husky Oklahoman who was a part-time taxi driver and a full-time drinker of hard whiskey. He was heavy-chested, heavy-lipped and jowly, a grumbler rather than a talker and a man of great ingenuity with tools and automobile engines. Under him I learned to drive the Fordson tractor on the place, man the gasoline pump, feed the calves, check an irrigation ditch, make lug boxes for grapes and many other tasks on a small farm....

And Roy knew how to handle boys, which he showed in an episode that could have cost me my life or my self-confidence. He had taught me to drive the tractor, walking alongside during the lessons as I maneuvered it, shifting gears, stopping and starting, turning and backing, raising a cloud of dust wherever we went. Between drives Roy told me about the different working parts of the machine, giving me instructions on oiling and greasing and filling the radiator. "She needs to be took care of, Ernie," he admonished me, "like a horse. And another thing, she's like to buck. She can turn clear over on you if you let 'er. If she starts to lift from the front even a mite, you turn her off. You hear?"

"Yes, sir," I said, meaning to keep his confidence in me as a good tractor man....

Except for food and a place to live, with which Jose provided me, I was on my own. Between farm jobs I worked in town, adding to my experience as well as to my income. As a clerk in a drug store on Second and J [Street], in the heart of the lower part of town, I waited on chicanos who spoke no English and who came in search of remedies with no prescription other than a recital of their pains. I dispensed capsules, pills, liniments, and emulsions as instructed by the pharmacist, who glanced at our customers from the back of the shop and diagnosed their ills as I translated them. When I went on my shift, I placed a card in the window that said "*Se habla Espanol.*" So far as my chicano patients were concerned it might as well have said "Dr. Ernesto Galarza."

From drugs I moved to office supplies and stationery sundries, working as delivery boy for Wahl's, several blocks uptown from skid row. Between deliveries I had no time to idle. I helped the stock clerk, took inventory, polished desks, and hopped when a clerk bawled an order down the basement steps. . . .

But like my uncles, I was looking for a better *chanza*, which I thought I found with Western Union, as a messenger, where I could earn tips as well as wages. Since I knew the lower part of town thoroughly, whenever the telegrams were addressed to that quarter the dispatcher gave them to me. Deliveries to the suites on the second floor of saloons paid especially well, with tips of a quarter from the ladies who worked there. My most generous customer was tall and beautiful Miss Irene, who always asked how I was doing in school. It was she who gave me an English dictionary, the first I ever possessed, a black bound volume with remarkable little scallops on the pages that made it easy to find words. Half smiling, half commanding, Miss Irene said to me more than once: "Don't you stop school without letting me know." I meant to take her advice as earnestly as I took her twenty-five cent tip.

It was in the lower town also that I nearly became a performing artist. My instructor on the violin had stopped giving me lessons after we moved to Oak Park. When we were back on O Street he sent word through Jose that I could work as second fiddler on Saturday nights in the dancehall where he played with a *mariachi*. Besides, I could resume my lessons with him. A dollar a night for two hours as a substitute was the best wages I had ever made. Coached by my teacher, I second-fiddled for sporting chicanos who swung their ladies on the dance floor and sang to our music. . . .

It was during the summer vacation that school did not interfere with making a living, the time of the year when I went with other barrio people to the ranches to look for work. Still too young to shape up with the day-haul gangs, I loitered on skid row, picking up conversation and reading the chalk signs about work that was being offered. For a few days of picking fruit or pulling hops I bicycled to Folsom, Lodi, Woodland, Freeport, Walnut Grove, Marysville, Slough House, Florin, and places that had no name. Looking for work, I pedaled through a countryside blocked off, mile after mile, into orchards, vineyards, and vegetable farms. Along the ditch banks, where the grass, the morning glory, and the wild oats made a soft mattress I unrolled my bindle and slept.

In the labor camps I shared the summertime of the lives of the *barrio* people. They gathered from *barrios* of faraway places like Imperial Valley, Los Angeles,

Phoenix, and San Antonio. Each family traveling on its own, they came in trucks piled with household goods or packed in their secondhand *fotingos* and *chevees*. The trucks and cars were ancient models, fresh out of a used-car lot, with license tags of many states. It was into these jalopies that much of the care and a good part of the family's earnings went. In camp they were constantly being fixed, so close to scrap that when we needed a part for repairs, we first went to the nearest junkyard.

It was a world different in so many ways from the lower part of Sacramento and the residences surrounded by trim lawns and cool canopies of elms to which I had delivered packages for Wahl's. Our main street was usually an irrigation ditch, the water supply for cooking, drinking, laundering, and bathing. In the better camps there was a faucet or a hydrant, from which water was carried in buckets, pails and washtubs. If the camp belonged to a contractor, and it was used from year to year, there were permanent buildings—a shack for his office, the privies, weatherworn and sagging, and a few cabins made of secondhand lumber, patched and unpainted.

If the farmer provided housing himself, it was in tents pitched on the bare baked earth or on the rough ground of newly plowed land on the edge of a field. Those who arrived late for the work season camped under trees or raised lean-tos along a creek, roofing their trucks with canvas to make bedrooms. Such camps were always well away from the house of the *ranchero* [farm owner], screened from the main road by an orchard or a grove of eucalyptus. I helped to pitch and take down such camps, on some spot that seemed lonely when we arrived, desolate when we left. . . .

Like all the others, I often went to work without knowing how much I was going to be paid. I was never hired by a rancher, but by a contractor or a straw boss who picked up crews in town and handled the payroll. The important questions that were in my mind—the wages per hour or per lug box, whether the beds would have mattresses and blankets, the price of meals, how often we would be paid were never discussed, much less answered, beforehand. Once we were in camp, owing the employer for the ride to the job, having no means to get back to town except by walking and no money for the next meal, arguments over working conditions were settled in favor of the boss. I learned firsthand the chiseling techniques of the contractors and their pushers—how they knocked off two or three lugs of grapes from the daily record for each member of the crew, or the way they had of turning the face of the scales away from you when you weighed your work in.

There was never any doubt about the contractor and his power over us. He could fire a man and his family on the spot and make them wait days for their wages. A man could be forced to quit by assigning him regularly to the thinnest pickings in the field. The worst thing one could do was to ask for fresh water on the job, regardless of the heat of the day; instead of iced water, given freely, the crews were expected to buy sodas at twice the price in town, sold by the contractor himself. He usually had a pistol—to protect the payroll, so it was said. Through the ranchers for whom he worked, we were certain that he had connections with the *autoridades*, for they never showed up in camp to settle wage disputes or listen to our complaints or to go for a doctor when one was needed. Lord of a rag-tag labor camp of Mexicans, the contractor, a Mexican himself, knew that few men would let their anger blow, even when he stung them with curses like, "*Orale, San Afabeeches huevones* [Lazy sons of bitches]."

As a single worker, I usually ate with some household, paying for my board. I did more work than a child but less than a man, neither the head nor the tail of a family. Unless the camp was a large one I became acquainted with most of the families. Those who could not write asked me to chalk their payroll numbers on the boxes they picked. I counted matches for a man who transferred them from the right pocket of his pants to the left as he tallied the lugs he filled throughout the day. It was his only check on the record the contractor kept of his work. As we worked the rows or the tree blocks during the day, or talked in the evenings where the men gathered in small groups to smoke and rest, I heard about *barrios* I had never seen but that must have been much like ours in Sacramento.

The only way to complain or protest was to leave, but now and then a camp would stand instead of run, and for a few hours or a few days work would slow down or stop. I saw it happen in a pear orchard in Yolo when pay rates were cut without notice to the crew. The contractor said the market for pears had dropped and the rancher could not afford to pay more. The fruit stayed on the trees, while we, a committee drafted by the camp, argued with the contractor first and then with the rancher. The talks gave them time to round up other pickers. A carload of police in plain clothes drove into the camp. We were lined up for our pay, taking whatever the contractor said was on his books. That afternoon we were ordered off the ranch.

In a camp near Folsom, during hop picking, it was not wages but death that pulled the people together. Several children in the camp were sick with diarrhea; one had been taken to the hospital in town and the word came back that he had died. It was the women who guessed that the cause of the epidemic was the water. For cooking and drinking and washing it came from a ditch that went by the ranch stables upstream.

I was appointed by a camp committee to go to Sacramento to find some *autoridad* who would send an inspector. Pedaling my bicycle, mulling over where to go and what to say, I remembered some clippings from the Sacramento Bee that Mr. Everett had discussed in class, and I decided the man to look for was Mr. Simon Lubin, who was in some way a state *autoridad*.

He received me in his office at Weinstock and Lubin's. He sat, square-shouldered and natty, behind a desk with a glass top. He was half-bald, with a strong nose and a dimple in the center of his chin. To his right was a box with small levers into which Mr. Lubin talked and out of which came voices.

He heard me out, asked me questions and made notes on a pad. He promised that an inspector would come to the camp. I thanked him and thought the business of my visit was over; but Mr. Lubin did not break the handshake until he had said to tell the people in the camp to organize. Only by organizing, he told me, will they ever have decent places to live.

I reported the interview with Mr. Lubin to the camp. The part about the inspector they understood and it was voted not to go back to work until he came. The part about organizing was received in silence and I knew they understood it as little as I did. Remembering Duran in that camp meeting, I made my first organizing speech.

The inspector came and a water tank pulled by mules was parked by the irrigation ditch. At the same time the contractor began to fire some of the pickers. I was one of them. I finished that summer nailing boxes on a grape ranch near Florin.

When my job ended I pedaled back to Sacramento, detouring over country lanes I knew well. Here and there I walked the bicycle over dirt roads rutted by wagons. The pastures were sunburned and the grain fields had been cut to stubble. Riding by a thicket of reeds where an irrigation ditch swamped I stopped and looked at the red-winged blackbirds riding gracefully on the tips of the canes. Now and then they streaked out of the green clump, spraying the pale sky with crimson dots in all directions.

Crossing the Y Street levee by Southside Park I rode through the *barrio* to Doña Transito's, leaving my bike hooked on the picket fence by the handlebar.

I knocked on the screen door that always hung tired, like the sagging porch coming unnailed. No one was at home.

It was two hours before time to cook supper. From the stoop I looked up and down the cross streets. The *barrio* seemed empty.

I unhooked the bicycle, mounted it, and headed for the main high school, twenty blocks away where I would be going in a week. Pumping slowly, I wondered about the debating team and the other things Mr. Everett had mentioned.

PART 2

MEXICAN LABOR, MIGRATION, AND THE AMERICAN EMPIRE

LIFE IN THE UNITED STATES FOR MEXICAN PEOPLE
OUT OF THE EXPERIENCE OF A MEXICAN

Ernesto Galarza, "Life in the United States for Mexican People: Out of the Experience of a Mexican," in *Proceedings of the National Conference of Social Work [Formerly National Conference of Charities and Correction] at the Fifty-Sixth Annual Session Held in San Francisco, California, June 26–July 3, 1929* (Chicago: University of Chicago Press, 1929), 399–404.

In 1929, when he was twenty-four, Galarza presented this paper at the National Conference of Social Work in San Francisco, California. It was one of the first times he questioned U.S. policy toward Mexican and Mexican American labor in a public forum. In this paper he points out the hypocrisies of harmful U.S. labor policies toward a people whose labor was instrumental in building an American empire.

Notable life events during this era:

- 1927: Galarza receives a bachelor's degree from Occidental College in Los Angeles.
- 1929: Galarza receives a Master of Arts degree in Latin American history and political science from Stanford University.
- 1929: Marries Mae Taylor, a teacher, who becomes his lifelong partner in activism.

The chief interest in the Mexican immigrant in the United States at the present moment centers around the question of whether Mexico shall be placed on the quota basis. . . . The restrictionists have mustered the familiar artillery of racial dilution and the color flood, while those who seek to keep the gates open, as they have been for the last eighteen years, are once more pressing the equally old argument that the very economic structure of the United States rests on the brawn and sweat of the immigrant.

Whatever may be the relative merits of the contending theses, one effect of the controversy has been to obscure the very fundamental proposition that something must be done in the way of social and economic amelioration for those Mexicans who have already settled in the United States and whose problem is that of finding adjustment. Thus far in the discussion the Mexicans who have settled more or less permanently here have been taken into account negatively; that is, restrictionists have found ample material for controversial argument in the group behavior of these people in their new environment. It is the central idea of this paper that the needs and interests of the Mexican immigrant already settled in the United States must be consistently taken into account; my object is to present the case of the Mexican who is with us.

For the moment let it be accepted as true that everyone has presented his side of the case except the Mexican worker himself. Later on we shall consider the reasons for this, whether it is desirable to make this considerable body of human beings articulate, and, if so, one or two suggestions as to the steps necessary to bring this about.

I speak to you today as one of these immigrants. I have only a simple and merely suggestive statement based on a knowledge of the community life of these people and of what goes on in their minds concerning the economic aspects of "the Mexican problem."

First, as to unemployment. The Mexican is the first to suffer from the depression in industrial and agricultural enterprises. He does not watch the market returns because he could not read them if he would; but he has a keen ear and ready understanding of the neighborhood rumors that speak of the stricken crops or prospective lay-offs. Something that borders on desperation grips many of them and the old familiar phrase, packed with a penetrating helplessness, goes the rounds: "Va a estar duro el invierno"—"It is going to be a hard winter." I flatly disagree with those who maintain that there is enough work for these people but that they refuse to work, preferring to live on charity. On the contrary, it is widely felt by the Mexicans that there are more men than there are jobs. The women storm the canneries of the Sacramento Valley by the hundreds in search of the jobs that are counted by the dozen. By and large, it may be true that the sum total of available work tallies neatly with the number of Mexicans looking for it. Thus far, however, the worker and the work are not to be found in the same locality. Again, the precariousness of the job in the face of so much competition has brought home to the Mexican time and again his absolute weakness as a bargainer for employment. He therefore takes what he can get and is devoutly thankful for that.

He has also something to say as to the wage scale. If you wish to touch the lowest reaches of individual bargaining in the labor market, go to the Mexican and learn his ways. It is often said that he is satisfied with enough to buy a pound of beans, rent a hutch, buy a quilt, and have a little left over for bootleg goods. The Mexican is not innately married to an animal standard of living. What happens is that he recognizes his absolute inability to force his wage upward and by dint of necessity he shuffles along with a standard of living which the American worker regards with contempt and alarm. . . . Unfortunately, when a Mexican family contrives to increase its income and to extend its range of necessities and comforts, invariably it begins with the wrong things. Radios, roadsters, and Chesterfields, and jewelry leave a trail of debt long after they have been pawned, worn out, or sold for a fraction of the cost to tide over a hard season. Before so many blanket charges are made against the Mexican on the score of his standard of living, something should be known of the high-pressure salesmanship to which he is practically always a victim.

The distribution of the labor supply is felt by the Mexican to be inadequate. At present he has to rely mainly on hearsay or on the information of unscrupulous contractors who overcharge him for transportation. Entire families move up and down the valleys of California in the orchard and hop field districts only to suffer repeated disillusionment. In one case several dozen families camped on the edge of a hop field two months waiting for the picking to begin. Less than one half of them were finally employed. Furthermore, these migrations are undertaken entirely at the cost of the Mexican. The lowly and disreputable Ford has been extolled now and then as the solution of the seasonal labor problem, since this type of conveyance has been almost universally adopted by the Mexican. But the Mexican well knows by this time that the Ford is not a perennial flower; and he also knows that far too much of his meager income is left in the tills of gasoline stations and the tire shops in his long treks along the Pacific Coast.

To these three aspects of the question—unemployment, wage scales, and seasonal migration in search of work—should be added two others about which the Mexican is concerned. They are the education of his children and the persistence of race prejudice.

The public schools have a distinct effect on the second generation of the immigrant group. The children begin to feel contempt for field labor and disdain for the sweat and grime which permeate the life of their parents. Along with this goes a cooling of the loyalty to the home country. Pride of birth is forgotten and in its place creeps in a desire to imitate playfellows in what appeals to them as distinctly American. What is worse, they forget the mother-tongue. And while this is going on they fail to find a secure place in the social scheme of their adopted country. . . . As Mexicans, they are denationalized and they find themselves in a difficult borderland through which it seems that all second generation immigrants must pass. Incidentally, I wish to state that as far as my own experience extends, the Mexican parent is uniformly grateful for the educational opportunities offered to his children in this country.

Finally, the Mexican immigrant feels the burden of old prejudices. Only when there are threats to limit immigration from Mexico is it that a few in America sing the praises of the peon, stating that he loves his family, has a passion for red flowers and soft music, drinks discreetly, and obeys implicitly. At other times the sentiments which seem to be deeply rooted in the American mind are that he is unclean, improvident, intolerant, and innately dull. Add to this the suspicion that he constitutes a peril to the American worker's wage scale and you have a situation with which no average Mexican can cope. . . .

My suggestions are that, first, some order should be brought out of the chaos of the seasonal labor supply, preferably by state initiative. As long as the present haphazard arrangement continues, surplus of laborers will be needed to compensate for the lack of correlation between the supply and demand for farm workers. Control by private organizations of this phase of the question is subject to too many abuses to be recommended.

Second, a bilateral accord with the Mexican government should be sought to iron out the immigration question. . . .

Third, whenever feasible, social service agents working with Mexican groups should use workers of Mexican extraction to make the firsthand contacts.

Fourth, there should be more real understanding of the adjustment which the Mexican is making to his American environment. For example, often I have seen statistics setting forth the high birth rate of the Mexican as an indication of the dilution of the American stock. Never yet have I seen in juxtaposition a statement of the death rate. How scientific can such analyses be when they ignore such vital information? Something more should be known also about the Mexican lives and why before the stigma of a low standard of living is fastened on him.

Last, I would ask for recognition of the Mexican's contribution to the agricultural and industrial expansion of [the] western United States. Here I am treading on holy ground where many have worshiped but few have spoken. It is amusing to read the praises of those opposed to the restrictions of immigration. From Denver to Los Angeles and from the Imperial Valley to Portland, it is said, an empire has been created largely by the brawn of the humble Mexican, who laid the rails and topped the beets and poured the cubic miles of cement. But this acknowledgement is misleading and tardy. For some obscure reason these builders of colossal fortunes have done their jobs and gone their ways still clothed in rags. If this wealth beyond counting is the result of enterprise, of foresight, and of vision, let it so be said; and let it be added that the men who have sweated into the mortar and driven their existence, inch by inch, into railroad ties were but the generous raw material of abundant Nature, and as such have received no more than their due. If it is true that the Mexican has brought to you arms that have fastened a civilization on the Pacific slope, then give him his due. If you give him his earned wage and he proves improvident, teach him otherwise; if he is tuberculous, cure him; if he falls into indigence, raise him. He has built you an empire!

What I ask, of course, at present is nothing but economic romanticism. But I ask it, speaking for those who cannot speak for themselves. And I conclude by repeating that unless the Mexican immigrant in the United States is made articulate, unless his economic contribution to the development of [the] western United States is recognized and rewarded, unless his needs and interests are considered from his own point of view, any attempt to solve the problem will lack the most vital of all values, the human value.

PROGRAM FOR ACTION

Ernesto Galarza, "Program for Action," part of a special section titled "The Mexican American: A National Concern," in *Common Ground* 9, no. 4 (Summer 1949): 27–38.

Common Ground was a publication of the Common Council for American Unity (1939–1959), a progressive organization whose purpose was to conduct research and do outreach to promote inclusive citizenship. One of their stated purposes was "to help the foreign-born and their children solve their special problems of adjustment, know and value their particular cultural heritage, and share fully and constructively in American life."

The list of barriers to societal, political, and economic parity for the Mexican American that Galarza outlines are almost identical to those that activists and progressive academics speak of today. The solutions he offers to ameliorate the Mexican American condition include participation in trade unions and the reform of federal labor and educational laws.

An interesting part of this article is his discussion of the migration to the interior United States that had begun by 1949. The Mexican American community was no longer staying in traditional border regions and states (California, Texas, Arizona, and New Mexico) but had successfully settled in new states such as Illinois, Michigan, Ohio, Pennsylvania, and Kansas.

It is important to address Galarza's use of the words "wetback" and "illegal" to refer to undocumented Mexican immigrants. These terms were part of the popular discourse of the time and were commonly used by progressive academics, reporters, and others involved in the labor movement. After carefully studying Galarza and his work, we believe that if he was alive today he would be part of the movement to denounce these terms to refer to any human being.

Notable life events during this era:

- 1947: As a result of the 30-month strike of fruit pickers against the DiGiorgio Corporation, growers urge the House of Representatives to create a subcommittee to investigate the organizing activities and job actions of the National Farm Labor Union (NFLU). One of the three representatives on the subcommittee is Richard Nixon, who for two and a half days cross-examines Galarza and other witnesses of the strike on behalf of the growers.

- 1951: Galarza leads a strike of cantaloupe pickers in the Imperial Valley of California.
- 1953: With H. L. Mitchell, co-founder of the Southern Tenant Farmers' Union, Galarza helps organize and participates in strikes by sugar cane workers in Louisiana.

The conditions of life and work of the Spanish-speaking minority in the United States are no longer a problem only of the borderlands. A historical process has been at work lifting this problem above local and sectional concern. It now involves communities as distant from the United States–Mexican border as Chicago, New York, and Detroit. It shows up in the rural slums that lie on an arc stretching from Arkansas to northern California. It is documented in federal reports on employment and in community conferences on human relations in the urban industrial East as well as in the rural agricultural Southwest. It has become a skeleton in the closet of our Latin American policy.

The Mexican agricultural migrant and itinerant railway maintenance worker have been the primary agents in this process. Over the past fifty years they have moved into practically every state of the Union. Today, while the bulk of over 2,500,000 of this minority is still anchored in California, Texas, Arizona, and New Mexico, thousands can be found in Illinois, Michigan, Ohio, Pennsylvania, and Kansas.

Within the group, the inferiority complex has been disappearing. From the uncomplaining ranks of Mexican "stoop labor" have emerged trained men and women to spoil the myth of the innate servility and incompetence attached to this group, with some romantic concessions, by the finance fanners and railway corporations that long have exploited them. Two world wars proved the courage, tested the loyalty, broadened the experience, and tempered the will of young men born and bred in a no-man's-land of social rejection and lack of civic opportunity for adult citizenship.

In the cotton fields, the truck farm, and the corporation ranches, as well as in the armed services, the Mexican has mingled with other minority groups more experienced in the defense of human rights and dignity, especially the Negro. He has rubbed shoulders with the militant Nisei GI's who did not come back from [the battle of] Monte Cassino to take it lying down. Through these contacts, methods of action have been learned and technics of organization have been discovered and communicated. The language of protest, pure and simple and almost always unheeded, has been supplemented by self-education and the discovery of the methods of redress available in the larger society by which he is surrounded. In this process not a few Mexicans have discovered the weaknesses of civic and political organization, locally and nationally, as well as the mirages of international relations which have affected their welfare. For half a century they have experienced, intuitively rather than rationally, the red tape, obscure diplomatic deals, misrepresentations, and legal taffy in which the civil liberties and economic opportunities of Mexicans in the United States have been entangled. But as the American school system has inevitably rescued a few of the more fortunate ones from the *colonias* of the rural countryside or the gashouse districts of the large cities, understanding has become more rational, supported by knowledge and experience.

As the individual capacity of certain Mexicans has been developed and as their collective insight has become sharper and more meaningful, the attempt to stop the clock on them by some social groups has also taken on different forms. In Washington an Associated Farmers' lobby prevents the extension of social security, minimum wages, and other forms of protection to the Mexican rural workers. The same lobby inspires highly confidential agreements with the Mexican government for the recruitment of Nationals or *braceros*, whose major strategic function is to depress wages in California and Texas. Men who are highly sympathetic to the policies of the Associated Farmers sit securely in control of the machinery of the Inter-American System, thereby heading off constructive multilateral action to tackle the problems of inter-American labor migration at its roots.

On this and other aspects of the changing context of the problem of the Mexican minority in the United States, an abundant literature has developed. This literature runs all the way from the serious, compact, and sustained scholarship of Dr. Paul Taylor's studies to the articles, newspaper accounts, and books of the "protest" type. In between are the shelves of catalogued masters' and doctoral theses, government reports, case studies, and monographs numbering thousands of items. Bibliographically, at least, the Mexican minority has come of age.

II

But now the time has come for this minority to find the connection between the library card index and life. In the living and working conditions of this group certain problems have been isolated, defined, studied, and analyzed. Now they must be resolved. Which are most urgent?

Wages and income. The Mexican agricultural workers, as well as those who work in the manufacturing, transport, and service industries, fall into the lowest income class. The purchasing power of semi-stable agricultural workers in

California and Texas is comparable to that of the sharecroppers of Arkansas and Mississippi. As a group the Mexican workers have not been able to shake off the tradition of "cheap labor." Wage discrimination based on race has been uncovered by federal investigators even in the mining industry. In the absence of adequate wage and income studies of the group, the economic status of the Mexicans can be verified by simple observation of their community life. Slum housing, child labor, inadequate food, school absenteeism, indebtedness, unpaved streets, and the almost total absence of decent recreational facilities for the whole family immediately type the average Mexican community.

Employment. In the urban centers, the Mexican still finds barriers to the better-paid jobs. In industry individual skill is not infrequently discounted because of color. Employers in the service industries, where "the customer is always right," yield to prejudice and close certain avenues of economic advancement to dark-skinned citizens of Mexican ancestry. In agriculture the employment situation is somewhat less subtly arranged. The Mexican field workers, by and large, are dependent on contractors, whose controls of the total social life of the group are all-pervading. These contractors are the bridge improvised by the boss-culture of the employers and the servant-culture of the workers. The labor power that passes back and forth over that bridge pays a heavy toll in the form of petty larceny, short-weighing, usury, wage competition, rent gouging, company-store profits, alcoholism, and other types of catering to starved human needs. Even where the contractor happens to be a decent fellow, or where the corporation ranchers go into the labor market themselves, the Mexican farm worker fares little better. He may expect, as he has found in California, that the corporate interests will move into the machinery of farm-employment placement, through which, in part, the labor market can be kept in a profitable state of over-supply.

Foreign labor. Since 1942 a new element has been added to the wage and employment situation of the Mexican farm workers in the United States. This is the recruitment of *braceros* or Mexican Nationals, through agreements between the government of Mexico and the United States. These agreements were originally signed as a wartime measure, but they have been continued under the insistent pressure of the agricultural employers' associations who were looking for a counterpoise to the wage demands of Mexican workers long resident in this country.

Stripped of technicalities, the recruitment of Nationals is a new phase of the old quest for sources of low-cost, inexperienced, unorganized mass labor power. The original intention of the agreements as understood by some of their early advocates—the protection of wage and living standards as well as civil rights of imported workers and domestic labor in time of great national stress—has been sidetracked[.] Instead, there is now the concept of "task forces" of Mexican Nationals, maneuvered in divisions of 5,000 or more, and assigned to duty in any state of the Union where local Mexicans, Negroes, Filipinos, and Anglo-American whites threaten to organize or ask for higher wages.

The negotiation of these agreements, practically behind closed doors, and the determination of the conditions of such employment by self-appointed arbiters in Washington and Mexico City, establish a form of international economic government practiced without the consent of the governed—in this case the millions of agricultural workers whose wages and standards are immediately affected by such agreements. Relief from this kind of misgovernment has not yet been found by the Mexican workers in the United States, either through Washington officialdom or through the present administration in Mexico City.

Inter-American standards. Since the wartime *bracero* agreements have been repeatedly hailed as a shining example of the Good Neighbor policy in action, their essential function and results in peacetime must be pointed out to be a glaring violation of the spirit of that policy. This is indeed the opinion of the former Secretary of Foreign Affairs of Mexico, Jaime Torres Bodet, stated publicly in October 1948.

By all the standards for decent living and working conditions laid down in the Chapultepec Conference and later in the Inter-American Conference of Bogotá, the agreements have been an economic Trojan horse, an administrative subterfuge, and a long-run political boomerang. Here was an area in which the Inter American System, through the Pan American Union, could have taken over administrative responsibility on a truly multilateral representative basis. These agreements could have been drawn up with the participation of legitimate trade-union representatives. They could have been administered without yielding to special interests or political expediency. But, as it has turned out, the Pan American Union, which the workers support directly through public funds appropriated from taxes, has proved an utterly useless instrument for the maintenance of inter-American standards of work and living. In public affairs the misuse of a symbol must be challenged as promptly and as decisively as the subversion of a human right or a constitutional liberty. In this case, the kidnapping of the Good Neighbor symbolism by those who have shut the door of the House of the Americas on the workers is something to which the organized Mexican workers in the United States will have to give special attention.

Illegal labor. There is also the widespread exploitation of Mexican workers brought to this country illegally. These so-called wetbacks (*see Hart Stilwell's "The Wetback Tide," earlier in these pages*) number probably not less than 60,000 in southern Texas alone. In some border areas—Imperial Valley, Brownsville, El Paso—the bulk of the unskilled farm labor is done by these people. In the San

Joaquin Valley between Bakersfield and Modesto there are probably not less than 20,000 illegals. People who talk about labor pools could well describe these reservoirs of bootleg manpower as labor quicksands, for in them all efforts to raise income for the agricultural worker flounder.

Up to the present, the burden of blame and punishment for violation of the immigration laws of the United States falls on the wetback himself. He pays the penalty in the low wages he must accept, the mistreatment he must put up with, the constant fear of arrest, the loss of wages if he is picked up, and the hostility of the local Mexican community. That he is a symptom of a basic maladjustment in the economies of the two countries and a victim of the feebleness of inter-American standards is not generally recognized. Moreover, it is not only the bootleg contractor and the grapevine headhunter who paves the way for the wetback. In a sense he is forced to seek better conditions north of the border by the slow but relentless pressure of United States' agricultural, financial, and oil corporate interests on the entire economic and social evolution of the Mexican nation. Inflation, rising utility rates, the agrarian stalemate, and the flank attack on oil expropriation are some of the major causes of the persistent exodus of Mexican workers.

Racial tension. The Mexicans, by tradition and custom, are a racially tolerant group. The acute sense of personal dignity, a Spanish legacy, strengthens the notion that no man should be judged according to his color or his race. Normally, Mexican communities in the United States have preserved remarkably well this valuable cultural trait.

But the operation of the present wage system of contracting and employment and the strategic use by corporation agriculture of race blocs to maintain and encourage racial jealousies as a means to competitive wage bidding, is injecting bad blood into normal racial tolerance. Today there is emotional dynamite lying around loose between Mexican local workers and Mexican Nationals, between Mexican Nationals and Mexican illegals—not to mention the possibilities for racial misunderstanding between Mexicans on the one hand and Filipinos, Negroes, and white Anglo-Americans on the other. Fortunately, this encouragement of racial antagonism is being held in check by the responsible leaders of all these racial groups. But for how long? Will their influence be strong enough to counteract the effects of prolonged unemployment?

Discrimination. In many communities Mexicans are still excluded from parks, from motion picture theatres, from swimming pools, and from other public places. Certain neighborhoods exclude Mexicans, however acceptable they may be culturally and professionally. There are still schools for Mexican children separate from those maintained for "white" children. In some important towns Mexicans do not patronize certain barber shops or stores. There are no "Keep out" signs, but instead of having a pleasant greeting for Mexican customers "they make one a bad face," as the saying goes. This type of social exclusion has been responsible for a good deal of the northward migration of Mexican workers and their families. Like the Negroes of the Deep South, the Mexicans have sought the more friendly towns and cities of central and northern California, Colorado, Wyoming, Indiana, and Ohio, where prejudice does not make a specific target out of them.

Closely tied to this problem is that of segregation. The location of the hundreds of Mexican colonies—invariably marked by the railroad tracks, cactus patch, city dump, and employment bureau signs—is in itself one huge, ubiquitous case of segregation.

Housing. This leads directly to the problem of housing, typically resolved by the Mexican workers in their patchwork neighborhoods commonly called *colonias.* Usually lying outside the corporate limits of the towns and cities to which they are attached, these neighborhoods cling to the surrounding countryside like gray desiccated barnacles, from which some unseen inexorable hand constantly squeezes the vital humors and amenities of community living.

A trip through one of these *colonias* is easy to make. Any motorist traveling along US 99—California's Main Street, as it has been called—can see these typical California rural slums from the windows of his car. From the upper stories of the better hotels in Fresno, Modesto, Sacramento, or Bakersfield, good views can be obtained of shack rows, tent settlements, and privy subdivisions occupied by Mexican families. In the Shafter colony of Mexican agricultural workers the stench from backyard toilets in summer is intolerable. In the heart of the Mexican colony of Bakersfield, young children play barefoot in sewer water backed up by winter rains. The *colonias* rarely are taken into account in public-housing projects. They have become normal sights. But public agencies and social workers know that these areas are foci of disease. On the tuberculosis maps the black dots are heaviest in the Mexican colony.

Education. The educational problems of the Mexican minority are of two basic types—the extension of educational opportunities to the young, and the creation of adult education programs adapted to the needs of these communities. So far as the children are concerned, education and child labor are waging, now as in past years, a bitter struggle for the young mind. The tent schools of San Luis Obispo County in California are better than what most counties in that state provide for the children of wandering Mexican pickers. But they are also mute reminders of the inability of local, county, state, and federal authorities to provide these young American citizens with decent facilities for learning.

The adolescent and college-age Mexicans today represent a reservoir of possibilities for leadership that has not been recognized. Hundreds of young men and women who have somehow survived the attrition of the crops and the economic pressure on the home and have finished high school can go no further. They represent what the American way of life can do at its best, even against the underlying resistance of finance farming, the international traffic in low living standards, and the other complexities of the boss culture.

Civil liberties. The degree of enjoyment of civil liberties and constitutional rights varies with the nature of sub-groups within the Mexican minority. Lowest in the scale are the wetbacks, the illegals, for whom there are no rights. Next come the Nationals, whose rights are defined by contract and occasionally enforced by a weak bureaucracy of United States and Mexican officials. Then there are the long-resident Mexicans who have never become citizens. They are reluctant to demand protection or to insist on their constitutional prerogatives because their status, too, is vulnerable.

The Mexicans have probably not missed any of the forms of mistreatment and violation of civil liberties that have been visited on the other minority groups in American life. Thus far, however, they have failed to develop strong institutional resistance to such invasions.

Community relations. The relationship between the Mexican minority and the dominant elements has generally been a punitive-inquisitorial one on the part of the latter. It is interesting to note how the Mexicans shrink from contact with even those agencies of the dominant group that are intended to "do good."

These agencies too often approach the Mexican client with a questionnaire in hand. Being questioned, for the Mexican worker, has too often been but the first step toward being arrested. Hence the reluctance of the Mexicans to ask for relief, to apply for medical assistance, or to have any truck with the formidable apparatus of any federal agency. The machinery of government, to the Mexican, has been something to avoid. It must be met only when it comes at one aggressively in the war dress of a cop. What lies across the railroad tracks can be left well enough alone.

But the dominant community is there. And so is the Mexican *colonia.* What adjustment there is has been worked out by the contractors on the economic level, by the survival of patriotic and cultural traditions that have worn thin, and by a silent skepticism toward the questionnaire-state that lies across the tracks and runs the show.

Rural and urban relations. Many important Mexican communities lie in the heart of metropolitan areas. In Los Angeles, Chicago, and San Antonio they have often been engulfed, sometimes bulldozed out of old quarters to make way for swank subdivisions or modern highways. Mexican centers of this type play a multiple role. They are winter havens for the migrant workers that criss-cross the land in spring and summer. They provide a stepping-stone from farm to industrial employment. They bring the young people into closer and more intense contact with the dominant culture. Here the rural attitude dissolves into an urban resentment and a mental confusion created by the economic and social conditions which face all city workers. One result, for the Mexicans, has been the separation of the urban from the rural groups, so that the full force of the Mexican community has never been brought to bear on the problems they have in common. The urban Mexican has never reached, as has the urban Negro, toward the rural Mexican so that both could improve their status. This gap is one that has not been sufficiently noticed by Mexicans themselves or by non-Mexicans who have attempted to work with the group.

Political impotence. From what has been said, it is not surprising to find that the Mexicans are a political nonentity in the United States. Though many thousands of them are citizens by birth or naturalization, they keep clear of political obligations and therefore do not take advantage of political opportunities. There are counties in the Southwest where the Mexicans could theoretically swing the results of an election if they registered and voted. But too often they do not. This in turn means that state and federal legislation rarely takes them into account. Even in municipal affairs it is uncommon to find spokesmen for the Mexican. Therefore all pleas to the state governor, the President of the United States, the legislature or Congress must be based on considerations of high human senti-ment. In the American political system, however, such sentiments have always been found by precinct organization and votes in the ballot box.

Trade-union organization. Perhaps the most serious weakness, and by no means the least important of the problems of the Mexicans in the United States, is their lack of economic organization.

The Mexican workers, both in industry and agriculture, have given sufficient proof of their understanding of solidarity among workers. They have shown that they can take every form of violence which vigilantism in this country has been able to devise. Mexican workers in Imperial, Salinas, and Orange have sustained industrial disputes single-handed against the combined police, political, and propaganda resources of finance-farming and corporation ranching. But as yet they have not solved the problem of union organization. The attempt to set up separate unions on racial lines has been disastrous. There is a language barrier. The labor movement itself until recently has taken a somewhat benevolent interest rather than an active organizational concern in Mexican workers.

In the field of agriculture, there are still other difficulties. There is the myth that farm workers are unorganizable and Mexican farm workers twice so. Farm wages are so low that the monthly union dues seem a heavy tax on the workers. There are long periods of unemployment when union obligations can be met only at considerable sacrifice. A trade-union of farm workers must face and meet assaults on its security ranging from local irritation, through state legislative attacks, and up to international maneuvers to swamp local living and working standards.

Nevertheless, the problem of union organization must be solved. The economic education of the Mexican worker is much more advanced than his cultural assimilation or his political experience. The union is his most vital point of contact with the larger community.

III

Here, broadly speaking, is the situation. Left to themselves, the Mexicans in the United States will undoubtedly continue to devise their own defenses against pressures of the kind I have described.

But what distinguishes the present moment is the growing feeling, in and out of the Mexican group, that future adjustment does not have to be left to laissez-faire, that it can be accomplished much more intelligently through widespread information about the group among Americans generally, through mutual counsel, planning, and concerted democratic action on the part of all those concerned with bringing all elements of the American population into participating partnership in American life.

To help give some direction to that feeling, or at least to outline an agenda for discussion, I offer the following suggestions:

The postwar economic relations of the United States with Mexico must be examined to determine whether they have strengthened or weakened the possibilities for democratic control of the human and natural resources of that country. The signs of the last ten years all too plainly point to the taming of the Mexican Revolution and the shelving of its fundamental economic reforms which so displeased and alarmed foreign corporate interests. Until Mexico can offer a far larger degree of economic security to its people, thousands of them will seek relief by migrating over the border, legally or illegally. Thus it becomes of primary importance to determine whether the economic policy of the United States is fostering or hampering the chances for creating a Mexico able to employ, feed, house, clothe, and educate its workers on a rising standard of living. To ignore this basic premise is to overlook the roots of the problem.

It must be established as public policy in this country that no agreements for the recruitment of workers in Mexico for employment in the United States are to be made without participation by the legitimate representatives of the trade-unions representing the workers. Specifically, this means that notice should be served on the Department of State, the United States Employment Service, the Immigration and Naturalization Service, the Department of Labor, and the Department of Agriculture that the time for confidential one-sided negotiations, based on proposals representing the views of finance-farming only, is over. In their place there should be tri-partite negotiations with full public hearings and adequate safeguards for the maintenance of living and working standards, the enforcement of the individual work contracts, and the protection of the organizational and collective bargaining rights of both the Mexican and United States workers affected.

The United States immigration law should be amended to make it a felony to transport, harbor, conceal, or employ an alien who is in this country illegally. When such aliens are picked up for deportation, their earned wages should be paid by the employer before they are returned home. The burden of responsibility should be placed by law where it belongs—on those who profit from the poverty and need that drives the wetbacks into illegal exile.

Likewise the authority of the Attorney General of the United States to admit or exclude certain types of labor under present legislation should be revised. At the present time this authority is the only legal ground on which the present drive of corporation farmers in California to beat down agricultural wages can be even remotely justified. It is a discretionary power which, because it affects vitally the lives of hundreds of thousands of people, should be brought within the immediate influence of public opinion and the frequent review of the legislative branch of the national government.

FEPC [Fair Employment Practices Commission] legislation, federal and state, should be fostered and specific efforts made to bring the Mexican minority within its purview. This should include much more attention to job discrimination against this particular group of the nation than has heretofore been given.

Legislative action and court action against rank practices of discrimination should continue. The recent successes achieved with regard to the elimination of double-standard education point the way. Many discriminatory practices against citizens of Mexican ancestry can and will yield to legislative remedies.

Federal agencies, especially the Department of Justice, can be better equipped to deal with violations of civil liberties involving Mexicans than they are at present. Trained Mexican American citizens are available for positions in these agencies to see to it that the Mexican minority is fully advised of its rights under law and to provide the legal means for assuring the enjoyment of those rights. Particular attention should be given in these agencies to the postwar experience of ex-servicemen of Mexican ancestry in relation to employment, government assistance, and other services to which the GI is entitled, irrespective of color or race.

The drive in Congress to include agricultural workers in the federal minimum wage law should be sustained. Such inclusion would immediately put a floor under the feet and a roof over the heads of thousands of Mexican families who work on the land.

Similarly the effort to include farm workers in the social-security system should be carried to a successful conclusion.

The facts on housing in the Mexican colonies should be laid before federal and state housing agencies and legal provision made for the correction of this blight.

Federal and state agencies likewise should work out, and legislative bodies approve, joint programs for the protection of the educational rights of the children of migrant farm workers.

State employment bureaus should be re-examined and administrative changes made to bring these public agencies as much in line with the needs of the farm workers as they are now in line with the interests of corporation farming.

Legislative action should also be mapped looking to the more stringent regulation of contractors who exploit the workers on the side.

An analysis should be made by competent persons of the relationship of social-welfare and public-service agencies with the Mexican minority group. This analysis should work from within the group outward, rather than from outside the group toward it. Its purpose would be to isolate and overcome the barriers that stand between the various community services and facilities that exist today and the Mexican group.

Service scholarships should be created, from public funds or otherwise, for the further training of promising young men and women of Mexican ancestry in the various branches of public welfare.

Above all, union organization must go on until it has brought the Mexican workers fully into the stream of the American labor movement.

To develop the details of such a broad program, and to keep it under constant adjustment to the needs of the Mexican minority, new functions should be given existing agencies and certain new agencies created:

The Pan American Union should be given research and administrative functions with regard to the negotiation of inter-American labor agreements, which should be withdrawn from the internal politics of governments participating in them. If a major reform in the Organization of American States is required to accomplish this, let such a reform come. It is long overdue.

Trade-union organization programs should extend beyond immediate economic aims to those dealing with the elimination of maladjustments between the Mexican minority and the larger community.

A Federal Advisory Council on Human and Civil Rights should be created with representation of the Mexican group. This council should have adequate informational facilities and should primarily concern itself with inclusive research on the major problems that affect the conditions of life and work of the minority groups.

State committees on human relations should be created where they do not already exist.

If they can be financed, there should be a series of conferences on the problems of Mexican Americans held during the next year in the three areas centering around Los Angeles, Chicago, and San Antonio, in which experienced leaders from the Mexican communities as well as representatives from other minority groups and private and public organizations working actively in the field of human relations and civil rights should come together to exchange information and extend mutual support and discuss specifically the organization of Mexican Americans for improvement of their status.

The matter of a national organization of or for Mexican Americans is not a simple one. The National Association for the Advancement of Colored People and the Japanese American Citizens League come immediately to mind. But the example of the NAACP in the fight for Negro rights is not wholly applicable, for Negroes in America have had the advantage of a cultural base which the Mexicans who have migrated here do not have. While for the most part they have been kept outside the main American cultural milieu, Mexicans in this country have undergone considerable cultural dilution—language, values, music, press, education—which is everywhere to be seen. This dilution is not altogether deplorable; it represents, in my view, an opportunity to move into synthesis with the rest of the American culture eventually. Again, there is the important problem of language. The higher one goes toward national organization, the greater the preference of Mexican Americans to express themselves in English and to use symbols that mean something only to English-speaking people. Reverse the direction and one finds the more intense symbolism and greater use of Spanish at the grass roots. This weakens both the organizational strength and the emotional strands upon which organization depends.

There should probably be a national body whose main concern is the Mexican American minority, but I am convinced it cannot be created by adopting ready-made patterns. I think it possible that joint committees of Mexican Americans and other minority groups can be organized locally for co-operation on issues which affect any or all members of those minorities. Perhaps such groups should decide whether the Mexican element should then set up separate local organizations to take advantage of strong minority consciousness where it exists, and then whether the Mexican Americans should move on separately toward a national organization of their own.

Whatever the decision on whether or not to push for a national organization, I am convinced of two things. One is the necessity for trade-union organization. Nothing that is done must interfere with this; everything that is done must stimulate and encourage the Mexican Americans to organize for their economic defense. This is the only way a self-sustaining base for a broad program on the whole front of the problems which face them can be created. Second, the international aspects of the matter can and should be used much more forcibly and persistently than in the past. By this I mean that the individuals and organizations who are violating every tenet of the Good Neighbor policy in the flesh and spirit of the Mexicans of the borderlands should be openly challenged and called to account. Here, I feel, is one important channel for the non-Mexicans to enter realistically the area of democratic international relations.

CALIFORNIA THE UNCOMMONWEALTH

Excerpt from Ernesto Galarza, *Merchants of Labor: The Mexican Bracero Story; An Account of Time Managed Migration of Mexican Farm Workers in California, 1942–1960* (Santa Barbara, Calif.: McNally and Loftin, 1964).

Though *Merchants of Labor: The Mexican Bracero Story* was originally self-published in 1964, the demand far exceeded Galarza's printing capacity, and he contracted with McNally and Loftin Publishing for a second printing that same year. An updated third edition was produced and released by the publishing company in 1978.

This chapter outlines the political economy and historical development of corporate agriculture in California. Galarza masterfully weaves a narrative that refers to historical and contemporary events to demonstrate how agribusiness built an industry of labor exploitation with the use of legal structures.

Notable life events during this era:

- 1963–1964: Galarza is chief counsel in the investigation of the tragedy that took place in Chualar, California. There, while laborers were being transported from the field to a bracero labor camp, an accident took place in 1963 that claimed the lives of thirty-two braceros; an additional twenty-seven were injured. He is appointed to this position by Congressman Adam Clayton Powell, chair of the House Committee on Education and Labor. Powell, the first African American to be elected to Congress in New York, was a champion of civil rights and the rights of workers.
- 1964: The Bracero Program comes to an end after existing for twenty-two years and contracting millions of Mexican men to labor in U.S. agribusiness. Galarza aggressively campaigned to end this program through action research, testimony, and direct organizing.

California was given its name by the Spanish writer, Rodrigues de Montalvo, early in the 16th century. He wrote of a fabled island inhabited only by women who waited somewhere in the imagination of chivalry for the coming of the *conquistador*. Three centuries of exploration finally brought soldiers and priests to the real California—Alta, a massive addition to the colonial empire bordering the Pacific for a thousand miles; and Baja, a stringy peninsula dangling off the west coast of New Spain.

California remained unsettled and undefended. While feudalism marked time south of the Rio Grande, the Americans marched on north of it. As their traders and scouts explored the continent to the water's edge they thought of possibilities other than those of commerce. William Shaler, a Yankee skipper, wrote in 1808 after a business voyage to the Pacific Coast: "The conquest of this country would be absolutely nothing. It would fall without an utterance to the most inconsequential force." And it did. The American armed forces landed in Monterey Bay in July, 1846, occupied the town, raised their flag and proclaimed California a part of the United States.

About a third of the area they annexed was embraced in the great Central Valley. This unbroken alluvial plain spread from the Tehachapi range in the south to the foot of Mount Shasta in the north. The Sierra Nevada raised a snowcapped windbreak against the winter winds from the east, while the coast ranges bowed low to give passage to the beneficent Pacific rains. The valley was nearly 400 miles long and 100 miles wide. More than a dozen rivers—the American, Mokolumne, San Joaquin, Kings, Kern and others—scoured the mountains and laid deep sedimentary deposits on the floor of the elliptical bowl, endowing it with a solid underfooting of rich earth.

To the south and west of California's Big Dish a fringe of smaller valleys, pocketed by the hills, added to the agricultural potential of the state, extending the range and variety of its soils and climate. Farming was possible somewhere almost throughout the year. The Americans soon discovered to their great delight and profit that the growing season in many parts exceeded 240 days. In the level deserts, once water was brought to them, plants could be cultivated and their fruits harvested throughout the year.

The Spanish kings had given away this land to their deserving subjects in abundant lots. Rancho San Antonio, whose boundaries included the land on which the cities of Berkeley, Oakland and Alameda were to rise, was given in 1820 to Sergeant Luis Peralta, a veteran of the DeAnza expedition of 1776. Jose de la Guerra's four ranches in Santa Barbara totaled more than 215,000 acres. Over 400 grants were issued under Mexican rule between 1833 and 1846 for small tracts of 4,000 acres and large ones of 300,000. In 1848 something like 8,000,000 acres were held by 800 *rancheros*, who called their little empires by names holy, hopeful, mocking or vulgar—Las Virgenes (The Virgins), Buena Vista (Pleasant View), Salsipuedes (Get Out if You Can), Las Pulgas (The Fleas).

These generous portions of real estate passed into the hands of practical, ambitious men who had only a limited interest in the past. The rancho way of life, so far as the earth and its uses were concerned, died fast. Its memory remained embalmed only in romance—the yearly pageants of Santa Barbara, the cool seclusion of the missions, the musical place names of cities and resorts, and the schmaltzy revival of bandit tales like those of Joaquin Murrieta and Tiburcio Vasquez.

The new land plungers and speculators impressed on California its characteristic of land ownership on a large scale. Men like Henry Miller and William G. Chapman appreciated two things about the *ranchero*: that he had owned the earth in a big way and that it was not too difficult to separate him from it by force, cunning and politics. They appropriated the most and the best of the public domain. Six operators, including the well-known Chapman, Miller and Lux, laid out and made good their claims to 1,250,000 acres.

Between the speculators and the railroad companies, which received more than eleven million acres of real property in grants, practically all of the public domain in the state was absorbed. The prior rights they held, the volume of capital they controlled and the political influence they enjoyed gave them the commanding lead in California agriculture which they never lost. From them descended such enterprises as the Kern County Land Company, organized in 1874. In 1883 the Newhall-Saugus Land Company put into modern production a tract of several thousand acres in Los Angeles County. Coming much later but in no wise handicapped for that reason[,] Joseph DiGiorgio in 1919 staked out a farm of over 10,000 acres in Kern County, southeast of Bakersfield. The perimeter of this ranch, which was one in a chain of large holdings running from the Imperial desert to the upper Sacramento Valley, measured nineteen miles. These "places," like the El Solyo Ranch and the orchards of the California Packing Corporation, became the hubs of resources, production and influence. In 1889 the larger commercial farms were already showing what such advantages were worth. One-sixth of the farms in the state produced slightly more than two-thirds of the crops, by value.

Corporate commercial agriculture abandoned the narrow base on which the farm economy had rested in the two previous stages of stock raising and grain production. The possibilities were grasped of the single cash crop produced with hired labor at relatively high cost in the expectation of large profits. This became the way of life. Farming, taking the state as a whole, developed into a variety fair of domestic staples and exotic delicacies—wheat, corn, beets, Chilean clover, Ararat olives, Andalusian oranges, French prunes and Mexican avocados.

The speedy success of commercial farming settled these important matters: (a) It consigned the family farm to a diminishing place in the economic scheme of things; (b) it bound the industry to the mass markets; and (c) it made harvesting dependent on high seasonal peaks of hand labor.

It had been expected that the completion of the railroads would bring an influx of settlers who would work the land in small holdings. This migration, so it was supposed, would break up the large estates. Land squatting was for many years the means by which it was sought to bring this about, but squatting was bitterly fought by those who had already tightened their hold on the shattered heritage of the *rancheros*. American agrarianism of the eastern variety did not succeed either in fighting or buying its way into a respectable partnership, much less a leading position, in the basic economy.

In this new economy individual subsistence or local self-sufficiency had no place. These were the traits of the backward *hacienda* system, with its traditional plaza fairs, its barter for use, its petty bargaining, its niggardly balancing of limited production and still more limited desires. Commercial farming on a technological basis required the mass market already being provided by industrial areas at home and abroad. The farm wealth with which California began to burst after the gold boom flattened demanded proportionate outlets in national and international consumption.

Technology was making the necessary connections. The ice-making machine was invented in 1851 and the refrigerated freight car in 1868. A year later the Central Pacific Railroad was finished and in less than twenty years entire freight trains with iced produce were moving over the Sierras toward the great common market of the east. The threat to the unity of this market was turned back by the victory of the North in the Civil War. The defeat of the plantation system with its chattel slavery secured for industrial agriculture an open market for its cash crops as broad, wide and rich as the nation itself.

The dependence on seasonal farm labor in numbers out of all proportion to the year-round work force became a characteristic of commercial agriculture. This necessity could diminish only as mechanization was able to take over the harvest tasks of picking, cutting, pulling, topping, sorting, sacking or boxing; and mechanization was slow in adapting itself to many of these tasks. The result was a highly characteristic curve of demand for seasonal labor with sharp peaks and long depressions between. This pattern became fixed. Technology improved, but production also expanded, and the specialized croppers of California seemingly could never match their everlasting manpower shortages at harvest time. In 1946 the figures for Kern and Fresno counties and for the state recapitulated the trend of decades. Kern County needed 1,750 seasonal and transient workers in March and 15,880 in November. Fresno County had work for 250 seasonals in April and for 32,710 in September. For the state as a whole the extremes of seasonal hiring in the fields ran from 68,000 in March to 244,880 in September.

This peculiar range of job opportunities required adult workers whose level of living was on a par with the limited income that they could make in four or five months of employment. Between the harvests such workers were expected to drift back to the "skid rows," the shanty towns and the grubby settlements that ringed many cities. This was the pulse beat of work and life for the California casual, and it had been familiar so long that farmers came to regard it as "one of the natural laws of economics."

What commercial agriculture had to offer its seasonal laborers in the way of a living was determined by the employers. These terms seemed attractive to Mexico's poor. Indeed, in the light of the conditions they faced at home, they were enticing. They stimulated the current of migration that set in before the close of the Diaz regime and rose by leaps thereafter.

MIGRATION BY DRIFT

The Treaty of Guadalupe-Hidalgo of 1848 left between the two countries a barrier to migration consisting of a desert 400 miles wide. From the south the Mexican central plateau slopes into the Rio Grande Valley over rugged terrain through which neither rivers nor pleasant prairies make passage convenient. Northwestward the Sierra Madre Occidental encloses the nation, its ranges backstopped by badlands of mesquite and sand. The narrow strip of coastal plain between Mazatlán and Guaymas, a possible migrant route, also is sealed at the northern end by the desert. Along its length population was sparse and roads non-existent. Passage was barred by hostile tribes and the hot climate was uninviting to the dwellers of the temperate uplands.

Thus the two nations remained back-to-back until Porfirio Diaz and foreign capital opened pathways through these barriers. Between 1880 and 1910 nearly 15,000 miles of railways were constructed to carry gold, silver, copper, lead and other minerals abroad. Some of these export routes connected the mines of Durango, Zacatecas, Chihuahua and Sonora with the American terminals of Eagle Pass, El Paso, Douglas and Nogales, which became the gateways as well for the export of livestock, petroleum and agricultural products.

The freight trains that carried this traffic could not avoid disturbing the sluggish feudalism through which they rumbled. Railroading competed for the indentured peons who were often ransomed from the *haciendas* to work as track hands. Construction camps sprang up along the right-of-way in a lengthening chain of outposts along which ex-miners as well as ex-peons moved. The American smelters lying just north of the border drew upon these trickles of manpower for the dirty work of handling the ores, creating permanent settlements where the laborers could work, pause, learn a few English words and weigh their chances for better living farther north. The progress of construction and transport quickened a sense of looseness, an awareness of the possibilities of movement, along their course. At its far end there was dollar work to be found, no more agree able than the menial tasks of the *hacienda*, but payable in hard currency that outmatched the *peso* two to one.

As civil war spread over the republic after 1911 a major exodus from the countryside began. Landowners fled to the large cities, principally the capital, followed by hundreds of thousands of refugees who could find no work. This was one of the two great shifts that were to change radically the population patterns, until then overwhelmingly rural. The other current was in the direction of the United States, now accessible by rail. It moved in the dilapidated coaches with which the Mexican lines had been equipped by their foreign builders, in cabooses fitted with scant privacy, on engine tenders and on flat cars for the steerage trade. "*A la capital o al norte*" (to Mexico City or to the border) became the alternatives for the refugees from the cross-fires of revolution.

The dream of a few became a reality for hundreds of thousands. In 1902 migration to Texas of Mexican farm laborers was sizable enough to attract national attention. According to a contemporary report, 400 men left one community in Zacatecas to seek work north of the Rio Grande. In June of the following year 672 *braceros* passed through Ciudad Juarez on their way over the border and in February 1910 the number was 2,380. The total number of migrants reported at points of exit between Ciudad Juarez and Matamoros was 1,000 per month. In the last ten years of the 19th century 971 Mexicans were reported as immigrants to the United States. In the first decade of the 20th, more than 49,000 were admitted.

The Liberal Party of Mexico, which lighted the fuse under Diaz, declared in 1906 that "spoliation and tyranny" had brought about "the depopulation of Mexico" as "thousands of our fellow countrymen have had to cross the border in flight." The Party promised that "all Mexicans residing abroad will be repatriated and given land that they may cultivate."

It was a feeble promise and it was made too late. Emigration increased steadily. Between 1911 and 1921 the number of legal entries to the United States rose to nearly 250,000. From 1921 to 1930 a peak was reached with a total of 459,287 persons, the admissions receding to 22,319 for the decade 1931–1940 as a consequence of the depression in the United States. During World War I immigration had been stimulated by a liberal interpretation of the law. The Department of Justice suspended the contract-labor prohibitions, head tax and illiteracy test.

As a result of these concessions during the fiscal year which ended June 30, 1919, over 20,000 Mexican workers were temporarily admitted, many for employment in California. Altogether 72,862 agricultural laborers entered the United States during the war and immediately after. Of these 21,400 were reported as deserters by the Department of Justice.

Combining the numbers of immigrants officially recorded by the Department of Justice with those who entered illegally, well over 1,000,000 Mexicans crossed the border between 1900 and 1940. They settled principally in southern Texas, Arizona and California. Census figures for 1940 showed that over a million and a half Mexicans resided in the borderlands and the more remote states into which they had scattered.

This massive trend enlarged on an unprecedented scale the population of the towns on the Mexican side of the frontier. Between 1940 and 1950 Tijuana's population increased from 16,846 to 59,117 and Mexicali's from 18,775 to 63,830. Matamoros had 15,699 residents at the beginning of this period, 43,830 at the end of it; Ciudad Juarez, 48,881 as compared with 121,903 in 1960. Taken together these border cities formed a labor pool secondary to the *colonias* of California and Texas.

The centers of population strung along both sides of the border constituted the great farm labor reservoir of the southwest. Within the borderlands[,] recruiting, transportation, border crossing and contractor hiring kept the Mexican supply attuned to American demand. From the south the reservoir was continuously replenished by new arrivals, among them the seasonal cotton pickers who remained in the Rio Grande Valley after the harvest. On its northern front it was constantly depleted as the older migrants pushed on to get away from the lower wages and the harsh competitiveness of the areas nearer Mexico. It was here that the Wetbacks exerted the greatest pressure, spreading until they were to be found throughout California and in many central and eastern states.

The conditions for the development of the Wetback traffic were the following: the concentration of workers in large numbers and in dire need immediately south of the border; facilities to enter and remain in the United States for the duration of the job; the offer of employment by American farmers; the absence of criminal penalties for hiring persons who had entered the country clandestinely; the protective coloration offered by the Mexican *colonias*; the services of Mexican intermediaries; and a tolerant or indifferent public opinion.

Wages, of course, played an important part in stimulating the flow of illegal labor. However low they might seem by American standards they were more than attractive by Mexican ones. In the 1940s some farmers paid 60 cents a day without board or housing. Ten years later an official of the U.S. Department of

Labor noted that in the lower Rio Grande Wetbacks could be hired for 15 cents an hour, which was half the wage commonly demanded by resident local labor. In California wage rates in general were affected by what a Wetback would work for. He was glad to accept 40 cents an hour in the Imperial Valley as late as 1954. "The Wetback," Department of Justice agents reported, "was at the mercy of the employers in terms of wages and housing. He could be paid practically any wage his employer might choose."

Farmers found the Wetbacks as anxious to please as they were willing to endure. From among them the employer selected the more able workers for tasks requiring skill, such as irrigating or tractor driving. They became differentiated from the common run of illegals, serving in specialized operations and becoming stable, regular employees. The employer would make unusual efforts to keep them and to arrange for their return if by chance they were picked up by the Border Patrol. Many of these "specials," as they were called, eventually obtained immigration visas with the assistance of their employers. There are no reliable data on this class of farm laborers any more than there are on Wetbacks in general but it can be supposed that they numbered between 6,000 and 8,000 throughout California before the *bracero* program got under way in 1942.

Among the Wetbacks there were not only peasants but also miners, bricklayers, truck drivers, weavers, chauffeurs and other skilled craftsmen. They were often enticed from the fields by canners, processors and packers at wage rates which were likewise lower than those for which local semi-skilled labor could be obtained. This transition was made easier by the fact that often packing was done in the fields, where men could be shifted without regard for job classifications or wage differentials. The transfer of Wetbacks from fields to town was a natural one, although attended by greater risks of arrest and deportation.

Through these higher level employments many a Wetback discovered more promising chances to improve his lot. In the fruit and vegetable packing sheds he obtained a social security card, something which he had not been able to secure as a menial field hand. This, and the higher pay, encouraged him to seek work beyond the sheds, a search in which he was encouraged by nonagricultural employers who were themselves looking for men willing to accept lower than standard wages. Thus the Wetback soon was to be found in restaurants, hotels, laundries, garages, building construction, domestic service, mills, brick factories and railway maintenance. In short, the Wetback, growing in numbers and experience, tended to show all the adaptive powers of a capable human being, useful and exploitable in a variety of trades and occupations.

The Wetback infiltration was geographic as well as occupational. Its base was the borderlands and its range the central and northern counties of California, where the pay was higher and the climate more agreeable. Those who were not transplanted thither by labor traffickers made their own way, starting at dusk from their hideaways in the Imperial Valley to avoid the blistering sun of the desert. The way of the Wetbacks led around the Salton Sea and by the main irrigation canals, along which they could often be seen, trudging in single file through the twilight, the shadowy figures of an animated frieze framed by dusty tamarisks and purple mountains. From Imperial and San Diego the illegals set out, sometimes in autos or trucks, paying for the ride as much as $100 deductible from future wages. They spread to the lettuce fields of Monterey, the orchards of San Joaquin and the beet fields of Yolo and Sacramento. The number of Wetbacks in the state during the harvest peak of 1952 was probably not under 60,000.

The stable portion of the Mexican population, the people who called themselves *locales*, was to be found in the rural and suburban *colonias*. By 1940 there were over 200 of these communities throughout the state. The largest of them was Belvedere Gardens and the adjacent Boyle Heights, dismal suburbs within the city limits of Los Angeles in which more than 200,000 Mexicans had settled. Others were hardly more than hamlets, like Cucamonga in the heart of the citrus country and Mendota, a huddle of tents and shanties midway on the west side of the Central Valley. Hardly a town of any size or pretensions—Delano, Hanford, Brawley, Sacramento, San Diego, Fresno—failed to acquire between 1900 and 1940 its Mexican *colonia* on the weathered side of the railroad tracks. In 1930 it was estimated that 28,000 foreign-born Mexicans were living in the Imperial Valley; 96,000 in Los Angeles County; 16,000 in Fresno; 14,000 in Ventura; 10,000 in Santa Barbara and 10,000 in Orange. The Spanish-speaking population of California was given as 416,000 persons in the census of 1940. The settlements in which they lived had a well-defined economic and social function. They were relatively stable labor pools into which recent arrivals from Mexico fitted easily.

The period from 1900 to 1940 was one of migration by drift, in contrast with the administered migration of the *bracero* that was to begin in 1942. It was a migration propelled by political turbulence in Mexico, channeled across the desert and brought into junior partnership with the capital that was ready to transform vast and barren lands to the uses of commercial agriculture. Legally or otherwise the migrants crossed the border, *palping* [feeling] their way, seeking new roots, guided and manipulated by turns through no design or plan. *Locales* they became after a time, resident farm laborers who became less desirable as they grew in understanding of the ways of an aggressive and powerful industry. Mingling with the Wetbacks in the *colonias* they were, on the whole, an ignored generation, subdued clusters of individuals rather than men and women in or progressing toward community.

The farm labor force of California which had been put together between 1860 and 1940 in racial layers consisted in its larger part of Mexicans who were easily molded to the established requirements and controls. In normal peace times it could do well enough without industry-wide planning. Although the system was slack and wasteful it clung to the methods of management characteristic of the labor pool.

THE POOLING OF FARM LABOR

Located on the western edge of the continent and on the eastern rim of the Pacific basin, California agriculture is strategically positioned with respect to the manpower stocks of China, Japan, the Philippines, the Mississippi Valley and Mexico. The industry, with its heavy and abrupt peak loads, had particular reason to "never forget" George Santayana's reminder "that among the raw materials of industry one of the most important is man." The harvest hands that were to be found in those areas were both raw and plentiful. They were recruited in a succession of ethnic waves that displaced one another.

The first to be brought in were the Chinese, initially for work on the railways and in the mines. As the gold boom passed and the transcontinental lines were completed—and as racial hostility mounted—the "coolies" moved into agriculture. In 1886, according to an estimate cited by Carey McWilliams, 30,000 Chinese worked as harvest hands typically grouped in gangs under a headman. The passage of the Chinese Exclusion Act prevented the continuous renewal of this source of labor[,] and California farmers, after unsuccessful experiments with southern Negroes and a premature look at the possibilities of Mexicans, turned to Japan.

The Japanese became an important factor in agriculture between 1890 and 1910, during which period their number in the United States increased from slightly over 2,000 to more than 72,000. They served a long apprenticeship in the truck farms of Monterey and San Joaquin, spreading gradually over the state. Being not only indefatigable wage laborers but skillful farmers as well, they leased and eventually owned land, managing it in their own right. In 1920 they were established in Fresno, Los Angeles and Imperial counties. By becoming more intractable as field laborers and more numerous as growers the Japanese, like the Chinese, became the target of bitter racial hostility. Japanese exclusion in turn became a rousing political issue and again farm employers had to look elsewhere for harvest hands.

The successors to the Japanese were the Filipinos, recruited in the Islands or from the surplus of plantation workers in Hawaii. In the mid-1920s they were arriving in California at the rate of more than 4,000 a year. By 1930 they represented a labor force of 25,000 single men, concentrated in the San Joaquin and Salinas valleys, where they became the base labor force in asparagus, lettuce, grapes and truck crops. Though they never equalled in numbers either the Chinese or Japanese, the Filipinos were no less important as competitors for farm work at the low end of the wage scale. Ill feeling brewed against the wiry, agile "boys" who moved about in tight crews, working faster and harder than was called for by a fair day's wages for a fair day's labor. Before 1930 riots against them broke out in Tulare, Watsonville, Stockton and Imperial. Once again, agriculture had touched the limits of another alien reservoir.

At about the same time, however, the ill wind that was dusting the plains of the lower Mississippi began to blow providently for agribusiness. The great trek of southern Americans, white and Negro, out of Oklahoma and Arkansas was beginning. Nearly 130,000 entered the state as farm workers, concentrating on the south end of the Central Valley and spilling over into Salinas and Imperial. Steinbeck found them in the canvas and tin can tenements of Weedpatch, Arvin, Strathmore and Cotton Road. Their arrival, according to Professor Walter Gold-schmidt, brought for the first time native white American families to "the army of cheap labor that is requisite for the continued functioning of the industrialized agriculture of California."

The continued expansion of commercial farming, racial antagonisms, the inevitable maturing of greenhorns into canny sellers of their labor, and the seepage of discontented and experienced workers out of the labor pool became the indicators of a perpetual shortage of agricultural manpower. Clearly not more than one generation of newcomers could be counted on to accept farm employment on any terms. The experience of a few years at the most was enough to convince them that they were worth more than they were getting. But unlike the skilled craftsmen in industry and the service trades, the alien farm hands were never able to organize their own labor market in order to bargain on relatively even terms. The world of labor was for them a pool into which they were dumped in large numbers; within which they were impounded by effective barriers of language, custom, and alienation; and from which they escaped only when racial antagonism dried up their jobs or competing industries offered them a way out.

The pool was conceived in practice, if not in theory, as an allocation to California of a portion of a self-renewing stock of raw labor. It sources were international—Kyoto, Canton, Manila, Oahu, Michoacán and the Ozarks. Selection at the point of supply was merely a matter of sorting out enough hands to fill the vacuum at the point of demand in Lodi, Tracy, Watsonville, Delano or Brawley.

The labor pool so constituted was supposed to be, ideally, frozen at the periphery and completely fluid at the center. It was the common resource of an entire industry, not of a single enterprise. No particular worker was committed to a given employer; and all employers, within the limits of a gentlemanly understanding concerning wages and other conditions, could dip into the pool. This was an important condition, for it made the immigrants the concern and responsibility of no one employer. What happened to them and how they lived, or what burdens they placed on the community in general, could in no way be held against the industry as a whole or any of its members individually. The pool at its best was insulated from the general labor market. American workers would not normally be willing to enter it; the immigrants could not easily leave it.

The basic function of the labor pool was to assure a surplus of manpower. Its effects were therapeutic as well as economic. Commercial farmers suffer from an occupational nervousness around harvest time that is inflicted on them by two unpredictable powers: the weather and the market. The ups and downs of temperature and price determine the difference between a successful "deal" and a disastrous one. A margin of extra harvest hands offered insurance in two respects. It guaranteed the gathering of the crop and, by keeping the supply rather than the demand side competitive, held wages down. Thus, the normal fever of a harvest "deal" was reduced.

The concept of the pool became another one of those "natural laws of economics" which are the theoretical stock-in-trade of agribusiness. William J. Monahan, a journalist who understood the theory, defined it with unusual candor as "a multilayer system of workers, including a bottom echelon of poorly paid harvest workers who have been used in seasonal labor in a mass employment technique." This bottom echelon was described as "an ample and fluid supply of labor" by the voice of commercial farming, the *Western Grower and Shipper*. The Farm Placement Service of the California Department of Employment shared this point of view. In the Department's Bulletin on the Stockton labor market for April 1951 it was stated that "there is a need for migratory workers to build up the dwindling labor pool in the area."

Labor recruiting associations were a natural outgrowth of the requirements of pool maintenance. It was early realized that among the joint interests of all commercial growers was the encouragement of favorable conditions for the labor supply. There was general agreement on what those conditions should be, for specialized crops affected by them presented the same difficulties of labor pricing, recruitment, management and control. The farm labor association emerged out of these circumstances.

Among the earliest of them was the Valley Fruit Growers Association of Fresno, which in 1917 brought together 3,000 growers "for the distribution of farm labor in the raisin districts to meet distress labor requirements." The Agricultural Labor Bureau of San Joaquin County was incorporated in 1926 to assist its grower members in obtaining labor. In the southern part of the state the Agricultural Producers Labor Committee was constituted to serve the needs of producers and packers of walnuts, avocados, oranges, lemons and miscellaneous vegetables. Wherever seasonal labor was a prime concern similar agencies were established. By 1946 there were 74 labor bureaus representing the interests of growers in every major crop in all the important production centers of California.

The procurement and distribution of seasonal workers was by no means the whole of the task which the labor bureaus set themselves. Equally vital was the stabilization of wages, which tended to rise in spite of the pool effects when workers stayed only through the peak of the picking, when they were pirated or when they presented more or less concerted demands for higher pay. The standardization of wage rates to meet such difficulties became a primary object of the labor bureau. In 1921 the Valley Fruit Growers of San Joaquin announced a uniform wage scale in grapes on which its members had agreed.

From the outset the Agricultural Labor Bureau considered it as one of its most important functions to obtain the consensus of its associates on picking rates, which were then published as the rates that would prevail. A representative of California cotton interests described the procedures as follows: "There is a custom . . . for farmers to gather together prior to harvest and discuss a uniform picking rate of wages. . . . After that scale has been arrived at . . . not only us but other financing agencies . . . assist them to conform to that." "The proliferation," wrote Lloyd H. Fisher in 1953, "of wage fixing organizations in California agriculture is so extensive and all-embracing that there would be no reason short of illiteracy combined with serious defects of hearing for any farmer to be unaware of the 'prevailing wage' for any commodity in any season."

The labor bureaus found that they could keep most of the farm labor contractors in line by the use of the published wage rates. The yardstick was applied to individual farmers and to intermediaries, who would not ordinarily risk their standing with their patrons by deviating from the schedules. The contractors carried no weight in the labor associations and were regarded by individual employers chiefly as the instruments by which labor pirating was carried out. Usually the contractor played the role of apologist of the wage schedules to the workers, his stock arguments being that "the farmers have to pay what everybody else pays" and that "the market won't let them pay any more."

The containment of wages worked smoothly enough over the long run, but it was a standing grievance among workers, who also blamed the employers and contractors for encouraging Wetbacks and pitting one racial group against another in the fields. Occasionally passive resistance turned into angry protest and when there was leadership to direct it, the labor associations responded with systematic violence.

To organize such violence was, among others, one of the purposes of the Associated Farmers, constituted in 1934 "to foster and encourage respect for and to maintain law and order, to promote the prompt, orderly and efficient administration of justice" and to assist employers in securing the undisturbed picking and transportation of their crops. The Associated Farmers, a statewide organization, was joined by local committees of farmers and their retainers who during the emergencies practically enforced the dictates of the labor bureaus. Behind the Associated Farmers and the vigilante committees there stood the less conspicuous commodity federations, whose leadership was in close touch through interlocking directorates that extended their lines of communication into every major power center in the state.

The enforcers were unquestionably successful in keeping the labor pool under control and wages on the level. The 1928 strike of the Confederacion de Uniones Obreras [Confederation of Mexican Labor Unions] was defeated by arrests and deportations. The threatened loss of the melon crop in the Imperial Valley "led the local authorities," as Professor Robert Glass Cleland noted, "to use extra-constitutional methods in dealing with strikers." The cotton strike of 1933 was broken by organized violence. In Lodi the angry farmers, literally up in arms, declared themselves against trial by jury in labor litigation "as reminiscent of medievalism" and a pastime for boneheads. In Brawley in 1934 a meeting of workers was invaded by police officers who attacked with tear gas and clubs. Sheriff's deputies and special guards numbering more than 400 put down the 1936 strike in Orange County. The Filipinos in Salinas were overwhelmed by mass violence and backstage maneuvers. The Mexican strikers in Santa Paula were evicted in 1941 in large numbers and their places given to dust bowl refugees. Professor Cleland summarized his view of wage controls and their enforcement tersely. He wrote in 1947: "California's industrial agriculture can exhibit all the customary weapons . . . gas, goon squads, propaganda, bribery."

The labor force conceived as a pool, recruited from the surplus stock of people in Asia, Mexico, and the backward counties of the United States, held together by mass coercion, was adequate for the needs of a democracy at peace. A spreading world war, however, was drawing the United States into its vortex, and California agriculture was sucked mightily into it. Mobilization and the production crisis at once threatened to tax its manpower, upset its wage structure, possibly give a smaller and more compact labor force some measure of economic leverage, and unsettle in unforeseen ways the existing private controls. It was this crisis that led directly to the first migrant labor agreement between the United States and Mexico, and eventually to managed migration under Public Law 78.

THE MANPOWER CRISIS OF 1942

According to the United States census California had in 1940 a farm labor force of 243,000 persons, of whom slightly more than 105,000 were hired workers. Of the hired force approximately 25 percent were seasonal, principally resident Mexicans and southern Americans, migrants from out of the state, intra-state migrants and Wetbacks. Of the Asian laborers[,] the Chinese had disappeared as a factor in agricultural employment[,] but there remained thousands of Filipinos, Japanese and Hindustani who dedicated themselves to special crops in limited areas of their own choice.

These were the agricultural manpower resources of the state upon which the demands of war production pressed. Farm employers were aware that those demands would strain the imperfections of the labor pool, bringing new and perhaps far more serious worries.

Among those imperfections the worst was that the immigrant farm laborer, whether he came from Mindanao, Oklahoma or Zacatecas, could not be bound permanently to the industry or to any particular segment or member of it. Agriculture was being continuously drained of manual labor by manufacturing, transportation and the service trades. These offered opportunities for better jobs which alert farm workers bid for. Industry and the service trades were expanding, their draft on the farm labor bank threatening to keep pace with accelerating war demands.

Within agriculture itself, in spite of the watchfulness of the labor bureaus, competition for workers was never thoroughly stabilized. The gentlemen's agreements on wage schedules did not prevent individual growers from hiring away their neighbor's help in the pinches of harvest. Pirating continued, especially where Wetbacks were concerned, through intermediaries of employers who were either too busy or too sensible to give personal offense to their peers by being caught stealing.

The enticement of laborers was not limited to local raiding. California's employers had to be ever watchful against the lure of higher farm wages in Oregon and Washington. The war, moreover, disrupted one important sector of agricultural production when in 1942 the evacuation of the Japanese population of the Pacific coast began. This had the double effect of removing field workers who were notably industrious, and of displacing farm families whose labor contributed importantly in certain crops. These imbalances in the supply of labor and the demands of production were accentuated by the growth of war industry—shipbuilding, aircraft, steel and oil refining. The new plants and shops in San Francisco, Vallejo, San Pedro, and San Diego drew thousands of migrants away from the Central Valley.

From the point of view of commercial farmers, particularly of the relatively small percentage who used the major part of the seasonal labor, the war not only threatened to subtract from existing manpower but also to add to costs by breaking wages from their old moorings. Higher wages were almost certain to follow from the better competitive position of the men and women who remained at farm work. In the decade preceding Pearl Harbor[,] farm pay had indeed shown a tendency to rise, though not precisely in a breakthrough. The gap with industrial wages showed a mild but disquieting tendency to close.

To head off this trend district and area committees were set up under Federal authority, the committees being composed of prominent growers and processors "who were actually instrumental in setting out the policies for the administration of ceiling orders." Through these committees certain crops were given protection against wages pressures. The rising curve of the preceding decade was pegged. In asparagus and tomatoes wages not only levelled off, they were actually rolled back. The lower limit of the rollback was fixed at 50 cents per hour, deemed as the substandard minimum rate.

The success of agricultural employers in arresting wage increases for the duration of the war was an important accomplishment. Aside from the immediate economic benefits of the stabilization of the harvest costs close to or even below 1940 levels, the local area and crop committees were a device that permitted commercial farming to take over the structure of control while the labor bureaus and associations were in abeyance for the duration of the war.

This was, however, only a temporary state of affairs. The transition from war to peace could prove as difficult as the adjustment from peace to war. Farm workers might renew their pre-war organizing activity, which had in great part caused the rise in wages already noted. The migrant workers from the southern states had proved to be both clamorous and belligerent. Thousands of farm workers would be returning to the fields from the war plants of the coast with union experience and new ideas on how to get more for their labor. The Asian labor stock was closed for an indefinite time. Controls would be removed from prices, but so would they from wages.

However useful controls were in keeping things tidy while farm employers pondered these matters, they were not addressed to the most critical problem of all. New sources of manpower had to be found. This was not only because of the real drains on the farm labor supply by military service and the attractions of industry; the pool had to be resupplied if the anticipated tensions were to be avoided. In 1942 farmers were already complaining over the loss of crops that might ensue if the labor shortage became more critical; they were also aware that losses other than financial ones—the intangible perquisites that go with social class domination—could be sustained if the pool were not refilled with proper workers.

The decision to turn to Mexico for such a supply was not hastily made. It was no longer a simple matter of opening the border and allowing the Mexicans to enter wherever they might choose and at whatever seasons of the year. Deliberate planning was required in an economic area in which it had never been welcome. Such planning could not be carried out by the private agencies of commercial agriculture as they existed with the speed and in the manner which would respond to wartime needs. It required the participation of the Federal Government. This was a departure that would have to be carefully considered by men committed wholeheartedly to self-helping free enterprise.

It was necessary to consider with great prudence the terms and conditions upon which labor would be made available. Terms and conditions for the employment of agricultural workers had never been subject to question or negotiation in California agriculture. There had been occasional bargaining between farmers and crew leaders. In their dealings with some labor contractors there had also developed a semblance of hiring by contract. But these instances were not typical. What standards there were before the war, so far as wages were concerned, were set up by the labor bureaus. In matters such as transportation and housing, employers brooked little interference except such as they agreed to among themselves as gentlemen, or such as was tactfully exercised by state agencies under the law. Standards set up for foreign workers in particular could easily become standards in general, and it was strongly suspected by agricultural spokesmen that such minimum requirements would be used as an excuse for extending to domestic laborers forms of protection which had never been conceded.

PART 3

ACTION RESEARCH IN DEFENSE OF THE BARRIO

PERSONAL MANIFESTO

In Ernesto Galarza, *The Burning Light: Action and Organizing in the Mexican Community in California*, interviews conducted by Gabrielle Morris and Timothy Beard in 1977, 1978 and 1981 (Regional Oral History Office, The Bancroft Libraries, University of California, 1982), 107–112. Date of interview: December 7, 1978.

In this interview Galarza offers a detailed account of the models he used in labor organizing and economic and social justice campaigns. As a public intellectual, he vigorously championed meticulous research and documentation as part of comprehensive strategies that exposed economic, social, and political injustice. The research then acts as an agent of social change and keeps the issue alive because it is made part of the public record and thus can no longer be denied by the larger society.

Galarza often critiqued public and private K–12 educational systems and universities for their roles in perpetuating and reproducing inequalities. For this reason he chose not to enjoy the comfort of a formal academic position even though he had the academic pedigree to do so (degrees from Occidental College, Stanford, and Columbia). He instead chose a career path that included the roles of organizer, author, researcher, teacher, and poet. In this sense, he was a true renaissance man.

Notable life events during this era:

- 1979: Galarza is the first Mexican American to be nominated for the Nobel Prize in Literature for his his autobiography, his poetry, and his children's books.
- 1980: Galarza receives the Friends of the Volunteers in Service to America (VISTA) award for exceptional service and work to end poverty. President John F. Kennedy championed the VISTA program in the 1960s; it was later institutionalized in the Economic Opportunity Act of 1964 under President Lyndon B. Johnson. The program provided funding for volunteers from all walks of life to enter poor communities to help reduce poverty and improve the quality of life in those communities.

Ernesto Galarza, circa 1970. Courtesy of Henry P. Anderson, photograph by George Ballis.

Transcribers: Ann Enkoji, Marie Herold
Final Typist: Matthew Schneider

GALARZA: There is a limit to what you can ask one individual to do, and I think that limit has been reached with me. Fortunately, we have taken the precaution of leaving a record in various places—in Alviso, in San Francisco, Berkeley, Santa Cruz. So I don't feel that these are blank pages that still have to be written by *me*.

In fact, the whole theory on which I operated for years is that if I wrote *books* in detail, with documentation listed, and bibliographies, that that would be *my* contribution to the history of my time. But I keep getting calls from people who keep saying to me, "Come and teach. Come and give us a lecture. Teach us this. Fill in these gaps."

With all the young Chicanos who are in this now, who are taking courses, who are going into graduate school, who are looking for things to do, I'm saying to them, "The system is still there. If you're young and energetic and if you agree that something's got to be done, go do it! You have enough of a background in the records I've left behind to give you a start." But this is a tough assignment! The idea of reading the past in order to do something about the present and the future, is *not* something that you learn in institutions.

MORRIS: The kind of energy and dedication you've put in it is probably a little terrifying to some people who haven't—

GALARZA: That's right, and I want to keep them terrified.

MORRIS: They may wonder if they can put in it what you have.

GALARZA: That's right. Experiencing that terror is part of their education. Because it is a terrible thing to have spent most of your life working with people—with children, with adults, with parents—coming to a peak of experience as we did in the Consortium and the Studio Lab, and to be forced by circumstances to realistically analyze a social system that's there in front of you—it's terrible! It takes a kind of grit that the schools of education—graduate schools—don't tell you anything about.

You have to *experience* the *awfulness* of a stratified social system that will not become human.

MORRIS: Event though it's made up of individual human beings.

GALARZA: That's right.

MORRIS: Is it also terrifying to look at a social system and see that it's rigidified and needs change, from the aspect of how do you make a start?

GALARZA: I made my start. In my case, my life is well enough known to a number of people through my books, my writing, my letters, in the documentation I've left behind. You see, I've always had this concern for thirty-four years that this might be significant to people who follow me.

I'm not in the position that *most* people are who talk into your microphone. What I say into your mike is really a fringe benefit because the people who have left a record in oral history are not people who have written their course. They're not. I know many of them. And they're glad of the opportunity to live in oral history because they haven't taken the time nor had the interest nor the skill nor the opportunity to leave a record of documents and papers behind them. *I* have. And they are in archives.

In time, if these issues remain alive, it will not be difficult for them—for my successors—to find out from *me*—from what I've written—what happened and my *views* of what happened—my appraisal—my analysis—it's all there. Some of it is still too scattered, I'm afraid—but it's there.

This is what I find in young graduate students. They shrink when I talk to them this way.

"You want me to write a dissertation of what happened to the Studio Lab? You want me to go to Santa Cruz and talk to those people? You want me to shag teachers down who are now in Los Angeles—who are scattered all over the state? I can't do this. It's too much! I've got to have my dissertation in by next June!" I say, "Fine. Get your dissertation."

GALARZA: The terror which these people face is very real. They know that the reason why their Ph.D. degrees are becoming less and less a passport into a profession is because of the stratification that happened.

MORRIS: The institutional structure.

GALARZA: That's right. And there are young men and women here in San Jose—*fine* young men and women—very capable—some of them have been my students who are now facing that terror. They apply for jobs. They're turned down. They're not told why. They go back and take graduate courses. They apply again. They're turned down. They finally settle—I know of one young man in the community who has a master's in social work and some advanced courses at the school of education here—he's now washing dishes for a living. That's terror.

I haven't experienced this terror in that *way*. I have been very, very fortunate in my lifetime in the things that I have done—the opportunities that I have had to understand what I was involved in, but I still sense that it's a terrorizing experience to finish your graduate work, to know that you're competent, to be technically good in your chosen profession, and to be told that there's no room for you in this society.

In San Jose alone, the numbers of such young men and women—I don't know how many there are, but I've talked to at least a dozen—who are now scrounging, baby-sitting, washing dishes, taking graduate courses over and over and over again. It's from this kind of a fringe of rejects, social rejects, that there will come, I hope, a very strong response to the sealing off of opportunities that is going on, and here's an example of how it happens.

MORRIS: How do they find their niche to make an attack on—?

GALARZA: For one thing, they think that talking to me will help, but I stay away from *that* kind of conversation because I've talked to them about these matters innumerable times. There is a point at which conversation becomes a sedative. "I know Galarza. If I go back and talk with him, I know what he'll tell me and he'll make me feel good, and this will help me until the next crisis. Then I'll go back and talk with him again." This is a cycle that these people go through. I don't intend to baby them along. I feel that if there's ever an opportunity for me to say something that will *break* the crust of this resistance, I'd be glad to do so. But going to congressional hearings, and appearing before boards, and talking to these people who are encased in their professional precincts, is useless.

This is the real crux of the future. The increasing numbers of these people who have paid their dues to the system.

MORRIS: They've gone through the education—

GALARZA: They've submitted to the requirements and now they're being told that "There is no room for you."

MORRIS: Is what I'm hearing that it's not clear yet where the opportunities to make the action is?

GALARZA: To me it isn't. Short of a crisis that will bring enough of these people together and force them to change institutional arrangements— but I don't see that happening. The schools in this district—the administrators are busy trying to find ways and means to increase the size of classes, and the teachers' organizations are busy trying to find reasons why they should accept these new students in their classes.

MORRIS: Is there any possibility that the financial strictures might be an opportunity, in that if there's less money for the governmental institutions, people may find other ways of trying to accomplish change in education?

GALARZA: Some of that is going on, and I dare say, it will continue, but this will affect only a small proportion of economically—families who are economically fairly able to face the crisis. There are people here who are making $25, $30 thousand dollars a year who can afford a private school. Whether the private school will meet the needs of the kids is another question I haven't thought about. But there will be a fringe of people who are able to escape the penalties. I doubt that they're more than a very small percentage. The bulk of these kids will be left to the devices and the maneuvers and the politicking of the people who run the system, and the system has got to protect them, first of all.

MORRIS: Protect the children?

GALARZA: No—protect the *administrators*. They raise their salaries instead of cutting them. They refuse to touch the basic issues that are depriving these children of the only opportunity they'll ever have to make themselves competent citizens.

I may not live long enough to see a revulsion against the situation, but I do know that talking to seminars and giving courses and appearing before committees—I do know that I spent a lifetime doing that, and this is the result. This is the end product of that. I don't see, with the little time that *I* have left, I should continue to tread that mill.

MORRIS: I quite agree with you. I was seeking for my own illumination—not asking you to go back to—

GALARZA: The Alviso situation is different in that if you want to keep abreast of that, I think you practically have to *meet* the people on this committee who are—they meet somewhat regularly. What they've done in the past two years, I don't know.

They call me up occasionally and want me to give them more training programs. But their training is pretty adequate, I think. They make smart moves and adequate strategies come out of their doing. They're not going to be plastered over and they'll survive.

It's just that I don't want to be drawn back into more meetings and putting into it whatever meager resources we, my family, have been able to set aside for this over the years. In other words, I think in Alviso we've done our job. We've finished and there's nothing more we can do.

At the Studio Lab we didn't do our job, which failed for the reasons I've described, but I have no intention to let these people absorb and really command the rest of my life. No intention whatsoever.

MORRIS: I think you're entitled to relax.

I did not mean to take as much of your time this morning, but I really appreciate it.

GALARZA: Well, we covered the outline, which is what I wanted to do.

MORRIS: Thank you.

GALARZA: I'll keep your letter here. I'll keep it and add it to the other notes that we have. Now, do you want to drop in and visit these people?

MORRIS: I would like to if you tell me how to get there.

GALARZA: The hearings are being held at the student union at San Jose State.

[end of interview]

INTERVIEWER'S NOTE

At Dr. Galarza's urging, an effort was made to include comment on the then-current state of bilingual education in the San Jose area by interested citizens or education professionals. When the interviewer arrived, after some search, at the San Jose State University Student Union room where the meeting was being held, there was about half an hour's wait for the next session to begin. About fifteen people were seated around long tables loosely arranged in a hollow square. Eventually a quite interesting film was shown of various bilingual programs around the country; some for Spanish-speaking children, some for American Indian children.

No materials on the hearing or other aspects of bilingual education were available, and there was no evidence of arrangements for members of the public to speak.

THE REASON WHY
LESSONS IN CARTOGRAPHY

Ernesto Galarza, "The Reason Why: Lessons in Cartography," *Rural America* (September 1978). Courtesy of the U.S. Department of Agriculture.

This short piece notes the importance of human geography and maps the political and economic terrains that unfolded because of the borders the United States and Mexico share. Galarza's mentor at Columbia University was William R. Shepherd, a renowned historian and cartographer of the United States and Latin America. During the early twentieth century, Shepherd published *The Hispanic Nations of the New World: A Chronicle of Our Southern Neighbors* (Yale University Press, 1919) and a series titled *Historical Atlas* (Henry Holt and Company, 1911–1964), a collection of maps that illustrate watershed moments in the development of world civilizations, both of which influenced how Galarza viewed and analyzed society.

Notable life event during this era:

- 1977: With community members, Galarza founds the Community Organization to Monitor Education (COME) to assess bilingual curricula in the San Jose Unified School District and advocate for a full-immersion bilingual curriculum.

The making of political maps is one of the more comforting occupations of mankind. The neat designs in contrasting colors convey a feeling of an orderly division of habitats. Such maps are frozen devices that show how peoples and governments have arranged themselves on any given date. The difficulty is that the map is always outdated because men will not stay in place. Especially when they have been assigned by their governments and ruling institutions a habitat that constrains rather than liberates, will they devise ways of breaking through.

That, in essence, is the history of the borderlands between the United States and Mexico.

In theory these borders are a wall of containment between the two countries. In practice they are a sieve through which millions of persons move back and forth, more or less legally, more or less temporarily. The neat separation that

Ernesto Galarza in the classroom. Courtesy of the Seaver Center for Western History Research, Los Angeles County Museum of Natural History.

shows on the political map ignores bulges, breaks, pressures and displacements of rootless fugitives from want. They have produced a mass of workers crowded into potholes of poverty second to none, in numbers and deprivation, in the Western hemisphere. The closer one looks at the realities of life and work in the borderlands during the 1970s the less they fit into the trim precision of official cartography.

Among the underlying realities are the following:

- The Mexican border areas for 50 years have been principally way stations for refugees in flight. Rural Mexico has been slowly and systematically colonized by more efficient forms of capitalist control and management of land, with an eye on the more lucrative export markets abroad. Commodity exchanges move Mexican cotton, melons, sugar, tomatoes and many other foods and fibers to foreign markets to become important items in the international balance of payments.
- Correspondingly, the forms and techniques of production have changed in favor of machines, centralized management, credit control, mass transportation and consolidated production units of land assembled to the requirements of corporate control. The technical revolution in land tenure and culture that began in the late nineteenth century has moved forward. The disestablishment of peasants and tenants has become a condition of modernization, and the surplus of landless rural folk has spilled from the large metropolitan centers into the borderlands where they await the chance to migrate into the United States.
- With these radical changes the character of Mexican rural society is being revolutionized. The traditional marketplace, the *tianguis*, with its localized exchange and its direct connections with the area of production, becomes the metropolitan *mercado* [marketplace] and the international commodities exchange. Barter gives way to monetary systems of profit and loss on a scale beyond villagers' ability to conceive or city consumers to control.
- The loosening and collapse of the sensitive network of relationships in a rural society, whose members play their roles as economic and political persons in relatively open view of their contemporaries, are being completed as urbanism takes over. The massive export of the unemployed from the countryside to the metropolitan centers is followed by their emigration as surplus people from the crowded centers to the nearest exit—the borderlands.
- Such an exodus, increasing in numbers decade after decade, invents its own devices for escaping the control of government and business and the institutions they dominate, notably the police powers that keep watch over population movements. The administrative apparatus maintained to keep people in line within the official demarcations of sovereignty and territory becomes riddles with evasions. People and capital, skills and technology, penetrate the border.

- Finally, matters reach a stage where the sheer pressure of a growing population south of the border makes the formal divisions of sovereignty practically useless to describe the actual state of affairs. Clandestine traffic in people and goods is nearly incalculable. The national sovereignties of Mexico and the United States have become interlocked in a process that neither can fully control within their respective police domains.

For some time to come—years certainly, decades perhaps—both the Mexican and the United States governments will negotiate advantages to their respective national policies apropos of the conditions of social instability in the borderlands. Both have powerful pieces to play in the international politics of power: Mexico, its newfound petroleum resources; the United States, the torrent of tourist dollars that flows south year in and year out.

The decisions reached and the compromises made at the highest levels of the two governments will be arranged, on the record, to agree with the formal demarcations on the political map. There has been too much rhetoric on good neighborliness to permit otherwise. But the underlying national interests that focus outwardly on the borderlands have deep class roots north and south of the border.

More than a line on the map, the border marks potentially a seismic fault with many fissures showing already. When it slips, the shock will be felt both in Washington and Mexico City.

ECONOMIC DEVELOPMENT BY MEXICAN-AMERICANS IN OAKLAND, CALIFORNIA

Excerpts from Ernesto Galarza, *Economic Development by Mexican-Americans in Oakland, California: An Analysis and a Proposal* (Berkeley, Calif.: Social Science Research and Development Corporation, 1966).

This report is another example of Galarza's mastery of spatial sociology. This report combines economic, political, and cultural geography to give a detailed account of the Oakland Mexican American community and notes the impact of the decisions of governments, corporations, and elites on the community and the space its members occupy. He also explores the relationship between Mexican American and African American communities.

Galarza offers a set of action oriented recommendations to decision makers based on the research findings of his team. He argued that following his recommendations would stimulate the economic and civic development of Oakland. His primary recommendation is that the city create an economic development zone specifically for Mexican-American commerce and specialty manufacturing. In his estimation, this space would root the Mexican American community and increase the involvement of its members in the civic life of Oakland.

Notable life events during this era:

- 1966: Galarza is approached by Mexican American residents of Alviso, California, about issues affecting their community having to do with urbanization and the fact that they are not included in planning and decision making about the use of public land and other resources. He begins community organizing with the residents.
- 1967: Galarza boycotts the conference of the Interagency Committee on Mexican American Affairs titled The Mexican Americans: New Focus on Opportunity held in El Paso, Texas. President Johnson had formed the committee that year to study the problems that Mexican Americans faced. But Galarza, disillusioned about the possibilities for real change for Mexicans and Mexican Americans via traditional two-party politics, instead attends the first La Raza Unida Unity Conference held in the same city. He joins the political organizing efforts undertaken within the Chicano movement and helps create a third party, La Raza Unida Party, whose platform is based on the interests of Mexicans and Mexican Americans. Galarza is elected chair of the Raza Unida Unity Conference.

INTRODUCTION

A. Comment

Exposure of a demographic area significantly or heavily peopled by Mexican Americans, particularly for the purpose of taking an economic picture, is more than likely to produce a series of negatives. If these negatives are viewed by experts accustomed to analyzing and planning for institutional structures of wide scope and great resources, they usually find it time-consuming and often annoying to adjust the focus. It is becoming more and more apparent however that the time must be spent and the annoyance endured. The Central City is ailing badly, and minorities like the Mexican-Americans are at the core of the syndrome. They are holding a mirror up to the affluent society; and though the glass be a small one, like this monograph, it is worth looking into closely.

B. East Bay Spanish-Speaking Foundation Proposal

In February, 1966, the East Bay Spanish-Speaking Foundation submitted a proposal "for long-term planning and action related to developing fully the economic potential of Oakland's Spanish-speaking community." The proposal, addressed to the Economic Development Administration, included a request for funding of feasibility studies and economic development plans that would directly benefit the Mexican-Americans residing in the City of Oakland.

Many of the basic concerns of the Foundation were set forth in its brief presentation. The Spanish-speaking residents of the City, the Foundation said, "wish to be involved at all levels of economic activity." Among them are persons whose skills in various handcrafts are presently unused. Others possess managerial skills, but opportunities for the productive use of them are lacking. The cultural uniqueness of the Mexican-American community is not expressed or encouraged in ways that would bring it notice and prestige. Its share in the economic establishment is meager, almost non-existent. Mexican-Americans are not on public policy-making bodies. In the important decisions which affect their jobs, their educational opportunities and their residence, the Mexican-American minority is allowed no voice either through responsible spokesmen or through democratic community involvement.

Although the Foundation's proposal refers to manufacturing, maritime and air transportation now on the planning boards as areas toward which Mexican-American participation could move, the emphasis of the proposal is on the possibility of creating a commercial and specialty manufacturing center within the City of Oakland. The Foundation believes that such a center would meet the objectives of the Economic Development Administration—to improve opportunities for successful establishment or expansion of enterprises; to assist in the creation of long-term employment; to provide job opportunities for the unemployed; and to bring technical assistance within the reach of Mexican-American business enterprises.

The proposed center, viewed from the economic and social setting in which the Foundation places it, appears to raise two different areas of exploration. The first would relate to the economic possibilities of the center considered as a job-generating establishment. The second would deal with such an establishment as a point of departure toward an exploration of other possibilities for growth within the Mexican-American community and towards participation in the major affairs of the City.

In both these respects, the Foundation is stimulating research, analysis, planning and action to bring about the creation of an economic base in the small business sector of the Mexican-American community from which stimulus and organization could advance in other directions. Once resources are available, as they are under the Economic Development Act, the pressing question is, "Where do we begin?" This monograph is intended as an introduction to that question, and the many others that must follow it in any consideration of feasibility.

C. Giant Urbanism—The Shift Environment of the Mexican-American

During the past fifty years, Oakland, like other California cities, has received the overflow of insecure labor from Mexico, the Southwest and the deep South. They are people with no stake in the economic system, no equity in its productive apparatus, no role in its bureaucratic machinery and no part in determining the arrangements under which they must make a living. They are marginal people for whom the margins of livelihood are narrowing.

A careful watch over what has been happening in the Central Valley of California illustrates the main drift. Families who have no capital, but with long experience and detailed knowledge of the earth and the ways of working it, have no way of entering the agricultural industry. The Mexican-American, a skilled and diligent land worker, has never risen above the class of wage earner. From the mid-twenties to the late thirties, the manpower shape of the valley was clearly visible. This manpower, representing a fairly wide distribution of population, consisted of a chain of small-to-medium size labor pools, strung north and south along U.S. Highway 99. These *bolsas de trabajo* [pockets of workers] were Mexican-American *colonias*.

In the last twenty years, U.S. Highway 99 has become the main stem of freeway construction. This construction has drastically rearranged the physical pattern of many *colonias*. Residential building has overtaken former migrant campsites. Industry has expanded, exacting a tribute of space for plants, warehousing, parking and junk. The Central Valley Project laid its canals in a network paralleling the highways, making it possible, on a grand scale, to capitalize heretofore marginal wastelands. Between 1942 and 1965, a massive assault on the agricultural job tenure of domestic workers was maintained in the form of the *bracero* program. With this assault, farm housing patterns changed. A multitude of on-farm facilities for seasonal labor—barns, shacks, shanties, and garages—which small farmers had traditionally afforded their migrant help, disappeared, as small farming declined. Barracks for *braceros* took their place.

For the rural tracts of farm worker residence, this meant rearrangement, dispersal, removal, relocation—drastic changes in a way of life. One current of retreat led to [the] sandlot fringes of the large Valley towns—Fresno, Bakersfield, Sacramento; a second, to [the] already overcrowded tracts of East Los Angeles, San Pedro and Oakland; a third, to shoestring settlements such as West Tracy, Firebaugh and South Dos Palos.

For the masses of displaced workers who made it directly to Boyle Heights in Los Angeles and Fruitvale in Oakland, there is no turning back. For others, Fresno, Stockton and Bakersfield are half-way stations to Boyle Heights and Fruitvale. For even the less venturous, who fell back to Firebaugh and South Dos Palos, the end is probably not yet in sight. Again the dam builders at San Luis and the freeway builders in Sacramento will pour a double-flanking advance of water and concrete along the western apron of the Central Valley. Booming land values and higher assessments will follow. If the migration escalator continues to operate as it has traditionally, it will take many of the present residents of towns like South Dos Palos to Fresno and Bakersfield and Stockton, or to Watts and Fruitvale. For the remainders, there is no farther West; except, perhaps[,] the peaks and crags beyond Priest Valley, where the California condor, too, is making his last stand.

These suppositions have only the validity of possible projections from long-term trends that are a matter of history. Moreover, these suppositions may be viewed by some as generally good prospects. They would accord with the general acceptance of "giant urbanism" as an irreversible process.

D. Oakland in Transition

The urban drift of the Mexican-Americans must be counted as among the many significant events that have happened to the City of Oakland during the past three decades. Though not as numerous as Oakland's Negroes, Mexican-Americans are important enough to engage the concern of those who sense the strains that threaten the Central City. Oakland, like many other American cities that are acutely sick, is in the midst of an agonizing self-diagnosis. It is made so by a proposition which is rarely acknowledged, namely, that where the symptoms of the illness are people, the cure cannot lie in surgery.

If more historical perspective were present in planning philosophies, it would be clear why this malignancy exists. The Mexican-Americans who have drifted to the East Bay area, like the Negroes, have been for the most part the surgical cast-offs of economic and social systems in which they were the painful reminders of bad social health. Had these processes occurred once only, urban California might hope, by one major effort, to recover from the massive migration caused by economic deprivation and social denial in the Deep South, in the Southwest and in Mexico. Oakland, however, like Los Angeles, Fresno, San Jose and San Diego, has also failed to grasp the important fact that inter-regional or inter-national dumping of human beings is far from the same thing as the dumping of goods. The brutal surgery which has separated millions from land ownership, and from the technological progress of the last hundred years, has merely grafted the same living tissue to urban bodies. The operative treatment cannot be repeated. The minorities, now compact in slums and ghettos, will not submit to another operation. The City cannot survive it—economically or morally.

It is from this economic and social point of view that statistics and planning blueprints derive significance and direction.

Oakland presently occupies a land area of approximately 53 square miles. More land will become available for reclamation as San Francisco Bay shrinks beyond the dikes that mark the shallow fringes of the Bay.

367,548 persons lived within this area according to 1960 figures. Demographically, the City is almost in a perfect freeze, for in 1963 the population was estimated at 367,599. Statistical projections indicate that in the next 20 years, Alameda County and eight others in the Bay basin will hold 65% more people than they do now.

Oakland's wealth, reckoned by assessed valuation, in the same census year of 1960, amounted to $661,933,000. Of those sidewalk highrisers, called parking meters (that tell so much about a city's congestion and all its attendant irritations), Oakland had 7,751. It has been a growing city, physically, having expanded eight times between 1873 and 1960.

This growth has been a function of location; a magnificent dominance of the eastern slope of the San Francisco basin. Good portions of the overland commerce of America and the maritime trade of the Pacific were spliced onto

Oakland. Today, on the promotional maps, Oakland is pictured as the heart of a radiant sunburst of marketing opportunities whose rays touch Seattle to the North, Denver to the East, Los Angeles to the South and Hawaii to the West.

Yet, in one respect it is an uneasy affluence. The war in Viet Nam is an important provider of jobs. The war keeps the waterfront, and the plants that backstop it, busy. The view from the Industrial Development Commission is fogged by anxiety. "Again and again," the Commission has said, "the need for the creation of new jobs resulting from new industries and expansion of local industries comes to the fore." As in San Francisco, planners are pressed "to salvage the city from a sea of slums" in an economy that might fail them suddenly if mass employment at critical points should decline.

Understandably, planning is the dominant theme of city administration. Oakland has a comprehensive development plan, adopted in December, 1964. The plan is open-ended and costly—more than $1,000,000 for two years of research. The complicated web of situations that 367,000 people create every twenty-four hours, too taxing for human brains, is beginning to make instant sense thanks, among other things, to the electronic gear that abundant money can hire.

But the search, fortunately, is not only for technical sense. Beyond the "relationships of rapid transit, freeways and streets," which is the order the Oakland General Plan places [as] its top priority, there is concern for reciprocating between living areas and working areas, shopping centers and civic facilities. Of still greater significance, however, is the need for "a continuing process by which the city government and its citizens join in an attempt to guide the city toward a realization of its long-term goals."

Therefore, if these goals are to be reached, the center of attention in the general plan should be those unstable neighborhoods in which most of the Mexican-Americans are concentrated and where the "sea of slums" has already begun to engulf human lives as well as traffic.

It is in these areas that the Oakland General Plan proposes to set up some twenty community centers, thus posing at once the central issue of the City's dilemma. For "community" seems to be the fluid and self-choosing arrangement of the magnetic field of associations which group people in ways they like.

A part, but not all, of this field can be explored by computers. New physical space can be created along the bayshore flatlands. Planners have noted that the areas along the Lake Merritt channel and east of Jack London Square are largely still unused and available. Technicians who have studied the present layout of the Central City, and its traffic patterns have complained that such traffic patterns give motorists no indication where they might reasonably start being pedestrians. In a broader sense, through technology and proper land-use, Oakland may be able to mark where and how it may reasonably stop being merely a city and start being a community.

I. THE MEXICAN-AMERICAN IN OAKLAND

Mexican-Americans are vitally affected by urban planning because of their numbers, relative concentration, precarious economic resources and limited prospects of entering fully into the creation, consumption and enjoyment of Oakland's urban riches. Instability and environmental problems surround Mexican-Americans. Their neighborhoods fit the description of the target areas on which planners are fixing their sights.

The 1960 census reported 23,466 persons of Spanish surname living in the City. Of these, 7,905 were grouped as Mexicana if they were born in Mexico or had one parent who was Mexican-born. If Mexican ancestry for more than one generation is taken as the basis of classification, "Mexican" and "Spanish-surname" become practically synonymous. Together, in 1960, they represented close to 8 per cent of the City's population. This percentage has undoubtedly increased. One projection of 1960 data estimates the 1966 Mexican population at over 50,000. While this figure may be high, it is an indicator of the trend of growth in this ethnic group.

Mexican residents are distributed in an arc of census tracts extending from Emeryville to San Leandro Creek. Within this arc there is a bulge of concentration, notably in the Fruitvale area. According to the 1960 census returns, slightly more than 20 per cent of the Mexican population was concentrated in five tracts. Within these, saturations of 25 to 50% were found.

Needless to say, these are neighborhoods of low economic vitality. Income levels are in the lower brackets. Of 5,808 families tabulated in 1959, those with incomes of $6,000 or less numbered 3,175.

A. Migration

The tendency of the Mexican population to increase and to remain on the lower levels of the economic scale result from the operation of traditional migratory patterns. For decades Oakland has been attracting some of the overflow of agricultural labor pools of California. The bursts of employment during World War II and the Korean War occurred when the Mexican residents were already numerous enough to provide a "migratory grapevine" for friends and relatives. Of these new residents, many were able to obtain enough of a firm hold on the city's economy to settle in, and in turn become new connecting links in the same migration process. Moreover, as the Mexican *colonia* tended to grow, it offered a sort of collective anchorage to Mexican job seekers who had no personal points of entry.

A Mexican-American community of sorts emerged and multiplied, adding to itself more of its own kind—poor people seeking better ways to satisfy the basic needs of food and shelter. It is expected that the Mexican-American minority in Oakland will continue to grow, given the present trend of the California and Southwest rural economy, unless forces beyond its understanding and control disperse it.

B. Research and the Community

The urban districts that are most in need of renewal are precisely those with obvious economic and social handicaps. Here, it would seem, there is also the great need for information about the people who live in such neighborhoods. But this information is a need which has not been met. The annals of the poor, so it has been noted, are notoriously short and simple. Those of the Mexican-Americans in Oakland particularly are brief. A preliminary inquiry showed only three published reports on the Mexican-Americans in Oakland between 1943 and 1964. Further search may identify other sources, such as academic theses produced by students of the University of California. But [the] thinness and obsolescence of the data suggest that Oakland knows little about the Mexican-American neighborhood targets against which the City is massing its planning artillery.

It is pertinent to comment on one important cause of this ignorance: the incompatibility between the refined and neatly designed methods of research upon which official planning rests and the immediate concerns of the inchoate community of a minority such as the Mexicans.

The lack of connection, as far as a target neighborhood can see, between what the planner wants to find out and what the local residents need to know is more than a technical fault. The priorities are not the same at City Hall and in Fruitvale. This can be understood by anyone who has worked in a Mexican *colonia* and has learned why information is so valuable a commodity among the poor. Typically, the information sought is of immediate urgency—where jobs are opening, where a low-rent house is available, where a license or a permit can be obtained, how and where to process a wage claim. A habit of mind is established which is necessary to survival—the habit of paying attention to the immediate physical needs of oneself and one's family.

Information about resources and opportunities is organized and passed along by the *colonia* in its own fashion. It is by no means a "structured system," put together for the convenience of planners. Long-term research is an intrusion. For the day's or the week's needs, it is also highly irrelevant.

If this incompatibility is thought of simply as a research gap that can be closed by inventing sharper tools, the prospects of "a continuing process by which the city government and citizens can join to attempt to guide the city" do not appear to be good. It is rather an important clue to what may be termed the systems-resistance of the poor, of which reluctance to give information is a manifestation. The resistance operates in varying degrees against administration, supervision, enforcement, policing and inquiry. There is among the poor a sort of collective privacy, the invasion into which is resented. There is good reason for this resentment. Privacy is the last refuge of pride and self-respect. It is the condition in which choices can be made or changed without risk of ridicule or punishment. It is also the chance to weigh those choices and their effect on personal security before they are expressed in words or actions.

The Mexican-Americans in Oakland may be buffeted rather than helped by urban renewal if all the reasons for their resentment are ignored. It is sometimes held that ghetto and slum dwellers are in that condition because they have a limited range of urban-life skills. The contrary is true. But their skills are of a different order than other urban dwellers. They possess survival skills imposed by individual and collective deprivation of long standing.

The "research gap" will begin to close when planning proceeds by stages sensitive to the priorities that the target community itself accepts. Progress will stimulate the community when it feels and sees movement toward community priorities. Both require organization from within and for the group.

C. Mexican-American Organization

Organization from within and for the group is at present running a losing race with urban redevelopment, a force that is outside of, alien and even potentially hostile to the residents of the Mexican-American tracts. Spontaneous organization of these residents is weak and helpless relative to the problems they face.

There is no up-to-date directory of Mexican-American civic and social associations, and information about such groups by direct inquiry is not easily forthcoming. Existing organizations include funeral societies, sports clubs, adult leadership centers under religious auspices and ad-hoc committees to sponsor Mexican holidays. In addition, there are chapters of the Mexican-American Political Association, the Community Services Organization, and the G.I. Forum, which offer their small memberships the encouragement of state-wide connections and emulation. Mexican-Americans also gain a small share of organizational experience through trade unions, but the leadership opportunities in this area are limited, and they have not generated rallying points and personalities for the community at large.

Even a superficial look at organizational activity among Oakland's Mexican-Americans indicates its weaknesses and the reasons for them. They are an ethnic group which is still undergoing continuous dilution through in-migration. There is probably a high rate of internal mobility, normal residential turnover having been stepped up by the drastic inroads of freeway construction. The professional and small business segment of the *colonia* is very much occupied [with] making and holding a place for itself, with little leisure and no wealth to spare for Mexican-American civic crusades. Connections with the intellectual world are almost non-existent, there being no visible channels between that power house on the hill, the University of California, and the Mexican flatlands.

The initial spurts toward organization of any kind—social, economic or political—run short of funds for elemental requirements: a place to meet, telephone and postage money, some semblance of continuing communication between meetings.

The opportunities for gaining prestige as a community leader, under these circumstances, are not numerous. Mexican-Americans endowed with the qualities for leadership soon find themselves in narrow competition with one another for very small prizes of status, small in relation to the issues of survival which the *colonia* is facing.

D. Social Services and Community Landmarks

If social services were offered to the Mexican-American residents through facilities within their own neighborhoods there might be some semblance of community form. These services would provide some point of convergence for the residents, at least in time of need. However, even in the supply of available services, the Mexican-American tracts show neglect. Mexican-American welfare clients must go to the downtown offices of welfare agencies to receive help. To be sure, the casework system reaches into the neighborhoods in the person of the social worker; but the house-call nevertheless is institution-centered downtown. Like so many other services, charitable or otherwise, the material evidence of community will and purpose—the walls of buildings in which they are housed—cannot become familiar landmarks in some subtle way belonging to those who use them.

In listening to conversation in the Oakland Mexican-American tracts, one misses references to familiar places from which citizens take their bearings and to which in time they attach their confidence and pride. It is remarkable that sophisticated connoisseurs of the great cities of the world forget this. The Eiffel

Tower, Piccadilly Circus and Times Square immediately polarize the feelings and direction of millions. They provide dramatic moments of identification. But these moments are few and far between. In the familiar life of the neighborhood this identification can and should occur every day, as it still does in the Mexican cities which have not been engulfed by progress. Even a Mexican consulate, which can provide a transition sense of identity to those residents of the *colonia* who retain Mexican citizenship, is missing in Oakland; a city with one of the largest concentrations of the Mexican-American minority in California.

E. Community Building Potential

With respect to community-building potentials, the Mexican-Americans are disorganized. To worry public charity with the perplexities of community organization would seem unreasonable. But millions of its dollars flow into the Mexican-American tracts each year. There may be some by-products of such large expenditures which have not been explored, and in which the Mexican-American residents could have a part.

"Pointing with pride" is more than a folk saying. It is a clue to collective confidence based on successful efforts in the past. In truth it can be said that in the Mexican *colonia* of Oakland, as in its counterparts in other California cities, there is a constant "pointing with shame" based on the continuous failures of poverty over decades. The shame is heavily accented with discouragement.

This discouragement is not the apathy usually attributed to the Mexican-American minority. It is not a lack of so-called Time Orientation, but rather an abundance of it. But it is past, not future time, and its lessons are vital to those who have only the thinnest margins of security to spare for community action. These considerations have to be kept in mind by all those who despair after their first efforts to involve the Mexican-American tracts in urgent public affairs.

F. Mass Communications

The public media of communication—radio, TV, newspapers and non-periodical publications—offer very limited encouragement to Mexican-American awareness and self-consciousness. What the public media exploit is simply identity of language. The fact that they carry their message in Spanish automatically opens a large public to them. It is mainly a listening and not a reading audience. The usual format is highly stereotyped and of narrow cultural range. In Oakland there are programs beamed to the Spanish-speaking by radio but none by television. Although the Mexican radio personalities are alert to technical innovations that lure listeners, their sponsorship looks for commercial returns, not community enlightenment. Consequently, there is no programming of documentaries, educational broadcasts or opinion forums in Spanish.

These observations apart, the fact remains that the Spanish-language radio is one of the enduring institutions that reach Mexican-Americans. Perhaps nothing else illustrates so well the appeal of spoken language as familiar sounds and symbols to an ethnic group that feels itself marooned within a larger society. Together, Mexican-American radio and the juke boxes that belt out recordings in a thousand restaurants, pool halls and taverns provide the lusty fare of nostalgia bravura that is the hallmark of *mariachi* music.

The printed media do poorly indeed by comparison. Oakland's Mexican-Americans and other Spanish-speaking residents do not have a single weekly or even monthly periodical, however modest, to reflect the doings and undoings of the "*colonia*." *La Opinion* is a Los Angeles daily that has some circulation in the City; its news stories have about as much relevance to Oakland's Mexican-Americans as they might find in the *Manchester Guardian*. *La Voz*, also a Los Angeles publication, reaches a very small number of Mexican-American Oaklanders, more as a political house organ and a medium for editorial comments on general themes and problems than as a comprehensive news source reflecting the life of the *colonia*. The incidental Spanish columns that appear at long intervals in non-Mexican-American publications only serve to emphasize this vacuum in communication. *The Post*, a Negro newspaper, has in the past reserved one page out of fifteen for news in Spanish.

The point intended to be made here is not that the deprivation of periodicals devoted to particular needs, requirements and tastes is peculiar to the Mexican-Americans of the City of Oakland. It is, rather, to question whether—allowing for all the obstacles that stand in the way—the printed word as a means to inform and to stimulate need be so utterly barren.

G. Cultural Centers and Activities

Within an ethnic minority of limited economic resources and of notorious transiency, enterprises that supply enduring fare to the community do not easily take root. There is nothing in Oakland that might properly be described as a cultural center for its Mexican-American population. The only cultural facility is a motion picture theatre that exhibits made-in-Mexico films. Even a Mexican bookstore is nonexistent. In lieu of a bookstore there are bookshelves in pharmacies and record shops, which no doubt reflect the low-reading interest of their customers.

Mexican-Americans, especially the young ones, show an enthusiastic fondness for social dancing, for which they are willing to pay. The *bailes* [dances] are for the most part commercial affairs, though they are also a standard device for charitable or philanthropic fund raising. In the large public ballrooms the dancing style is vigorous, a-la-mode, free-swilling and occasionally free-for-all. The customers are often treated to exhibitions of Mexican folk-dances, which they admire but which they do not perform. Patently, the Mexican-American youth want to dance. There is no reason why their enormous relish for the twist and the watusi could not groove them into the swing, the color and the variety of Mexican dances.

A mixture of culture and history survives in the annual celebration of Mexican anniversaries—the Cinco de Mayo and Independence Day. Official Oakland pauses on these occasions to defer to the *colonia*. Considering that Oakland stands on what was once Mexican soil, it might be expected that these observances would touch the purse as well as the heart of the City. But in 1965–66 the Entertainment and Advertising Funds of the municipal budget allowed nothing for the public remembrance of these Mexican holidays.

A cultural and information center has been funded for operation in Fruitvale, close to the largest tract concentration of Mexican-Americans. A special library project is also underway to "expand service and explore the needs of users with special language handicaps." It will cost $120,000 and will end with fiscal year 1967–68.

H. Mexican-American University Students

The Mexican-American students enrolled at the University of California are another close-by potential institutional resource for the Mexican-Americans of Oakland. An official count as of June, 1966 showed that there were only 76 such students. The figure is shockingly low, considering both the Mexican-American population of the state and the enrollment of the University. But among even this small number it is not improbable that there would be some who could find useful and stimulating roles in the *colonia*.

I. Planning vs. People

There is a hazard in attempting to explain the conditions of the Mexican-American people. It might be inferred that it is simply planning that is needed to bring around their halting folkways and cultural deficiencies. But urban redevelopment according to blueprint is dominantly a response to material and physical blight. There are run-down neighborhoods in which Mexican-American[s] live, but the Mexican-

Americans themselves are not run-down. Their collective modes of cultural expression are poorly funded, but they persist. This cultural expression should not be tampered with by well-meaning coordinators. What the Mexican-Americans may ask of a society that can well afford it is the institutional support necessary to assist them to be more and better of what they are and a material environment in which they can become part of what the City of Oakland wills itself to be.

Thus far the cultural expressions of the Mexican-Americans in the City have found no significant connection with the planning process. On the contrary, it would appear that radio, the press, language, music and dance will continue to surface in the daily life of the *colonia* in spite of urban planning. The collective basis of these expressions—neighborhood association and community consensus as to tastes and values—is reeling from the blows of rapid transit design and urban redevelopment. It has been said that "the fragmentation of the Mexican-American community" was produced by the construction of freeways through the bayside flatlands. After a decade, the community is still trying to knit itself together.

This process of massive attrition threatens to continue. The routes already fixed for transit construction pierce the tracts most densely populated by Mexican-Americans. Along these routes a relatively narrow band of commercial and residential change will take place, pulling land values up and deteriorated family dwellings down. Beyond this belt corresponding changes will follow. At the main stations of the system, highly capitalized shopping centers will discourage the "mom and pop" corner stores.

A figure of speech comes to mind which is not as forced as might appear at first reading. The Mexican-American occupied tracts lie roughly between the projected extensions of transportation, port development and industrial relocation. These extensions can be visualized as huge rollers of steel and concrete, moving parallel along the narrow apron of the bayside. Between these rollers the Mexican-American tracts seem to wait like so much *masa* for a *tortilla* machine . . . except for one important difference: It is known in what shape the *masa* will be after it has passed between the rollers. As much cannot be said, as current conditions exist, for the Mexican-American community.

J. Citizen Participation in Policy Making

Citizen participation in the planning process is the officially declared policy of the City of Oakland. Participation, however, is an organized process. Information, discussion, even debate and controversy, have to move along channels open to all if understandings are to be reached and decisions made with a broad base of participants.

These channels are the means for communication between different parts of the City. As long as the Mexican-American ethnic group is repeatedly churned out of shape and forced to leap-frog over itself in a never-ending search for shelter, it can neither seek out nor respond to meaningful participation. There are no sure ways for outsiders to enter into the ethnic enclave; and those who live in it have no devices to reach out. This is the frustrating and familiar story of private and governmental agencies when they seek to relate their programs to the Mexican-American.

Understandably, this condition makes citizen participation in the low-income tracts a very appealing but meaningless slogan. The masses of the poor continually seem to be breaking camp and running away from the serious business of conferring, consulting, meeting, convening and evaluating complicated plans for the City Beautiful.

II. PROBLEMS AND TRENDS OF CHANGE

As the American city is no longer able to cope with its painful distresses without the help of the Federal Government, so the various organic parts of the city which are in trouble cannot forefend themselves singlehanded. The trends of change in California within which Oakland will be called upon to plan its future, and the lines of cleavage along which the City may fault, must be reckoned with.

A. Increasing Spanish-Surname Population

There is, first of all, the increase of Spanish-surname residents in Alameda County, which draws upon the continuing instability of the Mexican-American settlements in rural California. The way in which the migratory escalator works is well known. Families move in stages. Relatives and friends maintain a sort of scouting system and a grapevine through which job possibilities and housing conditions are explored. The information which is passed on is reflected in patterns of migration.

The pulling power of urban Mexican-American settlements will be, as it has been, in direct proportion to their population. Alameda County has become one of the major Mexican-American *colonias* in the state. It will undoubtedly continue to attract ethnic growth.

These facts, related to Oakland's geographic position, relate the City closely to what is likely to happen throughout the Southwest. Moreover, the great circle of Mexican-American population enclosing California, New Mexico, Arizona, Colorado and Texas must be extended to include northern Mexico. The Mexican population centers in this vast area contain many reservoirs of manpower. Migration, seasonal or permanent, flows between them, tending to roughly equalize the pressures of unemployment, mechanization and systems of land tenure and to fit the labor market to changing patterns of investment and technology. Northern Mexico has been, and is likely to continue to be, the advance wave that keeps the Southwest piped into the enormous reservoir of Mexico's unused manpower.

B. Mexican-American and Negro Relations

If urban planners are to be foreminded and forewarned of the future, other considerations than population trends must be explored. These considerations have to do with the attitudes, moods and emotional responses of growing masses of Mexican-Americans in the urban tracts.

The first of these considerations is the relationship of the Mexican-American minority to that of the Negro in cities, such as Oakland, where there is a large concentration of both. There seems to be two possibilities at the present time: abstention of the Mexican-American *colonia* from the Negro civil rights and related movements, or a coalition of both, on the level of spontaneous and vigorous reaction as well as on that of deliberate political organization. Some factors may determine the course of things in favor of abstention: the adroitness with which Mexican-American political leaders are won over to collaboration with the Anglo establishment; differential opportunities for the Mexican-Americans as to jobs and housing; the degree to which leading Mexican-Americans compete with leading Negroes for the favors of the Anglo; the possible fear of the former in the face of the demands of some Negroes for exclusive "black power"; and the separation of the poor into distinct and potentially hostile ghettos.

On the other hand, the black-and-brown minorities are not back-to-back. Younger Negroes and Mexican-Americans are talking to one another less about ethnic romanticism than about economic realities that affect them both. The techniques of civil disobedience are not rejected by all Mexican-Americans; the search for dignified identity is present in both minorities; the problems of community structuring are basically similar; the disappointment with anti-poverty programs is shared with a skepticism and often bitterness that is as deep among Mexican-Americans as among Negroes.

C. Planners and Dwellers—The Mexican-American Tract

Urban planning, in Oakland as in other beleaguered central cities[,] is a deliberate effort to avoid the perils, the losses, and the anxiety threatened by [those who are] adrift. The apparatus of planning can command high-quality techniques. But planning very likely reflects the private reluctance of the Anglo establishment to resolutely confront its values with its valuables. The people in the tracts will not be impressed as long as urban planning *merely* operates on the Mexican-American tracts to excise them as contaminated tissue—to measure its success by massive mobilizations of capital that brilliantly design the wiring and plumbing of megalopolis.

The sense of the tracts is, of course, not the science of the planners. In any dialogue between the two, if one could be imagined, given the present terms, it would be impossible to convince the tract dwellers that what to the planners is the promise of a booming city is not to them, merely the lowering of the boom.

What the tract dwellers cannot yet say in so many words has been inadvertently said for them. *Look* magazine editorialized in its California issue of September 25, 1962: "The powerful, almost incomprehensible new forces that are reshaping the lives of men everywhere are at their strongest here; the traditional patterns of institutions, community and class (which hold back change) are at their weakest."

If the family, and the neighborhood, is the shortest radius of communication and personal relationships, and if they are the environment in which persons as individuals can achieve their healthiest growth, then the central city suffers gravely. If it is not, then the science of planning is right and the sense of the tracts is wrong. There does not then need to be created, with the necessary costs, an escalated series of organizations that will be truly responsive to the people in the tracts. There will be no need to determine what it will take to make these organizations self-sustaining and self-propelling. Their hope will lie in the benevolence of powerful, almost incomprehensible forces, a benevolence not yet shown by its municipal works.

That the tracts will nourish such a hope is itself merely a hope. It is also a gamble that urban planning and all that it presently represents will have room for all—absolutely all—on the zipper path to leisure which, according to *Look*, Californians are excitedly pursuing.

III. A MEXICAN MERCADO

The commercial and cultural center does not deal with the other concerns of the Foundation, that is, the problems of the Mexican-American neighborhoods. Central to this different order of problems would be the following proposition: A marketing and trading-type of center, a Mexican *mercado* [marketplace], economically self-sustaining, could be designed to serve a wide range of needs of the Mexican-American population of Oakland.

A glance at the maps and blueprints of impending urban renewal shows that tracts with the heaviest Mexican-American population lie in its path. The City has been acting, in respect to these neighborhoods, in accord with a policy which has not been formally announced or stated. To have done so would have raised a serious problem in public relations. This policy has been to build and scatter; the planners doing the building and the residents of the tracts doing the scattering. This bulldozing process has meant dispersal of thousands of people of limited resources during relatively short periods of time. It has been a policy. And that policy makes certain assumptions. They are: that a sudden and drastic destruction of neighborhoods demolishes only dilapidated buildings; that cleaner, healthier open spaces are available for those who are evicted; that there is an increase in the material and social wealth created by urban renewal which will somehow be shared and enjoyed by those who must move on.

From the standpoint of the Mexican-American low-income tract residents none of these assumptions are true. More than old houses are demolished in a condemned neighborhood; a hundred supports of psychological security are scooped up with the rubble. Especially to a minority like the Mexican-American, constantly diluted by contingents of newcomers, the *colonia* is in much more than a material sense a "port of entry." Under the crushing handicap of language differences, entry into a new society is a groping, often fearful process. It necessarily requires reliable information, for which a high price is often paid. It leans on empathies of speech, color of skin, manners, eating habits, and similar tastes. The Mexican *colonia* has provided much of this cultural mesh. The social agencies that have dealt with the inadequacies of the *colonia* have classified it as a sub-culture. But for those fully immersed in it, and utterly dependent upon it for jobs, shelter, food and enjoyment, it is simply their culture.

Like all cultures the Mexican *colonia* grew in a particular material environment. This environment was invariably marginal to the surrounding society. Both its security and its integrity as a culture depended upon its continuing to be marginal—that is, continuing to be undesirable, from the standpoint of those who could afford better.

But desire, locked solely to the price per square foot of a building site, is taking another look at the rundown tracts. The land space of the City has shrunk alarmingly, relative to the population. The tracts which threaten to become slums, or already are, provide the most inviting and profitable solution.

If, however, values were to be as carefully weighed as valuables, the question would be asked: What can be done in the design of progress to protect the spirit, the sense, the psychological mesh that more or less relate and bind the people now living there?

B. A True Community Center

This question does not seem altogether out of place in the present framework of urban planning in Oakland. It should be noted that its master plan provides for "community centers" placed throughout the city. Here, it would seem, is the sprouting of the concept which lies emphatically behind the question raised in the preceding paragraph. But it is a seedling that requires utmost care if it is to root in the genuine, spontaneous social life of the neighborhood, and to grow in response to the community which centers around it.

This care is all the more necessary, as it appears [that] all the Oakland planners have in mind is a token salute to the community in the form of the proposed community centers. These exist in other cities, and they show quite similar characteristics. Usually they are small clubhouses erected in unobtrusive places in which small meetings can be held and some recreational services offered to the young. They are usually well maintained; some are charmingly landscaped. Their management is assigned to an existing municipal agency as a fringe benefit to the neighborhood.

These "community centers" are, of course, a credit to the spirit of civic service. They are, nevertheless, in the nature of memorials to something that has declined and fallen in the American city—the spirit and structure of community.

C. Lost Community

The fault for this community decline, if it is a fault, must be blamed on progress. Rapid transit by automobile, by rail and by air, make it possible for the householders in one city block, if they are on the proper level of income and opportunity, to relate to different clubs, lodges, unions, associations or societies five or five hundred miles from the street on which they live. This is an exhilarating crisscrossing of voluntary associations made possible by swift technical advances in transportation and by rising incomes. Its delights, once the privilege of the transatlantic set, and later of the jet set, are now enjoyed by middle-class America.

And again this way of life is the nature of American society. It has added enormous mobility and variety to the lives of millions. America's migratory poor—not all of them farm workers by any means—have shared in this mobility, if not variety, of experience.

This kind of detachment from the homestead and the hearth has been the required counterpart of massive economic development, pushing people out where capital and technology no longer require as many "hands," and drawing them in where it needed more. Economic man, it would appear, has become an aerobic creature, survival becoming more dependent on antennae than on roots.

The way propertied and managerial America moves about its colossal apparatus of credits, capital, materials and machines has made it quite natural for managerial America to take for granted that human resources can be moved about in much the same way. The logistics of volume are applied to those of quality; the quality of human society.

D. The Barrio

Ethnic revolt in the central city is challenging these assumptions. The resistance has failed thus far. Over and over Mexican-American *colonias* have collapsed and disintegrated in the face of the overwhelming force of redevelopment. Could it be different, and does Oakland really want it to be different?

If the answer is "yes," there is room for experimentation with a Mexican *mercado* in Fruitvale. How should such a proposal be approached?

To begin with the approach would require acceptance of the idea of helping the Mexican barrio, the neighborhood, to maintain its hold on the particular portion of the urban landscape that it presently occupies. There are no open spaces in the Bay area, or in California for that matter, to which the Fruitvale tracts could be transplanted *en masse*. Nor has such an outlandish idea ever occurred to the planners. The reason is that they already had a more workable idea at hand. [The plan being] Individual replanting with each family on its own, relocation services not-withstanding.

The reversal of the planners' policy would be basic to the practicality and usefulness of a *mercado*. A relatively stable Mexican *vecindad* [neighborhood] continuously absorbing newcomers and thus renewing the peculiarities of its style of life would be the market toward which a *mercado* would be oriented.

It is suggested that on this basis the *mercado* be conceived as a combination community and shopping center.

A *mercado* of this nature should be physically planned as "a unified urban space" connected by channels for traffic with a surrounding community close by and daily accessible to the goods and services offered.

Such a solution of the problem of location would no doubt rescue, and perhaps invigorate, small Mexican-American business establishments tabbed for destruction. It would bring together the proprietors so threatened—a beginning of organization in this sector of the neighborhood.

Though dependent thus upon a local demand, the location, if close to a major station of the rapid transit system, could be brought within shopping-distance of Mexican-American residential districts lying along its route.

E. The Mercado

For a predominately Mexican-American clientele, the goods offered for sale in the *mercado* would cater to its needs and tastes. In the food lines, manufacturing could be added, especially those that are increasingly dependent on the "export trade" of Los Angeles processors. Bulk buying of such items as rice, beans, sugar and lard might be restored without economic sacrifice, thus bringing back to low-income families a measure of relief from high-priced packaging. Whether or not handcrafts could be produced would have to be based upon a closer analysis of the *mercado* and its neighborhood as both become profitable ventures.

The *mercado*, considered as a structure appointed to certain ends and uses, should have developmental funds as well as developmental space from the outset. Both would have to be adequate and flexible.

The number and types of workers for whom employment would be created would, of course, depend upon the amount of space allotted, the number of shops, the variety of goods, the emphasis on transactions over the counter, the size and effective demand on the supporting market area, and the presence of social services and facilities functioning on the spot. There is no reason why such services could not be cooperatively administered as a multiple-service center. A variety of indigenous neighborhood organizations, centering in the *mercado*, could bring together needs and resources. These organizations could bring order out of the confusion of community relations, where resources and needs have to make their initial acquaintance.

In this connection, something more has to be said about the problem of penetration of an ethnic minority community. With uncommon accuracy, these communities are designated as "target areas. The term is accurate only in that it describes a mode of approach by a public agency to a minority neighborhood. These agencies, each assigned to carry a special piece of the nation's social policy to low-income clients, and often within the deadlines of a crash program, must "penetrate" the target area for their particular purposes. This penetration is not simply a matter of communication which can take place effectively only after familiarity and confidence have been established.

What is happening today in the Mexican-American *colonias*? The growing number and increasing variety of services of the Great Society is sending the agencies into hasty consultation with a small number of interpreters, guides and experts who know, more or less accurately, the Mexican-American community. Eventually, of course, an agency may be expected to develop or hire such interpreters and experts. But neither the staff specialist nor the ad hoc community aide can organize and sustain the special interests of the clients so that they may become voluntarily involved in programs. Agencies up to now have not been enthusiastic about community organization in this sense. They seem to fear that they might become "penetrated" by their clients instead of themselves "penetrating" the communities.

The relationship between self-organization, responsiveness to needs, democratic processes of involvement, and communication founded on confidence is illustrated close at hand by the Oakland consumer cooperatives. Whether something from the cooperatives' experiences could be useful in the organization of a *mercado* ought certainly to be explored.

One feature which the Spanish-Speaking Foundation believes is desirable in their proposal is the creation of a Spanish-speaking atmosphere. The *mercado* has great possibilities in this respect. An atmosphere congenial to customers who are at home only in Spanish, and there are surely thousands in the greater *colonia* of Alameda County, would almost certainly be an important part of the sales pull. The *mercado* could be the one place in Oakland where Mexican-Americans could speak in Spanish without self-consciousness and non-Mexican-Americans eavesdrop without embarrassment.

One is tempted to imagine what a Mexican *mercado* might offer with regard to supermarket design. The four-walled, tar-papered, strutted barracks for packages surrounded by acres of barren blacktop is surely not the last word in these matters. A narrow-gauge train encircling the *mercado*, transportation rebates for shopping tours, and other bonuses to lessen demand for parking space, might be tried. The shopper, too, as a person, could be taken into consideration. A vista of walls not plastered with bargains and loss-leaders and convenient rest points would make routine shopping not less expensive but possibly less exhausting.

Some of these possibilities are not altogether fanciful. The Grand Central Market, located at Third and Broadway in Los Angeles, offers, by chance and by accident, some hints. The market is in an inconvenient location; parking space is expensive. Public buses make no allowance for the lugging of bundles and shopping bags. The corridors between the stalls are too narrow for the traffic at peak hours. Shoppers may have to travel seven miles or more on the busiest streets.

Tired customers lean on counters and railings for a momentary rest. Young children in the stream of buyers must be piloted through the crowds because there is no child-care facility.

Yet the Grand Central Market is popular and prosperous and about as typically Mexican as anything in Los Angeles, in spite of the ethnic mix of its clients. Prices are competitive, sometimes highly so. The quality of the fresh fruits, vegetables and other merchandise is good to excellent. The produce is generally fresh. Standard and specialty food items typical of the Mexican diet are displayed in abundance and variety. The service is prompt and friendly.

In the market, shoppers are met with human clerks, not by stacks of packages. The clerks are facile in Spanish, since many of them are Mexican-American. The snack counters are patronized by people who eat tamales and drink coffee as they stand chatting unhurriedly. This is the Mexican style of conversation, *platicando*. Three generations of one family can be seen moving together from stall to stall, each member carrying a bag or a package. On the sidewalks contiguous to the market people pause, in spite of the bustle and inconvenience of pedestrian traffic, to pick up bits of gossip broken off last week or last month.

No one can shop in the market without knowing at once that it is a Mexican place. Amidst the urban sprawl of Los Angeles which has swallowed hundreds of thousands of Mexican-Americans, this market is indeed "a unified urban space" holding and nourishing community. A dozen blocks to the north, Olvera Street, with a different market orientation of high-priced restaurants and novelties for tourists, seems to prefigure the commercial and cultural center that the Spanish-Speaking Foundation images for Oakland. It is quite possible that a feasibility study for such a center and for a *mercado* could find useful data in Grand Central Market and Olvera Street.

IV. A SERVICE AND RESEARCH UNIT

How much genuine interest there is at present, or could be tapped in the future, among Mexican-American businessmen with regard to the proposals of the Spanish-Speaking Foundation is, at this time, a matter of speculation. Such interest will have to be discovered, if it already exists. In addition to a series of preliminary discussions, ways and means for stimulating interest into viable organization calls for much broader contact with the community[,] and ultimately such discussions must lead to a commitment of specific goals and distribution of responsibilities.

Keeping in mind how often in the past potentially good proposals have floundered during the research stage, a dual-purpose service-and-research unit would be worth considering. This unit would have two assignments: to provide small businesses with the assistance that is necessary to lay the foundations for cooperative action; and to conduct the feasibility and development study which has been requested by the Foundation.

The desirability of carrying forward services, organization and research simultaneously needs to be emphasized. These services are the three strands out of which realistic patterns of community organization emerge. Services make it immediately evident that research and organization are intended for action. Research designs invariably change as organization and action enlist new people and reveal new possibilities for creative relationships between them. Action can both make demands on research and be disciplined by it. Failures in program planning can often be traced to the separation of these elements into arbitrary time-stages. The gaps between research, organization and services can be so wide that interest, motivation and opportunities can fall into the gaps and disappear.

However careful an economic and technical analysis of the feasibility of the Foundation's proposal might be, the initial and primary question still remains: Does the Mexican-American business community want the proposed centers? If it does, the next question is what resources of time, energy, interest, experience and capital is it willing to commit on rising levels of participation.

The possibility of creating a Mexican-American non-profit corporation to create and manage a commercial and cultural center and possibly a *mercado* would have to receive high priority in a feasibility study. The planning and completion of the study could itself become the first undertaking of such a corporation.

This approach would have a number of advantages. It would at the outset create the institutional device by which the Mexican-American business sector would organize itself around a concrete program, specific goals, available operating facilities, and contractual obligations. Through it the circle of contacts with the community could be widened, making it unnecessary to launch still another assault on the "target area." Personal attention to the details of planning, research, organization and action would provide a range of new experience to the members of the corporation which would be of great value to the individuals, and if competently applied, to the community. At the conclusion of the study, the decision whether to support or not support the proposals would be the decision of persons within the community, and not outside of it.

ALVISO

THE CRISIS OF A BARRIO

Ernesto Galarza, *Alviso: The Crisis of a Barrio* (San Jose, Calif.: Mexican American Community Service Agency, 1973).

Galarza was commissioned by the John Hay Whitney Foundation and the Mexican American Community Services Agency to study and report on the political and economic inequalities in Alviso, California. His research team found that Alviso was undergoing an economic transformation that was manipulated by elite interests from San Francisco and the surrounding Bay Area. He referred to Alviso in later interviews and publications as a model case study for understanding what was taking place in Mexican American communities throughout the Southwest.

Galarza often communicated his belief in research and its ability to act as an agent for social change. For this reason he took extra measures to ensure that the research approaches he used were systematic and methodologically rigorous. The Alviso study set a standard of excellence in action research.

Notable life event during this era:

- 1973: Galarza receives a grant from the John Hay Whitney Foundation to study and experiment with bilingual education. As a result of this work, the Studio Laboratory for Bilingual Education is instituted in San Jose and a foundational literature that argues in favor of a bilingual curriculum based on applied first-language immersion is created.

INTRODUCTION

Physical space offers the possibilities and limits the conditions of the existence of a human society. The founders of a village, a town or a city begin by appropriating space. Its distribution, arrangement, uses, regulation and occupancy whether resting on conquest, domination, custom or law, determine the conditions of life of the occupants.

Where space is seized by conquest and its previous holders are destroyed or dispersed, or where it is claimed by discovery and primitive settlement, the appropriation of space is comparatively easy to observe and to record. With the emergence of western industrial urbanism in the last three hundred years the significant struggles for living room have been transferred to the city, typically the metropolitan complex. On this stage the human drama of the use and enjoyment of space is not as easy to discover and document.

In the case of the Mexican-Americans now living in the United States, particularly in the southwest, little attention has been paid to the process by which the Mexican communities—the *barrios*—are fast losing their precarious hold on the physical space that gave them a location, a presence in numbers, an identity, and a cultural refuge. This process is taking place almost entirely within the metropolitan networks of cities like San Antonio, Los Angeles and San Francisco. It is in the central districts of this urban mesh that the tides of migration set in motion by the massive evictions of the past—the dispossession of the *campesinos* [farmworkers] of Mexico, the importation into the United States of seasonal contract labor under government sponsorship, the displacement of men by mechanization of agricultural production—deposited the *barrios*.

Research has not documented this process. Social scientists have not concerned themselves seriously with its sociological significance to the Mexican ethnic group itself, its connection and relationship to the deep currents of American life that do not originate in the *barrio* but do destroy it physically and culturally. To understand it would require particular studies of what has already happened in Los Angeles, Albuquerque, Phoenix, Fresno, Sacramento, San Antonio and San Diego, to mention only some of the instances of barriocide.

This report on the experience of Alviso does not pretend to be a model for such research. If it does nothing more than call attention to the need for it, its central purpose will have been fulfilled.

AUTHOR'S STATEMENT

In the fall of 1971 and through the spring of 1972 the John Hay Whitney Foundation provided financial support for a team study of the crisis of the community of Alviso, which is the subject of this report. The members of the team were Robert A. Cervantes, Dorothy Ellenberg, Ernesto Galarza, Julie Hitz, Roy Eugene Lokey, Efraim Lugo, Luis G. Nogales and Juan S. Vigil.

The report draws heavily on the numerous discussions among the team members and their individual and collective research. The conclusions and opinions drawn from them, as set forth in the following pages, are entirely mine.

Ernesto Galarza, San Jose, California, February 1, 1973.

THE TOWN OF ALVISO

Alviso's territory is approximately 14 square miles of shore lands located at the southern tip of San Francisco Bay and about ten miles northeast of San Jose. It is an area of tidewater marshes that receive the runoff from a large part of the Santa Clara Valley. The resulting floods isolate the residences and business establishments that have been constructed on fill consisting of dirt and even rubbish. Indeed, because of its isolation and topography, Alviso had become a dumping area for San Jose, Santa Clara and other adjoining municipalities. Over some fifty years of persistent effort the Alvisans raised a compact area of high ground on which they built their homes. They still face a problem of soil subsidence due to the geologic structures on which the town sits. Siltation, tide erosion, a flood plain devoid of vegetation to break the wind patterns of the winter, and a shoreline that is for the most part inaccessible to foot traffic emphasize the impression of dismal marginality of the Alviso territory.

Indeed, until the abuses of man committed on the bay in recent years began to take their toll of marine life, Alviso and its environs were a natural wildlife refuge. The major commercial use of such an environment was the construction of salt evaporation ponds, whose dikes separate the town from the South Bay basin.

SOME HISTORICAL BACKGROUND

Alviso's present unattractiveness as a home for man is the combined effect of the increasing inability of Alvisans to cope with the conditions imposed by nature and by social change. As one of the first incorporated cities of California, Alviso staked its hopes for a bright future on its geographic location and the enterprise of early residents touched with the speculative imagination of the Forty-niners. In the 1860's the town was an important link in the water and overland routes linking northern and southern California. It attracted weekend vacationers from the growing cities to the north. With these and other rosy prospects in mind the pioneer Alvisans developed schemes for real estate promotion not unlike those that characterized the urban burst of southern California in the 1920's. Alviso's urban bubble was baptized before it was blown: It was to be called New Chicago.

The 1870's and 1880's, however, bypassed these hopes. The new railroads did not choose the town as a railhead; the Santa Clara hinterland remained solidly agricultural, a festival of fruit blossoms in the spring and a canning and packing center that found other outlets to the national markets more economical and attractive than Alviso.

From the 1890's through the 1940's the town subsisted on the marginal spill of agricultural prosperity and miscellaneous opportunities for economic gain that the peculiar location and circumstances of the isolated community offered. Gambling clubs and the related amenities for weekend pleasure seekers attracted a certain clientele. Small shipyards for the construction of fishing and pleasure boats were built along the bayshore. On the landward side of the high ground pear orchards framed the Alviso flood plain[,] attracting seasonal pickers who made the shacks and weathered trailers of the town their summer headquarters. Alviso even became a convenient way station in the clandestine traffic of "wetbacks"— Mexican farm workers who entered the United States illegally. Principally the area settled into its role of a site for sewage treatment plants and for the disposal of dirt fill and industrial waste. With the exception of the high ground of central Alviso and its modest industrial fringe along the shore, the 14 square miles of its territory remained open and spacious.

THE MEXICANS IN ALVISO

Occupancy of such spaces, however unappealing to middle class families in search of suburban amenities and able to pay for them, proved attractive to another class of persons—Mexican families who were being displaced from agricultural employment and railroad maintenance and who were searching for cheap building lots, low rents and proximity to alternative chances for work. The Mexican discovery of Alviso began in the 1940's. It progressed through chance acquaintance with the community during a harvest season, connections with a family that had already established a foothold in the area, the offer at low prices of town lots that with patience and much labor would be filled and shored above the winter flood levels.

Another attraction for displaced Mexican families was the availability of residential buildings that were being discarded to make way for freeways and new residential tracts in San Jose. They could be salvaged and moved a few miles to Alviso. Compared to the outlay for a new house, the cost of moving one of these hand-me-downs was a bargain. Today the architectural style of the town is heavily accented by rows of homes with the unmistakable stamp of cultural transplants from another epoch and another place. The Mexican Alvisans have improved these relics. Many of the original structures have been remodeled, enlarged, painted and landscaped. There has been considerable slack in the enforcement of building codes, and within this tolerance ingenuity and the poor man's husbandry have provided passing shelter. Amidst the variety of remodeled and refurbished houses, single-room shacks, bungalows and farm-labor camp barracks there are no high-rise, high-rent apartments. On the whole, housing in Alviso presents a gray facade streaked by the seasons behind which families double up and ponder their chances of survival as a community.

This community presently has a population of approximately 1600 people. About two-thirds of them are of Mexican ancestry. Numerically Alviso is therefore a Mexican neighborhood or barrio. Any radical change in the political status of the town, its economic activities, its institutional forms or its demographic character would affect in vital ways the accommodations which its minority residents have been making precariously over some four decades.

In many respects, Alviso's past, present and future typify what has been happening to the Mexican communities of the greater San Francisco Bay area.

LIVING SPACE FOR THE MEXICAN BARRIOS

As one of California's important, agricultural areas, the Santa Clara Valley attracted Mexican farm laborers and their families who gathered in small, inconspicuous neighborhoods located in the rural spaces adjacent to cities not yet afflicted with growth. These neighborhoods were labor pools that served local farm labor demand adequately enough, supplemented by seasonal migrant workers from other parts of California and other states.

Around these *colonias* a work pattern developed consisting of seasonal or part-time employment in trades, crafts and services that hired workers with minimal skills. The critical factor in the stability of these employment patterns was housing. The Mexican workers were the lowest of the lowly paid. Buying a home was beyond their means. Low rents in unimproved neighborhoods within reach of the job site were a prime condition for making ends meet.

It was under these conditions that the barrios of the greater bay area were established in the early years of the present century. From Gilroy in the south to Hayward and Union City in the north—a spread of some fifty miles of farm land and light industry, of packing sheds and canneries—the Mexican *barrios* grew in spots of land rated low at the time for industrial or urban potential. In the center of this spread Alviso became a refuge for Mexicans seeking to combine a low-cost level of living with accessibility to a job mix within the range of limited skills.

The Mexican *barrios* that were thus dependent on marginal living space were in no way prepared to survive the advance of urbanism southward into the peninsula from San Francisco and Oakland. Cities like San Jose, Sunnyvale, Santa Clara and Hayward began to spread during the last quarter century, first in ripples and then in tides of advancing suburbs, raising land values and posing new problems of zoning and taxation.

What remains today of these social, cultural and ethnic enclaves is the residue of a many-faceted squeeze on the living space of the *barrios*. The progress of urbanization, with its attendant complex of freeways and airports, shopping centers and industrial parks, has ground the barrios inexorably. The history of all of them—South Oakland, Union City, Moran Hill, down-town San Jose, Hayward, Cupertino, is exemplified by the story of Alviso.

A TOWN BESIEGED BY PROGRESS

Only a person who is well informed and thoroughly documented on its history can read the present landscape of Alviso and interpret its meaning. It is a large and coveted parcel of real estate whose legal boundaries are still intact but around which urban progress gathers its pressures, and forces. A new freeway marks the boundary between Alviso and San Jose, from which lateral expressways are ready to penetrate into and through the residential high ground. A rapid transit system is making its way south from San Francisco, its projection to the vicinity of San Jose raising the possibility of another major dislocation. The extension of an airport which already covers Alviso with its flight pattern could bring about a massive encroachment from another quarter. On a map of the area one of the principal streets of San Jose, South First Street, is rapidly becoming the axis of light industrial, commercial, and trading development. The axis is anchored in the new financial district of down-town San Jose, and points in a straight line at the heart of Alviso. Pear orchards have been uprooted to make way for trailer parks that have already been laid out on the south side of the town. Within the town itself holders of large parcels of land are projecting the construction of apartment complexes. If and when the silted channels of the bayshore are dredged, a marina complete with lagoons, parks, beaches and seaside residences may replace what is now the residential sector of the community. A national wildlife refuge of some 23,000 acres has been created by an act of Congress with good prospects that Alviso may become the administrative headquarters and a source of employment, as well as an attraction for commercial enterprises that the foot traffic of the refuge is expected to bring. There are plans for a major international trade mart in the vicinity of the airport. Amusement parks of the Disneyland type are being projected on locations that are likely to make land values in Alviso soar.

The tides of progress that have been gathering momentum throughout the bay area during the past thirty years are now banked high around Alviso, waiting to break through and intrude on one of the most coveted portions of real estate in Santa Clara County.

ANNEXATION OF ALVISO

The political expression of the increasing interest in Alviso by private and public developers was the campaign to annex the town to the City of San Jose. Since the mid-forties the larger cities of the Valley had been competing strenuously to extend their boundaries and stake out administrative control of the anticipated economic expansion. During this period the City of San Jose succeeded in establishing corridors of control in all directions except Alviso. Two attempts to annex the town by elections failed.

The third attempt succeeded. In January 1968 annexation was approved by the Alvisans by a vote of 189 to 180. To all practical purposes local government ended with that election. Because of a series of lawsuits challenging the election filed by the losers, Alviso has remained in a twilight zone with respect to its legal status.

At this writing the litigation is in its fifth year. Its effect has been to halt in their tracks the private and public developers, who have been understandably reluctant to commit millions of dollars as matters now stand.

The aim of the plaintiffs in the litigation has been to gain time to plan and prepare for a different kind of future for the community than the developers have in mind. The important question for the Alvisans therefore is: What are the alternatives? But before a choice of courses could be proposed to the opponents of annexation[,] two conditions had to be met. First, the research and planning sources that affected Alviso had to be opened to the Alvisans: second, there had to be organized a citizen's group that would commit itself clearly and firmly to effective, democratic, autonomous local control.

PLANNING FOR ALVISO

Because of its strategic location, Alviso unavoidably has occupied a good deal of the attention of the official planning agencies of the City of San Jose. It can be said, in fact, that research and planning for drastic changes in the land uses of the town were simply the technical arm of a political goal that had already been settled—annexation. The official studies strongly emphasized the blight of the town and drew up proposals and blueprints of the familiar urban renewal type. Reflecting the diverse and sometimes conflicting interests of private and public developers, the planners projected marinas, industrial facilities, public attractions and high-cost residential promotion.

These proposals were competently documented, but no one was briefing the community about them. In any case, the Alvisans were concerned with issues to which the planning bodies did not address themselves—rezoning, code enforcement, assistance to the present residents to avoid relocation, economic development that would tend to stabilize rather than disperse the present community.

In these matters the Alvisans had no experience prior to the election of 1968. After that event some token representation on planning bodies was conceded. A few local residents were co-opted to serve as planning advisors: but the basic goals of the planning process as settled in San Jose were not changed.

ALVISO—NEGATIVE SURVIVAL FACTORS

- Low income: The Mexican families of Alviso stand on the lowest income levels. At those levels the prevailing concern of day-to-day living is simple survival. Men and women who live under the constant pressure of poverty have no surplus of material resources or psychological confidence to spend on the demands and risks of responsible citizenship. Alleged apathy, non-involvement, acquiescence and even submissiveness are the effects of that double condition of the poor.

- Dependency: Family resources very soon reach the point of exhaustion in Alviso, creating the conditions of dependency on public welfare without which living levels in the community would fall even lower. There does not have to be an overt threat of losing welfare benefits to make dependent families prudent in their dealings with those who hold so much of their precarious welfare in their power.

- Institutional guardianship[:] Low income and dependency create the opportunity for agencies external to the community to set up their services on a case load basis. The effect is to separate individuals and families from the economic class to which they belong. The result is a sort of welfare individualism that does nothing to encourage collective action to improve a common lot. There is no public agency giving social assistance in Alviso that is committed to the proposition that the community must survive as a community.

- Political guardianship: For many years prior to 1968 Alviso was governed as an incorporated town by a self-perpetuating group of decision makers. The Alviso Mexicans were denied political experience, which they did not trouble to demand.

- Institutional aimlessness: Alviso and its Mexican residents are a very distant by-product of a cultural disintegration of the collective sense of community. This disintegration has been produced by hundreds of years of conquest, expropriation and exploitation. The tribal foundations of group survival ceased being a part of the cultural traditions of the Mexican people. By the beginning of the 20th century these traditions had been replaced by a characteristic version of western, individualistic society. The Alviso Mexicans are an infinitesimal example of this historic process.

- Limited equities: In the situation in which the Alvisans presently find themselves the indispensable credential for admission into the circle of decision-makers is property. Not including those who own the bayfront industries of the town, the Alvisans probably own less than ten per cent of the assessed real estate. The Alvisa Mexicans do not own Alviso.

- Transient tenancy: The individualistic role of the homeowners and their frail share of the wealth represented by real estate is weakened further by the transient character of the house renters. It is a floating population prompted by no sense of permanent connection with the fortunes of the community as such.

- Co-optation: Lacking their own public institutions to bestow prestige on its more prominent members[,] the Alvisans respond to opportunities offered by outside interests to play the part of "community leaders" or spokesmen. This role has been assumed by persons who are not related by a network of responsible relationships within the community itself. Without a strong element of trust monitored by accountability, co-optation has become a process of isolating the more able or ambitious citizens from their neighbors.

- Public misinformation: Information which importantly affects the present and future of Alviso has typically circulated only among the co-opted leaders, the alien planners and the agents of welfare administration. As a community the Alvisans had no way to screen facts from rumors. Nor have they had agents of their own to pursue inquiries neglected by outside interests.

- Undercapitalization: The high value placed by private and public developers on the potential land uses of the Alviso territory explains why these interests have been ready to mobilize very large amounts of capital to realize that potential for private profit. Even if the Alvisans had had before them an alternative model of collective community organization and action, they would still have been totally incapable of funding economic actions that would credit such organization with concrete accomplishments and visible benefits.

- Negativism: Among the Mexican population of the town there are a number of elders whose views on the effectiveness of collective community action are extremely negative. These residents have the leisure to visit and spread their opinions about town. To them Alviso is the final refuge for a people whose history is one of unceasing displacement, migration, and relocation. This negativism is often expressed in public meetings and supported by reference to experiences known to be true by the listeners. Speaking through such voices this negativism comes through with the persuasive overtones of a bleak ancestral wisdom.
- Economic pluralism: As stated above, the Alvisans do not own Alviso. Ownership of property is unevenly distributed between homeowners, small industrial establishments, municipal utilities, corporations, and developers of various categories. All except the homeowners can expect some form of increment in their stake if the town is annexed. Only those who make their home in Alviso and who value familial and cultural ties sense the disaster for them that would follow such an event.
- Grantsmanship: Reacting to protests and grievances among the Mexican minority throughout the nation, federal, state and local governments have responded with a variety of programs that have in common a rhetoric of concern for the *barrio* as a community. In reality the rhetoric is misleading. Alviso's experience with such programs[,] as will be explained in more detail below, has been that public grantsmanship creates new forces of fragmentation within the community. Grass roots participation in these programs in practice means the co-optation of a few of the more aggressive or more capable residents who are endowed with budgets and powers and bureaucratic authority that set them apart from and above their neighbors. In the process the local bureaucracy has been gradually converted into a delivery system of services that fulfill the requirements of federal policy rather than those of minority community besieged by progress.
- When, in an open democratic society, opposing interests face each other, two factors are decisive: the personal ability of the individuals who serve those interests, and the institutional support they can depend on. The Alviso Mexicans drifted together. The negative elements of social drift—what might be called its statics—have been indicated above. The positive factors from which a survival strategy might have been devised should now be indicated.

ALVISO—POSITIVE SURVIVAL FACTORS

- Cultural identity: The most promising of these is the cultural identification of the majority of the Alvisans with one another by reason of their common Mexican ancestry and the survival of certain cultural traits, principally language and religion, durable familial structures and values, the familiarity of close daily contact in a small neighborhood and a class status of low-income workers shared by most of the residents.

- Class status: Up to the year 1968 no single group of Alvisans held class control over their neighbors with respect to their jobs or their standing in the community. Neither from the welfare payments received by many families nor from their modest wage income was it possible for a few to emerge as job givers, or patrons of their neighbors. Both wage earners and welfare dependents easily identified their common social needs, and both readily understood that the resources to meet those needs lay outside the community.

- Ethnic relations: Although the Mexicans were numerically dominant they did not develop political or social power domination with respect to the Anglo minority in their midst. Between families, there was a degree of familiarity and easy contact which maintained a favorable talking distance between the individuals who worked out their lives on the Alviso scene.

- Bilingual communication: From both the Mexican and the Anglo sides the ethnic contacts were made easier by a marketplace bilingualism of little academic distinction but great practical utility. In either language there were enough Alvisans who could follow the drift of conversation or public discussion and thus avoid the uneasiness and wariness of persons who do not understand what is being said in their presence.

- Black-brown ethnic relations: Alviso has no black population and therefore no base for a black interest group to make its presence felt in the politics of the community. There has been no trace of the black-brown competitiveness and suspicion that has developed in other communities where an ethnic mix produced rival claims on grants for public projects.

- The neighborhood scale: Of the 14 square miles of the town's territory only a small area of a few hundred acres has been filled and conditioned for construction. Sprawl has been discouraged both by poverty and the terrain. Except as out-of-town job commuters, the Alvisans have lived within sight and sound of one another. City Hall was only a few blocks from any household.

- Stability: Among the homeowners the economic attractions of low land costs have outweighed the inconveniences of flooding, dumping, unpaved streets and the lack of other public amenities. The refugees have become settlers. Up to very recently there were no industrial or agricultural booms to upset the low-level equilibrium of a community living, literally and figuratively, on marginal resources. There was a continuity of residence of Mexicans creating a presumption that Alviso would continue to be a place where they could cope with living. The Mexicans were comparatively recent comers to the town but they readily identified themselves with a tradition of municipal autonomy of more than a century.

- Geographic insulation: Communities, like individuals, seem to require a sense of identity, of distinct selfness, which is greatly helped or hindered by the local geography. Entering or leaving Alviso is a distinct physical experience. The territorial boundaries created by nature are as distinct as the political boundaries around which in the past industry and urbanization have detoured. In a society in which geographic distinctness of a separate home ground of social groups has become blurred, institutions weave a new mesh of social cohesions that may be much less visible to those who are not certain of what they belong to, if anything. The Alvisans benefitted from the strong sense of geographic identity even as they suffered from the absence of indigenous institutional vigor.

- Benign polarization: Helped by geography, the Alvisans' sense of cultural and ethnic identity produced enough polarization to reinforce an awareness of local interests different from the interests of those who merely used Alviso as a present place of business and pleasure or as future opportunity for private gain. Until 1968 this polarization included the substantial property interests of the town, the political elite that governed Alviso, the agriculturists, the small industrial entrepreneurs and the homeowners. This informal coalition, which tended to keep the town poor and in disrepair, began to fall apart around 1968 when it became clear that the participants in the coalition could stake out disproportionate shares of the promised bonanza for themselves. Those who seemed least likely to profit from the future were the Mexican homeowners.

- Foreign alliances: Taking the word "foreign" in a parochial sense to mean factors existing or operating outside of Alviso, the community's connections with individuals and groups of outsiders was a favorable survival factor. Alviso's problems were well known to institutions such as the Santa Clara Council of Churches, through which a considerable body of church-affiliated opinion was enlisted in support of the Alvisan's efforts to help themselves. Members of the faculty and students of San Jose State University had served over the years as volunteers and community organizers. The Coalition Against Poverty, undoubtedly the most widely connected network of contacts between civic organizations composed of middle and higher income citizens of the county, gave Alviso a high priority on its organizational and lobbying agenda. Through academic and other channels the plight of the Alvisans as a Mexican *barrio* under sentence of extinction became known to sympathetic and influential individuals and organizations in San Francisco, Los Angeles, Chicago, Washington and New York. To a greater extent than most Alvisans realized this outer circle of sympathetic interest in their plight offered a forum from which their case might be made known to a wider audience.

Balancing the negative and the positive factors bearing on the chances of community survival which have been summarized above, the prognosis was not positive. It was abundantly clear by the time the annexationists succeeded in 1968 that Alviso was caught squarely in the process of urban change that had already physically destroyed many Mexican *barrios* in the southwest, not a few in California itself.

THE PROGNOSIS FOR SURVIVAL

The Alvisans, for historical reasons peculiar to them, are a people who have never participated fully in citizenship[,] as they have never participated in a distribution of income and wealth that would have provided opportunities to exercise citizenship.

It is important to stress that the Alviso Mexicans have sought help from outside the community and that they have received assistance during the past ten years with an abundance of good will and a minimum of financial support. The first response to the Alvisans that was in any degree viable was a Study Team funded by the John Hay Whitney Foundation.

THE ALVISO STUDY TEAM

After the Foundation had approved in principle the basic concept of grants to teams that would address themselves to the critical problems of a particular community, conversations were started in San Jose among persons who had credentials to take part in a team that would concern itself with the Mexican-

American community of Alviso. These conversations led to the conclusion that initially the team would have to direct its efforts toward creating a repository of data and information vital to an understanding of what was going on in and about Alviso and to make this information available to the Alvisans themselves.

For the first ten months of its existence, therefore, the term Alviso Study Team accurately described the character of the group. It was composed of seven persons, all of them residents of Santa Clara County and all of them with personal knowledge of one aspect or another of Alviso's contemporary experience. These persons were: Dorothy Ellenberg. Luis Nogales, Juan Vigil, Ephraim Lugo, Eugene Lokey, Robert Cervantes and Ernesto Galarza. The combined experience of the team members professionally made it possible to bring to bear a serious interdisciplinary judgment to the problems and issues that were of vital importance to the Alvisans.

From the outset the team members agreed that they were not assigning themselves a research project of an academic nature; that the information that would be sought should have high relevance to the vital issues facing the Alvisans; and that the study phase was an unavoidable initial step in view of the control of documentation and information, especially relating to policy decisions, that planners and others closing in on the town had established.

When the project was approved by the Foundation[,] the team estimated that the initial study phase might take two years. The previous familiarity with the Alviso situation and the number and diversity of contacts which the team members collectively had access to made it possible for the team to conclude its studies in ten months.

As the team was being assembled it was obvious that it would be composed of "outsiders". A team of resident Alvisans would have been preferable, but it was not feasible for several reasons: (1) No group of Alvisans could have been formed with the connections and the experience to accomplish a quick and reliable breakthrough into the sources of information required to equip the community with important facts; (2) at that point the Alvisans had no legal resources to gain access to planning records; (3) even if the information were available to the affected citizens, they needed counseling on the meaning of such information; and (4) there did not exist within the community an institutional agent subject to democratic restraints that would guarantee its continuing as an inside team responsive to local interests.

The Alviso Study Team was sharply aware of these circumstances and was especially conscious of the possibility that it, too, could become manipulative. As the work of the team progressed and its influence on the Alvisans became noticeable, opportunities to deviate [from the original intention of the research purpose] did indeed present themselves. The team members had no difficulty in recognizing and declining them.

The team's goals for Alviso were laid down from the outset:

> The quest is for a social group small enough to balance freedom and responsibility and opportunity for all its members, if not guaranteed[,] at least encouraged by the way it is structured and the way it operates in daily life.

Further, the goal was a community

> that will look to the level and upward securities of all its members; the creation of an educational process that will run continuously and parallel to the public affairs of Alviso, but independent of private rewards and personal advantage; the enlistment of professional advisors to inform and train the residents to become competent in the discharge of their responsibilities to their community.

In brief, the team set out to examine in detail what would be required to apply Robert Dahl's concept of "neighborhoods of human proportions . . . territorial units that are small enough to facilitate participation and yet large enough to exercise authority so significant as to make participation worthwhile."

OPERATION OF THE ALVISO STUDY TEAM

The group met regularly, usually once a week on Saturday mornings. At these meetings information was exchanged and analyzed, assignments were made and reports were received. Each member of the team maintained his own personal circle of contacts in Alviso and in San Jose. There was a continuing discussion with Alvisans as individuals and groups[,] by means of which the information passed on by the team became part of the public opinion of the town. Important public meetings that had a bearing on Alviso were attended by team members.

From time to time the team prepared and published in its own name information bulletins in both Spanish and English in which important current issues were documented and analyzed.

The team did not set up a central collection of documents of its own. It did exchange copies and memoranda of useful papers[,] and the files on Alviso of every member were available to all. Groups with special interests to promote in Alviso and San Jose soon came to recognize the credibility of the team and the effect of its research on the formation of public opinion within and outside of Alviso. This credibility was never compromised by allowing such interests to make use of the team resources to serve their own ends.

The end that the team was pursuing was the formulation of a concept in the minds of the more influential Alvisans of a community institution that could eventually claim legitimate representation of the interests of the town; an institution that would not be a disguised hiring hall through which a few residents would receive special benefits and status. The team from time to time formulated and offered for discussion proposals and models for such an institution, and encouraged examination of the operational and legal forms that such an institution might take. These proposals in effect aimed to create an understanding of a model of a community commitment and a community process that was not similar to anything the Alvisans had ever experienced or that they could see in operation anywhere around them.

The team did not publish its research memoranda, but their contents were given to Alvisans when it was felt that the persons receiving the information would put it to uses compatible with the goals the team was pursuing.

After nearly ten months the informational work was practically complete. A more limited task was to keep the information current and the Alvisans up-to-date on the developments that were pressing upon them.

During the first quarter of 1972 it was decided to make closer contact with the Alvisans and encourage a sense of self-confidence which had been growing noticeably. A temporary office was opened in the town and more intensive discussion of the organization of a neighborhood council was stimulated. It should be said that the team consistently stressed that its role was to inform and counsel the residents to the end that they eventually create and maintain their own organizational means for advocacy and action. The result of this was the creation of the Ad Hoc Committee of residents.

THE AD HOC COMMITTEE

This was a new social grouping of Alvisans, mostly Mexicans, which originated and received its initial encouragement from the Alviso Study Team.

The Ad Hoc Committee in its early stages was a study and discussion group oriented more and more to the problems of community organization and action. Between fifteen and twenty-five residents attended its meetings, the effects of which were noticeable in the public opinion of the small town. The organizers of the Committee were solely concerned with development projects, proposed policies, schemes and programs that could affect the tenure of the residents. In this regard they understood that the proponents of such schemes and projects, whether they were private promoters or public agencies, could be dealt with only by a body of Alvisans whose credentials as community spokesmen were unclouded by partisan interest.

The Ad Hoc Committee was soon organized well enough to set up sub-committees that were assigned to fund raising, legal defense, public information and advocacy. The Committee initiated a service of door-to-door information and convocations of meetings to inform the townspeople of important matters. Eventually it was the aim of the Committee to organize a system of plebiscites through which the residents could express their choices in those matters.

Within a few weeks of its creation the Committee had become a pivotal influence group in Alviso affairs. Given the incoherence of community structure and the demands of the model the Study Team sought to encourage, the promising beginnings of the Committee should be understood as the cumulative effect of a number of factors. The educational efforts of outside volunteers had been going on for some five years. Independent research for the benefit of the Alvisans had been initiated with a small grant from the Southwest Council of La Raza in 1970. The Alviso Study Team had brought this research up to date and had found ways to put it to practical uses. And finally the team had offered its experience in organizational techniques and a strong bias toward democratic processes. Personal acquaintance over several years had created feelings of trust that made exchanges easy between the Alvisans and outsiders.

On this promising course, the Ad Hoc Committee was able to affect significantly two issues of vital concern to the entire community. One was the lawsuit challenging the annexation election of 1968. The other was the proposal to create within Alviso a New Towns development.

THE ANNEXATION LAWSUITS

By the time the Ad Hoc Committee appeared on the scene, the complaint against the City of San Jose had been tried, appealed and remanded for retrial by the State Supreme Court. At this point the Committee recognized that until the litigation was concluded plans and projects for development would be halted. It was clear that the Alvisans were buying time. Although the Committee did not file the complaint, it took the initiative for the prosecution of the case when its prospects had begun to sag. Many members of the Committee accepted liability for legal costs that might be assessed against the signers of the complaint, Jesse Canales and Everardo Resendez.

As an opportunity for public enlightenment the briefings on the progress of the case which were held by the Committee were in marked contrast with the secretiveness that usually surrounded public affairs in the town. The legal defense fund which the Committee raised through donations demonstrated the important point that the Alvisans should and could match with their own modest resources the help they were receiving from outside.

After the creation of the Committee, efforts continued on the part of the defendants to arrange a settlement of the suit. These efforts were addressed to the Committee, a circumstance that marked an important change in the center of influence in the community. Up to that time this center had been an organization called the Alviso Improvement Corporation, organized by a wealthy landowner, who had campaigned for annexation. The Corporation had signed a contract with the City of San Jose which, the Alvisans were told, established iron-clad obligations to make certain improvements in the town and set up the Corporation as the watchdog of those obligations. The contract was used effectively as a device to win supporters in the annexation election. When its terms and implications were explained to the community[,] the support for the lawsuit which the Committee encouraged had a double effect[:] it delayed the legal abolition of Alviso, and it showed that while the Corporation could and did deliver an election, it did not represent the interests of the town vis-a-vis San Jose.

THE NEW TOWNS PROPOSAL

In 1972 Federal funds became available for urban redevelopment through the device of special corporations by means of which public and private financing could be combined to build modern satellites to congested cities. The open spaces of Alviso are a natural spillway for the urban pressures moving in from all directions of the Bay area. The New Towns concept was suited to the development plans, many of them already in blueprints, that local promoters had in hand.

New Towns soon became a critical front in Alviso's prolonged struggle to survive. The strategy adopted to pave the way for the rise of a New Town in the heart of the old one was for the City of San Jose to sponsor state legislation to create a corporate body that would undertake the venture. The board of directors of that body, it turned out, was to be composed of the members of the City Council, acting in a dual capacity.

It was during the progress of the bill authorizing New Towns that the Ad Hoc Committee showed how quickly it had moved to the center of community awareness and influence. With the assistance of members of the study team, the Committee informed itself competently on the provisions of the proposed bill. A round figure of $40,000,000 was circulated as the reward for accepting a plan that would have prepared the ground for the extinction of the community. The Committee named its own spokesmen to appear before the legislature. It prepared amendments to the original bill which were negotiated step by step. On one occasion the Committee sent a delegation of forty residents to the state capital to support its views.

The resulting bill was not the one that had been originally introduced. And while it cannot be said that the approved text fully protects the tenure of the residents and the autonomy of the town, "maximum feasible participation" of the people most sharply affected by New Towns reached its peak with the Ad Hoc Committee.

The hopeful prosecution of the lawsuit, the successful intervention in the New Towns controversy, the continuing educational process, the open informational services and the growing self-confidence with which the Ad Hoc Committee spoke on the community's affairs indicated the beginnings of a political process that the residents had not experienced before.

These were noted by the team as encouraging signs and every opportunity was taken to formulate a more permanent type of community organization centered on the collective good and welfare.

The team remained aware that the cultural underpinnings for such an organization were frail indeed. Nevertheless, with the assistance of team members[,] various drafts for a Town Hall, a Mesa Redonda [roundtable], a Neighborhood Council, or a *cabildo,* were prepared and discussed. The defensive actions in the courts and in the state legislature could be meaningful in the long run only if in the time thus gained[,] enough Alvisans reached a level of understanding and personal commitment that would stand the increasing pressures from within and from without.

From the outside the most persistent of these pressures came from City Hall in San Jose, with its partisans in the community who were convinced that only annexation could lift the town out of its economic sloughs. Within Alviso the economic interests of the low income residents, particularly the homeowners, diverged more and more sharply from those of large landholders anxious to capitalize on the intense growth of the town that annexation promised to generate.

In spite of their promise, the holding actions of the Ad Hoc Committee were not neutralizing the forces that were centered on Alviso. The study team had become active late in the progress of this encirclement, and the Ad Hoc Committee had made a late appearance indeed on the scene. A much more adequate formulation of assistance to the Alvisans in the various directions suggested by the study team was as clear in the minds of the team members.

In the closing weeks of 1972 the progress of the Committee, guided by the team, came to a halt. It proved incapable of dealing with an agency in the community that increased divisiveness within the town and reinforced the negative traits of a community not culturally constrained to bend its members to serving the common good. This agency was the Alviso Family Health Foundation, the legal body that administered and operated the clinic for medical and dental health services.

THE ALVISO CLINIC

As a result of a community consultation in 1968 directed by outside volunteers, it was determined that the Alvisans' most urgent need was a local medical and dental clinic. Efforts to that end were making progress by the summer of 1969. A grant of $10,000 was obtained from the Ford Foundation to initiate construction of a clinic. The administration building of a motel that was being demolished in San Jose was purchased and moved across the city to Alviso. The town council provided a site on a long term lease. With volunteer labor provided by the residents construction began. The old motel building was remodeled. Design, planning and building proceeded with the help of engineers, contractors and doctors who volunteered technical advice and supervision.

These beginnings, modest as they were, aroused the enthusiasm of the community and attracted the attention of outsiders to an unusual example of community action at its best. Application was made to the Office of Economic Opportunity for a federal grant to enlarge the building, purchase modern equipment, hire trained personnel and provide training for junior staff and health counseling to patients.

The Ford Foundation grant had been requested and approved by the local chapter of the Community Services organization, affiliated with the statewide federation of the same name. The local chapter appointed a committee to administer the clinic[,] whose prospects grew with the favorable possibilities of federal funding. The first OEO grant of nearly half a million dollars was followed by larger grants. The current budget allots over $1,500,000 for a year's operation.

The physical appearance of the clinic, with its modernized central facilities and trailer satellites with administrative offices, became a dominant feature of the drab Alviso landscape. With a payroll of some 150 persons the clinic had become in less than three years the largest employer in the town. The outreach of its services now embraced hundreds of families who did not live in Alviso, and who were shuttled by a small fleet of buses. Young people were enrolled in courses to train them for paraprofessional service in the medical and dental departments. The staff was classified and organized in the unavoidable image of a small bureaucracy already displaying the frictions typical of all such establishments.

Outwardly the launching and the growth of the clinic were achievements worthy of note, especially to observers of community affairs in Mexican *barrios*. By the end of 1972 the clinic had become something of a showpiece of the Office of Economic Opportunity, visited by functionaries from other parts of the nation and of the world. The clinic was close to becoming a model of successful community action with genuine grass roots origins, with new jobs to offer the unemployed and opportunities to gain experience in the conduct of public affairs which the Alvisans had notoriously lacked.

THE TRANSFORMATION OF THE ALVISO CLINIC

The notable success of the clinic in so short a time and from such modest beginnings almost completely eclipsed the subtle conversion of the clinic from a system for the delivery of medical and dental services to something more. In the short span of three federal grants and with millions of dollars to spend the clinic was transformed from a medical center to a civic center. It assumed roles and took the initiative in matters such as urban planning, economic development, community organization, New Towns negotiations and community information.

In order to make the point unmistakably clear, there were two processes at work in Alviso. One was the organization and participation in a federally financed program to provide health service to a low-income community through and with the participation of the community itself.

The other process was the search for and the creation of an institution that would address itself to the fundamentally political strategies that would protect the community from extinction, contrive a degree of community power able to negotiate options, provide on a continuing basis reliable information on which the residents could make choices of public policy to be negotiated, raise the funds necessary for research and public information, finance legal services for defensive or positive litigation, plan for urban change and progress in a manner and through instruments that would not sacrifice one part of the community to another, and consider alternative possibilities for local economic development with a view to community sharing rather than individual advantage.

It was the second of these processes to which the Alviso Study Team addressed itself. In its judgment the clinic's services were appreciable and deserving of support. The clinic, however, was not so organized internally, or subject to community opinion externally or legally constituted or financed, to serve the broader interests of Alviso as a whole. Nevertheless, the clinic speedily assumed the role of representative of those broader interests, without an awareness of the requirements of such a role. It would be necessary to imagine a community program as well financed as the clinic, and capable of providing itself on a scale as adequate as the clinic's, with those technical support services which are no less essential for local community organization than competent physicians and dentists are for a Clinic.

The Alviso Study Team represented a first step toward such an image. If the word "political" is taken in its broadest context, two observations can be advanced at this point. The first is that encouragement and support for the model pursued by the Study Team is not a policy of the federal and state establishments. The second is that there is no source of private funding at present willing and able to accept the scale of financing or the continuity of support that could match the resources that are wiping out the Alvisos of America.

It is instructive to identify some of the more important factors that account for the preemption of a vital political role in a small Mexican community by what should have remained simply a specialized social service.

THE CLINIC AS THE NEW ESTABLISHMENT

The first step in this direction was taken when the Office of Economic Opportunity made it a condition for financing the clinic that its governing body be a legal entity separate from the local chapter of the Community Services Organization. The state CSO under its charter retained certain powers over the affairs of the local chapters that the OEO felt could be exercised by the CSO [in a way that would] interfere with the contractual relations between the OEO and the clinic. The committee that had been appointed by the local CSO to oversee the clinic in its first days was reconstituted into the Alviso Family Health Foundation, and it was with that Foundation that the OEO negotiated its grants.

Neither the new board of the clinic nor the legal experts of the OEO, in limiting the influence of the state OEO, took the pains to limit the potential intrusion of the clinic's bureaucracy into the fundamental political process of the community. The OEO's view of Alviso from Washington was narrow and distant, and it did not in any way take into account or show any sign of being aware of the negative and positive factors of the community culture which have been indicated earlier in this report.

Whether or not the separation of the CSO from control of the clinic was a conscious and self-serving move by the board of the new Foundation, the board very quickly sensed its powers under the federal grants. The expansion of these powers was further encouraged by a series of significant decisions made in Washington and accepted by the Foundation.

One of these was that the area of service of the clinic was to be expanded. Originally the residents of Alviso had indicated that they needed and wanted a clinic proportioned to the town of Alviso itself with its 1600 residents. This did not accord with OEO guidelines and the area of service was enlarged to include several thousand clients living outside of Alviso. This change raised a new set of problems of participation, representation, communication and administrative responsibility. It also meant that the residents of Alviso proper had to wait their turn for clinic admission as part of a much larger clientele of nonresidents. The identification of the clinic as a service for and by the Alvisans was lost. A program widened to include several communities and thousands of clients now required endless hours of board meetings to deal with the administrative problems of a much larger and complicated operation.

A second and significant difference that was introduced into the relations of Alvisans with one another was the power to hire and fire that was placed in the hands of the board of the Foundation. An employer-employee relationship was established between neighbors who had been economic equals theretofore. Patronage and even nepotism followed, as well as self-serving appointments by members of the board. The salaries and emoluments which were under the control of the board provided incomes for the favored ones that were considerably higher than the poverty level typical of the community.

Furthermore, as the clinic loomed larger on the landscape and in the concerns of the town, it became more and more favored by government agencies for funding programs in child care, consumer cooperatives, job training, housing, and youth guidance. In all of these projects the clinic took a hand. Institutional machinery can be bent to serve many purposes if those purposes meet with no competition. By the middle of 1972 the board of the Foundation was in that happy position. For all practical purposes, it was a convenient handle by which federal programmers could make immediate connections with a community that was otherwise amorphous.

These tendencies were sharply reinforced when the Economic Development Administration chose the Foundation as the recipient of a sizeable grant for a feasibility study of the possibilities for economic growth in the area. The staff for this study was selected and hired by the clinic board. There was little expertise on the board in this crucial area of community concerns, which in fact was the front line, so to speak, of the struggle for survival of the town. Neither did the EDA grant concern itself with the dangers of preparing an economic development program proposal totally devoid of community commitment based on full public information and citizen education.

The increasing dominance of the clinic group was strengthened by the prestige of personal connections with important state and federal officials, the authority to allocate jobs, the inside information which emanated from or led to critical decisions, and the status resulting from successful brokerage with unprecedented federal funds. The grass roots action that had made the clinic possible originally had been reduced to the power of less than a dozen residents. Within this small circle those who could cope with the complicated dealings with Washington were fewer still. Unable to explain and often to justify administrative decisions or to grasp the import of unfamiliar issues, the board avoided discussion with the community. Months passed without town assemblies where the board could give an account of its stewardship.

The Alviso Study Team lost no opportunities to identify these trends and to explain why, in its view, they did not fill the crucial demands of community survival. A dialogue of this kind with the grantors of funds and the dispensers of prestige in Washington was unimaginable, since there were no federal agencies actively concerned with this sector of the war on poverty. Such a dialogue with members of the community was possible and was maintained by the team, except with those who were more and more drawn into the tight circle of privilege and control of the clinic.

The Ad Hoc Committee was created by residents who were excluded from this circle, but in due course many of its key members made a fatal mistake in strategy, the explanation of which brings this report to its conclusion.

The gist of the error was that several talented members of the Committee decided to contest the control of the clinic on the stand that they could reverse its direction and make it genuinely responsive to the needs of the community.

THE CURRENT CRISIS OF ALVISO

Late in 1972 board elections were held and several Ad Hoc Committee activists, as a personal choice, campaigned for the posts. The result was the election of a majority of seven out of nine members who came from the membership of the Committee. It should be said that the team strongly advised against this course.

The risks were plain to see. The administration of the clinic had come to demand much of the time and energy that the board members could spare for community work. The new board, to reform the clinic, would have to make staff changes. Given the state of mind of the community such changes would be regarded as a takeover of patronage. Those who had been elected were among the most able of the residents who had given the Ad Hoc Committee its promising start. The demands of the clinic would drain their activity almost entirely in that direction. The aura of community dedication that had grown around the committee was bound to tarnish with the suspicion that the Committee had made a successful grab for power. The Ad Hoc Committee had not formulated a statement and a program along the lines recommended by the team to hold the new board to account. None of the successful candidates had run on the central issue—the assumption of multiple roles by the board of the Alviso Family Health Foundation. The new board would unavoidably become the successor in interest with respect to the advantages and responsibilities deriving from the contract with the federal agency. Finally, there appeared to be no possibility, short of a drastic reversal of Washington's guidelines, of reducing the area of service of the clinic to the scale of the town of Alviso proper. Nor was it likely that the new board would put into effect a retrenchment that would greatly reduce the number of jobs provided by the clinic.

In brief, the new board had not formulated and proposed to the community a program for stripping the clinic back to the limited role of a health service agency. The board elections proved to be a transaction that substituted new persons for old, not a radical change in the philosophy and strategy of community organization. It may be asserted that the only influence working for such a change was that of the study team and the team had to reckon with the material attractions and the appeal to the self-interest of residents with a latent capability to imitate and improve upon Anglo customs of manipulation fortified by money and status.

The transfer of control of the clinic to the new board was followed almost immediately by the publication of charges of improper use of funds by the old board. The charges were documented by an anonymous accuser who was evidently well informed. These charges brought federal investigators to Alviso. The executive director resigned in protest over changes in personnel policy intended by the new board. Key professional personnel gave notice.

ASSESSMENT OF THE ROLE OF THE ALVISO STUDY TEAM

Alviso must be identified as one of those Mexican *barrios* in which the forces in American society which are demolishing the physical base of the Mexican-American minority culture are at work. The process is not complete until the bulldozers have moved in, and it has not yet reached that state in Alviso. The team entered the scene when the process was well along.

Few Mexican barrios in the southwest have provided a detailed account of their decline and disappearance. If Alviso proves to be an instructive exception the work of the team would account for it.

That the team devoted the better part of a year to research and investigation is a clue to one of the major barriers in the way of understanding what is happening to the Mexican communities. This barrier is the nearly total absence of information resources open to the residents of the neighborhood. These barriers the team in good part overcame.

But the object of thawing out vital facts so that they might flow among those most affected by them is a colloquy, through which the habit of measuring proposals made or actions taken by public officials against alternatives can be established. This kind of dialogue the members of the team maintained through some fifteen months of active contact with Alvisans.

Communities like Alviso, when they begin efforts to discover collective ways of improving their lot, are hard pressed to make a choice of priorities. Among many pressing needs deprivation is stamped not only on their economic profile; it shows also in a proneness to exclude from these priorities the most important one of all—the creation of a community morale and structure that challenge the self-serving compulsions of outside agencies intent on viewing a community as a "target" and not as an organism. This distinction the team attempted to make as clear as possible.

It requires experience and some special skill for an observer to detect important and often decisive negative effects of the behaviour of agencies that offer relief to a community from its deprivations. This behaviour is not necessarily a conspiracy; it is perhaps something worse—a mindless and even naive acceptance of values, procedures and structures that ultimately will destroy the chances of creating communities on a human scale, operating in accord with American democratic ethics. In its analysis and constant commentary regarding the role of the clinic, the team attempted to understand and foresee the consequences of a cultural aimlessness on the local scene worsened by regressive guidelines imposed by the federal government.

It is also clear, in retrospect, that once the team completed the research necessary to understand objectively what was happening to the Alvisans the dialogue of the team with them did initiate a political process that the town had not seen before. This political process was not one of local partisan maneuvering, lobbying, coalitions or pressures. It was a demonstration of the conditions of operation of municipal democracy on a local scale, reliable information, education, open deliberation, simple devices to produce decisions, and techniques of organization.

The team avoided the danger of encouraging dependency [on] its services in the belief that such dependency provides the community merely with a choice of manipulators. The choices that an independent citizenry must make in a democratic society will never come easily. These choices will always be forced by competing interests of citizens for whom freedom must mean the options of forming, dissolving and reforming those sub-groups that speak for opposed choices. The search for community integration that the team sought to encourage was for the conditions of level dealing in this process.

CONCLUDING OBSERVATIONS

Time is passing quickly for Alviso. The informed opinion of those who are guiding the legal strategy of the lawsuit against the City of San Jose is that the decision on their appeal will be handed down in the near future. The prospects of winning the appeal and a new trial are considered [to be] negative. The City of San Jose continues to seek a settlement as Alviso's bargaining position weakens. The end of the litigation is in sight, and the Alvisans have been sidetracked from the promising course originally set by the Ad Hoc Committee, their energies and their critical powers now being centered on the scandal of the clinic.

Each of the major events in the struggle between San Jose and the Alvisans strengthened the view of the study team that those events, taken together, pointed to a syndrome of national, not merely local, proportions. One of these—federal grantsmanship—had made the crucial difference. Capable Alvisans were ready to succumb to its seductions. They emerged from the fog of ignorance of what was happening around them with the help of the team, but what was happening around them was in many important respects merely the rippling of a tide that is pushing all of American society toward super-urbanization.

Alviso has not yet been engulfed by this tide, but its fragile dikes have been breached.

With Alviso in mind it can hardly be said that America is free to choose as to the type, the style, and the values of the nuclear social unit of its vast and complicated society. America has been feeding on the vital cells of community. In the case of the Alviso Mexicans, typifying the experience of practically every Mexican-American barrio in the southwest, the cells were already weakened by the fact they were the carriers of a culture in exile, far removed in time and space from its indo-agrarian society past.

Societies like individuals, can't go home again. The Mexican Americans now living in the southwest of the United States have become urban villagers; it is in the urbis, and not the village, that they must work out their destiny.

Judged from the standpoint of what America presently prizes—a habitat of urban giants offering in exchange for the cultural and political forms of small communities[,] the dizzy mobility of rapid transit[,] and the illusions of revenue sharing—Alviso's immediate prospects are in doubt. When the legal bars to annexation are removed[,] the face of Alviso will change with new marinas, high-rise apartments, tourism, light industry and show business. Alviso will be in the mainstream of the American way. Its face will be different and it will not be brown.

The experience of the Alviso Study Team suggests that a team can play a significant supportive role in minority communities where there already exists an institutional structure with a strong cultural base. To such a community a team can bring organizational skills, information, legal insights and a variety of professional experiences. Since the tenure of a study team is short, the objective of the community must be immediate and clearly defined. In such situations a team can have the effect of a booster in some specific crisis.

Where, on the other hand, a community is in process of material extinction and where its minority status already indicates an almost incalculable shortage of resources for survival, the study phase of a team is merely a first step. The second would be a Community Assistance Team, sufficiently endowed to continue its supportive role, possibly over a period of years. Then support would have to be specifically in the area of organizational training, legal assistance, research, democratic procedures, community education, urban planning and economic development.

Between such an assistance team and a community there would have to be formal and legal terms of mutual responsibility and commitment. They would make explicit the goals and values of an urban process radically different from the megalopolitan cannibalism abroad in America today.

PART 4

POWER, CULTURE, AND HISTORY

MEXICANS IN THE SOUTHWEST

A CULTURE IN PROCESS

Ernesto Galarza, "Mexicans in the Southwest: A Culture in Progress," in *Plural Society in the Southwest,* edited by Edward M. Spicer and Raymond H. Thompson (Albuquerque: University of New Mexico Press, 1972), 261–297.

The following selection is a revised version of a paper originally prepared for a 1970 conference organized by anthropologist Edward H. Spicer devoted to the concept of a plural societies in the Southwest. Within the broad questions Spicer posed about "the nature and development of variant groups within dominant societies," Galarza outlines the transitional evolutionary nature of Mexican American culture within the Southwest.

Let me say at the beginning that this is not a research report carried out for scholarly purposes. It is more a loose meditation on some 40 years of field experience in "a land full of wonder but not much information," to borrow from J. R. [R.] Tolkien. My view of the subject is perhaps slanted by the fact that I have been in this land not as a participant-observer, but as a participant-adversary. I have not liked much of what I have seen in the intersection of cultures in the Southwest, where cultures do intersect, and I have been more prone to object than to be objective.

There is something else less personal that ought to be said. I have not been able to observe a Mexican Southwestern culture working itself out in isolation. On the contrary, at every point I have seen an infraculture in compulsory contact with, and subordinate to, a supraculture. For this reason I am continually unsure, when I imagine I am dealing with an aspect of the Mexican culture, whether it is an action of that culture or a reaction to its containment.

It is from these points of view and with these predispositions that I shall try to follow the scheme of discussion which Spicer has given us. We were to address ourselves mainly to: (1) the content of Southwestern cultures, (2) the historical experience of each of them, and (3) what he calls the self-concept or evaluation that sets the critical boundaries between cultural types. In this framework, he asks, can we recognize the processes that produce plural societies and maintain them or that undermine them and destroy them?

My effort to respond to these instructions divides this essay into its natural parts. First, I will attempt to explain what I mean by the concepts I use. I will then try to outline how the Southwest culture of the Mexican looks to me at the present time. Within this view, I will discuss the cultural implications of the Mexican's historical experience, as well as the cultural forms that he has preserved throughout that experience. This will bring me to a Mexican community whose profile is typical and illustrative of my theme. I will then deal with what I call the cultural reactivity of the Mexican and will try to suggest how this culture looks in action, rather than in reaction. Finally, I will make some observations on the two cultures face to face.

CONCEPTS FOR THE UNDERSTANDING OF MEXICAN CULTURE

The intellectual tools available to us in this connection are not as sharp as they might be. Terms like "minority," "acculturation," "traits," "primitive cultures," and "self-image" quite obviously derive from an anthropology that is itself a product of the culture that has overrun the world in the last 300 years—the culture of the western European white man. Is there, by chance, any bias in this of which we should be aware in observing the regional Mexican culture?

The word "minority" is a simplistic numbers test that does not explain some important matters. It does not remind us that there are minorities within minorities, which outsiders tend too often to regard as monolithic social groups. It is easier to explain them this way. Neither do numbers alert us to the fact that a Mexican can be and very often is a member of other minorities—as a trade-unionist, for example.

Further, the current terminology does not invite us to consider more carefully those select minorities, reckoned by economic influence rather than skin color, that wield enormous power over all the others. Both Learned Hand and Walter Lippman have hinted that we should not be so impressed by numbers: Hand, when he said that "we have come to think of the problem of democracy as that of its minorities," and Lippman, when he wrote that "every country is a mass of minorities which should find a voice in public affairs." And, I might add, every minority is a mass of individual human beings in more or less desperate search for security and identity.

We can see where the numbers method leads us. If a minority makes up ten percent of the total population, it should receive, some argue, ten percent of the available decent housing, ten percent of the jobs and so on. But why not ten percent of the civil liberties?

Acculturation

Let me next consider the term "acculturation." We are coming to the point where it means a sort of recapping process, a replacement of cultural treads. The implication seems to be that the reconditioning produces something as good as new. I do not believe that this is so. Acculturation, in my view, occurs only once in the life of any individual, during the early years when he is enfolded in the very tissues of the social group into which he is born. Later, he is conquered or he emigrates. Necessity or force compels him to learn different ways. This I would call "remedial acculturation," which I suspect is as inefficient, costly, and ultimately unsatisfactory as remedial reading.

Culture Traits

Identification of cultures by "traits" is convenient but hardly clarifying. To be sure we are able to associate individuals in groups by speech, intonation, address, and even by the way they walk. But this rule seems to be safest when the group we are talking about is small. Trait lists for Mexicans have been made and demolished. I have counted some 40 supposed traits offered as identification of the Mexican in the Southwest. As for Mexicans in Mexico, Monroy Rivera (1966) has offered just one, which I might translate as "runtism," from the title of his book, *El mexicano enano* (The Dwarf Mexican). He goes on to assign some 90 subtraits, but I must emphasize that his is a dour and sardonic list drawn with no scientific pretense.

Primitive Culture

Counting minorities by the numbers, regarding them as a *tabula rasa* for a second acculturation and reducing them to trait counts, belongs in the same category of concepts as that of "primitive culture." Primitivism is the conceptual child of contact between the overwhelming advance of the western European white man and the native societies of Africa, America, and Asia waiting to be conquered by him. In the Southwest we have a residue of it. "They live like savages," I have heard white agricultural employers say of Mexican migrants who were forced to live under conditions which were, indeed, primeval. Anglos who are less outspoken in their judgments than such employers nevertheless employ a language of sympathetic condescension. The Mexican minority is described as "disadvantaged," "culturally deprived," "underdeveloped." And since poverty appears to be self-perpetuating under the current American social system, we have become reconciled to separating the "little traditions" of the poor from the "great traditions" of the elite. Matthew Arnold would have gone mad, I dare say, in the Mexican Southwest. So might we, unless we remember that it is not the contrasts between cultures, but the inward consistency of each that makes them worthy of serious study, respect, and possibly imitation. For it is only from that inward consistency that we can hope to understand the multitudinous ways in which humanity has sought, and continues to see, the answers to its universal needs.

Let me underscore, without abusing it, this matter of inward consistency. After becoming lost in the painstaking explanations of culture handed down to us by the masters of anthropology I went back to Webster. I fingered my way down his column of definitions: *culture*, the intellectual content of civilization, a particular stage in civilization, the trait complex of a separate unit of mankind. Then I came to the biological connotation: *culture*, the cultivation of microorganisms in a nutrient medium. But why, I asked myself, should the biologists monopolize such a useful concept? Is it not as plain, on the basis of the data, that human beings, like microorganisms, cannot grow, cannot even survive without a passage into life through the nutrient medium of culture in a social group?

Here, I think, is the crucial difference between a cultural process and a cultural package. I have only a slight quarrel with those who have to deal in cultural packages for the sake of convenience—academic, ideological, or commercial—as long as we remember that it is for the sake of *their* convenience. And as long as we do not forget that the striving for an inward pattern of a culture is the projection in a social group of the strivings for security and identity of the individuals who compose it.

Self-Image

The foregoing offers, I hope, a more promising approach to the question of "self-image" or identity. I believe that both identity and security grow side-by-side in the individual life history. Both are embodied notably in the learning of language, which is only one of the vital social securities that group life offers. These social securities are inseparable from the web of a culture. To identify with them is to participate in them with a sense of security, trust, and reliance. If the original process of acculturation—and it happens only once, as I have said—provides, even as it imposes the bonds, restrictions, and prohibitions of the particular culture, a sense of enjoyment of those securities, then the foundations of identity are also laid. Thereafter the individual who is thus happily equipped is able to cope.

This is why I am not overly impressed with the cries of indignation from Mexicans, especially the younger ones, who bewail their loss of self-image. I find that they are almost always individuals with a certain ruggedness, or at least aggressiveness, of self. They are not asking "Who am I?" but "Why don't those racists like what I am?" It is those Mexicans who are *not* protesting a loss of self-image at the hands of Anglos who concern me more. These have indeed been damaged psychologically. Their self-security has crumbled step by step along with their self-identity. But I am not sure how much of this must be charged to the Anglo culture and how much to the Mexican. Physical violence to children is not unknown in the Mexican family.

CONSIDER ON THE MAINTENANCE OF CULTURE

As briefly as I can, I will now attempt some answers to the questions which Spicer has posed. What maintains a culture is access to an environment adequate to its survival and subsistence and shelter and freedom from outside constraints on its own forms of value, ritual, art belief, feeling, and institutional behaviour.

The significance of cultural activities—speech, thoughts, techniques, and the like—is that they represent the individual search for security and identity in a network of human relations. It has been said that there is nothing more useless than a single telephone, and it can likewise be said that there is nothing less functional and more desolate than a single individual. Kinship groups are widening circles of relations that provide basic security and identity for the individual. Once this core is established, a person will feel aggrieved or resentful in the face of derision, mockery, or affront, but he will not feel broken.

Historical experience has been stressed by Spicer as a bond of culture. I would say that the historical experience of the social group that makes the difference in the living generation is not so much the textbook record of its victories glorified and its defeats borne with dignity. It is the fabric of those cultural forms that have survived and again make it possible, today and now, for the individual member of that group to know his identity and feel his security. History tells us the origin of those forms and the common experience that lies behind them. It helps us not to confuse culture with ethnicity, which merely insulates it; or with society, which embodies it; or with the state, which likely as not will pervert it; or with government, which polices it.

Since so much is being said about community in the Mexican Southwest, I have to touch upon this subject also. Community means to me the social group living together in ways which somehow seem self-relevant, and which somehow keep to the human scale of social behavior. It appears necessary, for community to exist, that there be a resource for survival and security accessible more or less to all of its members. Communication also is on the scale, and a satisfactory compromise between the restraints of the community and the display of the individual ego appear most possible in community.

THE MEXICAN SOUTHWEST TODAY

In what follows I use the word "Mexican" as Spicer uses it, a cultural type existing in the Southwest which embraces five varieties: Hispano, Chicano, rural Norteño, urban Norteño, and Mennonite. We are talking about some five to six million persons living in five states: California, Arizona, New Mexico, Colorado and Texas. It is a vast area in which the Mexican population has distributed itself in seven fairly discernible regional groupings: the San Francisco Bay basin, metropolitan Los Angeles, the Central Valley of California, the Salt River Valley of Arizona, the upper Rio Grande Valley of New Mexico and Colorado, a less-defined area centering in Denver, and Texas. There is an eighth which affects in its own peculiar ways all the others, and which I will call the "Border Belt."

The present demographic shape of the Mexican population of the Southwest has been developing for 100 years or more. We might say that for a century men have been fleshing out the skeleton of communication and settlement marked out during the previous 300 years. The pivots of seven of these areas are San Jose, Los Angeles, Fresno, Phoenix, Denver, Albuquerque, and San Antonio. The eighth, the Border Belt, has no center. It is a narrow stretch of desert, some 1800 miles long, between Brownsville and Tijuana, located on both sides of an imaginary line drawn by treaty, ignored by nature, and transgressed by men.

Emigration and Immigration

We can call it a Mexican Southwest today mainly because through the Border Belt the northward migration of Mexicans has continued, recharging with population, not only the areas north of the border but those lying just south of it as well. The immigrants did not come to find virgin lands and to organize new societies in them, like the Mormons. Seeking work they scattered over the region, each man and each family in accordance with their own luck.

Since it was not propelled by kings, emperors, or presidents with national ambitions or by designs of aggression, this immigrant flow did not disturb the historic cultures which were already there. In these cultures, as in those of the Pueblos of New Mexico, differences in environment, resources for subsistence, and isolation made for differences in cultural forms. These survive today in the styles of the Norteño, of the Hispano, of the Indian reservations, of the New Mexico villagers, and others. This is why it is necessary to allow immediately for varieties of the Mexican type and why we must concede to local pride and tradition the possibility that even the varieties may break down into variants.

This explains a problem that contemporary anthropology has created for itself in looking at the Southwestern Mexican. The anthropologist feels compelled to order, classify, arrange, and tabulate human groups in a way that will make them understandable to him. As a purely intellectual and altogether commendable procedure—a necessity if we are to be tidy in our thinking—it seems to imply also an effort to place their subjects in an order of merit or a hierarchy of importance. This feeling, universal throughout the Southwest, is an important datum for the researcher, one which Spicer would probably deal with under the heading of "ethnic boundaries."

It would not surprise me if there is a storm of indignation when it gets around that a few of us have met here and agreed that there is a cultural type called Mexican. Some years ago Landes (1965) offered a friendly suggestion that the type be called "Hispanoid." She only succeeded in annoying many people. I suggest that we try for agreement not on a name but on a slogan. I borrow it from Mexican folk wisdom, in which there is a saying, "*juntos pero no revueltos*" (which, if you will pardon my translation, might be read as "sunny side up, not scrambled").

This suggestion is not as trivial as might appear at first. There is now emerging something called *La Raza Unida* [The United People]. It is in part a desperate attempt, in the political area, to link and coordinate a number of regional styles and many local varieties of those styles. These styles, and varieties too, have gradually taken shape in accordance with the local environment and the degrees of political starvation which the Mexican has been experiencing. As a political device, the slogan "*La Raza Unida—Juntos pero no revueltos*," could have interesting psychological effects and important practical applications.

Cores of Poverty

Going back to the Mexican culture, we find that within the eight major regions into which the Mexicans have sorted themselves we have to trace more detailed patterns. In each of these regions, not excluding the Border Belt, there are compacted cores of population in which the rural Mexican of 50 years ago is being transculturated into the urban Mexican of today. The heart of these areas are those census tracts into which Mexican poverty has been compressed. If, in looking at any culture, we must first notice its ecological setting, with the Mexican we must begin in these cores of poverty. Nearly 90 percent of the Mexicans are today living in or near them. There are variations in the pattern, but the differences are not in the quality of life. It would be hard to say who is poorer, the landworker of Tierra Amarilla or the chronically unemployed laborer of East Los Angeles.

Earlier in this essay I said that an important fact to grasp about any culture is its inward consistency. Following Benedict (1934), I now want to add that this consistency flows through a pattern or configuration which is peculiarly polarized. It is important to seek this pole because it leads us to the field of human energy around which other forms of that culture tend to arrange themselves. Victorian England gravitated around London, and London, around the culture of the City. The trade, politics, strategies, ideology, and weapons of empire gravitated around all three. We can draw concentric circles around this dynamic power, each in turn wider than the last, each embracing more marginal manifestations of the English way of life at that time, such as the slums and the coal towns. I am not trying to compare English culture and the Mexican situation here. All I am trying to point out is that the Mexican culture, too, has its polarization and its configuration; that its core is poverty and not power; and that the cultural ripples it sends out, therefore, hardly go beyond the limits of the census tract.

The massive immigration of the last 50 years, which accounts for the demographic pattern I have described, brought with it no formal institutions to perpetuate its culture. Of these the most important would have been schools. In the highly segregated barrios and *colonias* the Mexicans had to accept the educational agents of a different culture. And frequently these agents forbade the use of Spanish, gave unintelligible intelligence tests, adopted tracking systems by which Mexican boys and girls were switched permanently to a siding, and taught reading as ritual.

The lack of indigenous institutional anchors has been characteristic of Mexican culture in respects other than education throughout the 20th century. The church, Roman Catholic or Protestant, is still a proselyter, essentially the partner of an alien, secular power that long ago destroyed the economic and political autonomy of the original Mexican societies. In the arts and literature no peculiar institutions have emerged to train the artist and the writer in a Mexican tradition, to give him a base and a public. The Mexican has not even been able to defend and preserve his language. Altogether, the Mexican culture has been not a ship, but a raft coming apart, plank by plank, among hostile tides.

HISTORY AND CULTURE

Let me turn now to the Mexican culture in the light of its history and later to a notation on some of its cultural survivals. The opening line of the familiar Mexican song "El caminante del Mayab" [The Mayan Traveler] could be my theme for this section: "*Cuan lejos estoy del suelo donde he nacido*" (How far I am from the land where I was born). It is the song of a wanderer, a personal lament such as we can hear in many other cultures. In the Southwest today a loud note of cultural nostalgia is being sounded, not sentimentally but militantly. It comes mainly from those who were born on the northern side of the border but who are ignored in the history of the land of their birth and who now seek to find one in which they feel they belong. We have to examine the roots of this feeling from the angle of the two political systems which have divided that history between them.

The Two Conquests

For some 300 years what the indigenous social groups in Mexico had to contend with was the Spanish version of the eruption of western Europe throughout the world. Contrary to what happened elsewhere, the native Mexican tribes were not annihilated. They were rather kept in a servitude whose economic molds are well-known, such as the *encomienda*, the *hacienda*, and the *mita*. The native economic systems did not totally disappear. They survived in the out-of-the way places where the Spaniards found it too expensive or too inconvenient to bother about taking over. Elsewhere, the Spaniards dominated and domineered for 300 years as a minority, if we go by the numbers. There is an estimate that during those centuries fewer than a million white men emigrated from the Iberian Peninsula to New Spain.

To me the notable thing is that the indigenous Mexican survived and multiplied until he put his genetic and cultural stamp on the mixed society that emerged. But this is not altogether what the Mexican activists are emphasizing currently. Out of the period of servitude they abstract something else, the brand of bondage. "We are a conquered people," they are saying.

Less than half a century after Spanish rule was ended by revolt there came the shock of the defeat of 1848. By this time there was a Mexican Northwest, which by courtesy we can continue to refer to as the United States Southwest. Those who were living in this region came under American rule. Here was a second conquest reinforcing the first one, still remembered in bitterness.

This attempt to draw the line between the Anglo and Mexican cultures by reaching into the past is an ambivalent one. In the process the Mexican will be turning up skeletons along with precious jewels, like some digger in the ruins of Yucatan. But for now it is the jewels that count—the valor, the defiance, the gallantry, the science, literature, and art of a race that went down, and even the bronze color of the skin.

That an "inferior" culture, the white one, could have done in a "superior," the brown, was not only unjust, it was offensive. The offense and the injustice to the Mexicans continue in the domination of the white man. He owns the productive lands that once belonged to them, and he continues to appropriate the fruits of their labor. He drafts their youth and sends them abroad to be killed in the service of an ill-defined national interest. When the tourist trade or refrigeration or electronics or atomic energy make the desert increasingly possible for business, he comes back and picks up the pieces of it he had overlooked, not to make more room for the Mexican, but less. You can see what I mean if you will stand on the roof of a skyscraper in Phoenix and look around you.

The rewriting of the history of the Southwest which Mexican intellectuals are planning will not be a purely academic exercise. It will have an emotional drive as well. It will be an effort, not to live history again, which is not possible, but to feel it again, which is. Maybe this has advantages and disadvantages. The advantage may be that the Mexicans thereby are tempering their wills for still another test they do not clearly foresee. The disadvantage may be that, in fixing on the past, they fail to notice that the engines of their historic defeats have not spent their force. The high-energy industrial civilization of the Anglo-American, which is continuing its intrusion into the agrarian societies of the world, includes Tierra Amarilla, the Central Valley of California, the Salt River Valley, and the lower Rio Grande Valley in its sweep.

I would not say that the Mexican of the Southwest is on a pointless sentimental journey in his emotional appeal to history. His revivalism is valid on certain grounds. When a social group is conquered and continues to live dominated, its history, at least, should not be appropriated by the intruder. Moreover, that history is the only way there is for him to find out why the Mexican has no land base as part of his system of identification. And having no land base[,] where else will he find one? How, lacking it, prevent the slow erosion of the inward process of his culture—the forgetting of his history, the decline of his speech, the corruption of his manners, the starvation of his young?

How long it would have taken the Mexican emigrant peon of the 1910's to reconstruct his culture in the Southwest, is of course, idle speculation. In his numerous regional cultures he was essentially agrarian, a village man, with collectivist and communitarian traditions. The liberal political revolution of the 1860's neglected him and then gave way to the long dictatorship of Porfirio Díaz, whose alliances with foreign capital undermined even more the material basis of the native cultures.

Encounter with Industrial Civilization

It was this Mexican who was propelled into the migrant stream of 1910–1940, headed northward, bound for an encounter with a high-octane industrial civilization. In that civilization a combination of revolutionary changes was under way.

The railroads were creating an American common market. The telephone and telegraph were giving it unprecedented speed in communication. Agribusiness was laying its foundations. The legislative lobby as an instrument of politics was already demonstrating its ability to shape national policy. And the legal systems of the Anglo confirmed his title to the cream of the environment from which wealth was to be made. There was also under way a massive migration to the cities, into whose ghettos the Mexican would be driven.

I cannot stress too much that these technical revolutions offered jobs, and that mobility was the price of being hired. This was a mobility of individuals, or families at most, not of a numerous social group moving together and therefore keeping its culture more or less intact. By the 1880's, most of the former institutions of Mexican colonialism had been destroyed or reduced to mere relics by Anglo society, for example, the pueblo, the presidio, the mission, the rancho. After this, the two cultures could no longer coexist on equal terms. The California constitution of 1978 marked the end of true biculturalism, as it did of bilingualism, in the schools, courts, newspapers, and public administration.

All this, too, became a part of the historical experience of the Mexican in the Southwest, at least of the large majority of those persons who presently make up the Mexican cultural type. We have yet to study and understand more thoroughly two important chapters of that history which between them divide the last seventy years. Up to the early 1940's, the story is principally that of the Mexican land-worker, locked into an exploitative wage system by mob violence, police power, and legal process. After the 1940's, the story is mainly that of the displacement of these same people toward the cities, with still another cycle of drastic changes such as the shift from agrarian to urban vocations, the dissolution of the family as an economic unit, the loss of the communitarian sense of the rural *colonia*.

It is this last chapter which stands most vividly before the Mexican today, for he is experiencing it himself. I will merely catalogue some of those experiences. As a worker, he is finding that the economic ladder to the better-paying jobs is becoming more like a greased pole as industrial processes are automated and skills are refined. The public school system presents him with a dilemma of choice between vocational training that only leads into winding, if not blind, alleys on the one hand, and the liberal arts on the other, for which the Mexican community offers limited professional opportunities. In politics, wherever the enfranchised Mexican represents a critical swing vote, the two major parties have contrived to permit him to do just that—swing. His extended family is becoming more and more the extenuated family, with the wife-mother working, the young dissenting or revolting, and unemployment finally driving it into dependency on public assistance.

These are broad generalizations, of course. Nevertheless, I think the Mexican experience falls within them, and I now want to comment on some of the implications of this statement.

A CULTURE IN TRANSITION

Leon-Portilla has said that the reality of the *Norteño* culture emerged in the Northwest basically through the establishment of the villages, the mining towns, the presidios, the ranches, the haciendas, and the missions. As he takes the historic process at the flood, I take it at the ebb. The cultural reality of which I am speaking has submerged with the disappearance of these structures. Without them there were no alternatives to acculturation and assimilation by the Anglo. If it is true that it is the characteristic institutions of a society which most deeply affect human behaviour, then we are prepared to agree that the Mexican's behaviour in the Southwest has been most deeply affected by the disappearance of his own traditional institutions.

I want to look now at those cultural forms which have kept their vitality in spite of the disappearance of traditional institutions, and to indicate how and why that vitality has diminished.

The Endurance of Spanish

The first and most important of these is language. Spanish is spoken throughout the Southwest, in the family and on the streets. It is the language in which public meetings are conducted and in which a good deal of business is transacted. The closer to the Border Belt one moves the more Spanish one hears, the spontaneous kind that expresses promptly the spirit of the speaker. One can walk for blocks in Albuquerque, San Antonio, Los Angeles, San Francisco, or Denver and hear the continuous flow of Spanish conversation. Here and in innumerable smaller communities from Corpus Christi to Sacramento[,] menus in Mexican restaurants are printed in two languages as a convenience for their Anglo, not their Mexican, customers. The work talk on the job and the gossip of the town is Spanish.

We can attribute this endurance to a number of factors. One is the family in which the older members are native Spanish-speaking. Another is the continuous replenishment of adult newcomers who can speak nothing but their native Mexican tongue and who remain firmly attached to it all their lives. Their family ties across the border are likewise durable for at least one generation. Family visits to and fro are another strand of this familistic bond.

In ways which anthropologists and sociologists have not up to now observed too closely, Spanish serves more subtly to maintain the cultural network. It continues to be the medium, for hundreds of thousands of persons, by which important information gets through. This communications system operates through informal conversation groups which convey the names, locations and other sufficient data for finding work, obtaining social services, avoiding unwelcome contact with authorities, finding help in distress, or companionship in leisure. Insofar as the urban *barrios* have survived, they remain the centers of this interchange.

If we were to attempt to locate the area in which the Spanish language in the Southwest is most likely to keep its roots deep and vigorous, it would be in this non-Anglo world. As we move away from it the depth lessens and the vigor declines progressively, and both can be measured by generation as well as by area. By stages Spanish becomes a second language and finally a decorative fringe of the stepmother tongue, English, which takes over inexorably.

It is in the fringe area that we find the academic bilingual programs. They are an attempt to reconnect the speech with its cultural medium by Anglo institutional programs and educational devices. They face many obstacles. School administrators who are culturally monolithic and therefore monolingual make room for bilingual programs with reluctance or skepticism. Those who are more enthusiastic or sympathetic are obliged to filter Spanish instruction through curricula dictated by Anglos and not by the Mexicans. In spite of these initial difficulties, it seems possible, at least in districts where Spanish is the natural spoken tongue, to develop institutional support for a return to the bilingualism of the mid-19th century. The important question is whether the Anglo state is willing to settle down to an effort which will have to last for generations to accomplish that end. It is my estimate that the past five years and the next ten will be no more than an experimental stage, during which the Anglo intention will be tested and the technical problems worked out.

Changes in Family Life

When we look at the family we see again the importance of time in the formation of cultural forms. Complete family units are constantly being transplanted from Mexico to the Southwest and with these there come not only the original language but also the values, the rules of deference, the etiquette, the hierarchies, and customs.

Two or three generations after migration these break down. I think it is inevitable that they do. In the Anglo manner Mexican mothers go to work for wages outside the home. Where the educational opportunities have been better and the economic status is higher, the Mexican housewife begins to take part in public affairs, until a kind of separate *and* equal competence shatters the classic image of the dominant Mexican male, the *macho*. In this process first the children, then the grandchildren, have also slipped from the old molds and the generation gap is further widened by the cultural gap. So today the Mexican family in the Southwest presents a very wide range of familistic cohesion. One can hear Mexican youth refer to the father either as *el jefe* or as "the old man."

There is another variation in the family patterns. Where agricultural migrancy still exists, as in California and Texas, the Mexican family continues to transmit occupational skills to the young. That they are low-wage skills, and that they are accompanied by serious educational penalties, has long been known. I raise the point here only to make it clearer that the urban family has totally relinquished this role with regard to its young.

As the Mexican family acquired its cultural retreads in successive generations, an interesting situation came about that we can observe around us today. The family is no longer the most resistant barrier to Anglo assimilation. The resistance is now coming from the young, often the very young. It takes the form of public denouncement, not of private devotions to a traditional way of life. The young, in their passionate criticisms of the *gabacho* [pejorative term for a white person], every *gabacho*, accuse him of a plot, only a part of which has been deliberate and malevolent. The rest of it is the way of societies in interaction. The truth is that bars are let down as well as forced down, and it is important to be able to tell the difference. Not to be able to do so can lead to ethnic paranoia.

By forcing down of bars, I mean such acts of Anglo barbarism as the punishment of children in school because they spoke in their mother tongue, often the only one they knew. By the letting down of bars, I mean the substitution by the family of English-speaking television programs for Spanish ones, or the disuse among the younger adults of the relationships and the terms *mi comadre* and *mi compadre* [godparents or parents of one's godchild]. Nor have I heard in 30 years a Mexican bride defy her older brother for the first time in her life shielded by the possessiveness of her brand-new husband: "*Ya tengo otro que me mande*" (Now I have another who commands me).

Residence: Colonia and Barrio

It has been around the family and through the medium of living Spanish that the Mexicans more recently settled in the Southwest have improvised their patterns of residential togetherness. Some of these residential patterns have been ephemeral, like the farm labor and railway construction camps, which, for all that they may have remained in one place for 15 or 20 years, were nevertheless merely stopping places. Much more lasting were the *colonias* and the *barrios*, terms which have not always been mutually exclusive. The *colonia* once meant the settlement on the fringes of a city or large town, accessible to farm, railway, and industrial jobs. It also meant the whole of the Mexican community in a given district, usually urban, whether scattered or concentrated in one neighborhood. In the larger cities, such concentration easily adopted the original Mexican descriptive name of barrio.

It was in the *colonias* and the barrios that Mexican culture transferred itself more or less intact. In them the language kept its strength and its flavor. The food, the manners, the music, and the religion were original Mexican. The cooperative inclinations, as well as the belligerent individualism, were at home. Twice a year the *colonia* and the *barrio* celebrated Cinco de Mayo [Battle of Puebla] and Dieciseis de Septiembre [Mexican Independence Day], as they still do, with queens and *gritos* [shouts] of nostalgic defiance against invaders long since dead.

The out-of-the-way places where the agricultural *colonias* were formed early in this century remained safe from Anglo intrusion for several decades. They were built on useless or marginal land. As labor pools which filled or emptied with the harvest cycles, they distributed agricultural manpower conveniently at no cost to the industry. Of these communities many have disappeared. The economic development of the Southwest and the urban spread of the last three decades have obliterated them. Only on the fringes of this advance do they cling, diminished and parched.

The urban *barrios*[,] like the *colonias* of the countryside, started as cultural enclaves in the Anglo world. It cannot be said that the Mexican culture which they replicated on so small a scale flourished, but it did survive, replenished by continuing immigration. With little or no institutional life, the *barrios* stabilized a population of low-income wage workers from which the surrounding city drew manpower. In the *barrios* ethnic identity was strongly provided. The familiar words by which friends and kin expressed secure relationships came straight from working-class Mexico: *compadre* [godfather to your child], *paisa* (for *paisano*), *vale* [pal], *cuate* [pal], *tocayo* [person who shares your name], *carnal* [brother], *raza* [my people]. Likewise the words that set the ethnic boundaries between the Chicano and the Anglo: *gabacho, gringo, bolillo* [white bread], and *guero* [light-skinned person]. In the *barrio* the instruction of the young was, of course, turned over to the American English-speaking public schools, but their education, Mexican acculturation in manners, continued in the homes—at least as long as there was enough of the barrio to enlarge and reinforce the forms of behaviour demanded by the family.

It cannot be too strongly emphasized that the cultural vitality of the *barrio* depended upon the numbers of Mexicans living in close contact and the stability of its location. It also depended upon the retention of the successive generations within the cultural mold, and the resistance of Spanish speech and Mexican manners and customs to alien example. In other respects the *barrio* was always a dependency of the host society.

The barrio has begun to break down. In many cities it has been wiped out by urban reconstruction. From a distributor of manpower it is becoming increasingly a reservoir of unemployment. Its young are more and more anglicized in speech and in manners. Demolition, economic deterioration, and cultural dilution threaten the *barrio* at this point. How it can resist all three, if the Mexican is to retain it simply as the haven that it has always been, is the vital cultural question he must answer.

Wetbacks

It would seem, as something to speculate about, that the cultural mode to which Anglo society would like the *barrio* to conform is that of the wetback. This variety of the Mexican way of life in the Southwest is a direct product of public policy on the part of the two national governments. The border, more or less open to provide an escape hatch for millions of utterly poor Mexicans, is like a cunningly designed filter that separates the economic utility of the Mexican illegal entrant cleanly from the rest of his cultural makeup. Never a participating member of the community or society, as Samora (1971) describes him, the wetback lives anthropologically in a no-man's-land. Wetbacks hide throughout the Southwest by the hundreds of thousands, contributing only their labor power and receiving only their bargain basement wages. Yet as a group they represent the most authentic transplant of Mexican working-class culture in the United States. And as a person this particular Mexican shows how culture, the original acculturation, provides the real identity, rather than the labels that society invents for it. The wetback may have been a *bracero*, a border commuter, a "green carder," and he may and does become a resident alien, or finally a naturalized citizen. This, at any rate, is the ladder every wetback hopes to climb, and in the Mexican *barrio* he finds the first rungs among people who give him a little of their own cramped space.

ALVISO: A CASE IN POINT

At this point I am going to bring what I have been talking about into focus by an illustration. For this I have chosen Alviso, a town of some 1800 people located at the southern tip of San Francisco Bay. Its boundaries enclose 14 square miles of marshland, settling ponds that produce salt, orchards, and building sites that over the years have been filled with rubble, When the winter rains are heavy, the bay backs up to meet the floods of Coyote Creek and Guadalupe Slough, the waterways that meander by.

Alviso's population in 1966 was 68 percent Mexican and 31 percent Anglo. It has been a way station in the wetback underground, a *bracero* pool, a summer campground for harvest hands, and a dump[.] The Mexican families presently living there settled out of the migrant stream or moved from surrounding communities attracted by the inexpensive lots and the lower rents. Until recently the area has been isolated, marginal geographically and economically—one of those places where a typical *colonia* could take root, unmolested because of its dismal appearance.

In the late 1960's the community resembled a partially deserted, rundown boomtown of the 1930's, with poorly paved streets and rubble-filled vacant lots. The houses were dilapidated and overcrowded, and many did not have adequate plumbing. The one elementary school was the only educational and recreational facility in the city, with the exception of a park which was nothing more than a vacant, muddy lot without any grass or trees. A converted motel building housed a medical clinic, and a half-century-old building was used for the police and fire departments, as well as the city council chambers, a day-care center, and a community meeting hall. Roughly 70 percent of the families had incomes of less than $5,000 a year, and many were on public assistance. At the same time the entire city had an assessed valuation of less than $3,450,000, of which approximately $250,000 represented the assessed value of the homes of residents. The average level of educational attainment was the eighth grade.

In Alviso, Mexican culture did not flourish[,] but it did survive. The predominant language was Spanish. The ways in which people were congenial or quarrelsome were Mexican. Here the minority was the majority, and English was the second language of the neighborhood. Its religion was Roman Catholic. Individuals and families made trips to Mexico as often as their savings would permit, and visiting relatives from home found Alviso comfortable because of the familiar tone of life. Characteristically it was a talking and not a reading community. Town politics pivoted around kinship; cliques and factions were more significant than party lines. There were fewer than 400 registered voters in the town.

Such a culture could hardly have been the envy of outsiders concerned with power politics and progress. And so it was, until progress had soaked up all the available real estate in Santa Clara County, which includes Alviso. During the past two decades, down both sides of San Francisco Bay, a new megalopolis has been forming. Along the Nimitz and Bayshore Freeways, which between them embrace the bay, suburbs, electronic plants, an airport, light industry, and automobile assembly plants have closed in. Land values skyrocketed until prune orchards could be priced at $30,000 an acre for residential tracts.

The tide of investment polarized around the city of San Jose, the county seat. Under a shrewd, engrossing city manager, it annexed and consolidated wherever it could. The heart of San Jose itself was chopped up to make way for a grid of freeways, and in the process the barrio of central San Jose, an old Mexican community, was wiped out. The city boundaries touched those of Alviso to the north, and evidently the time had come for something to be done about so much unused land—14 square miles of it—occupied by so few Mexicans.

The strategy to annex Alviso to San Jose was launched some ten years ago. Annexation was rejected by the Alviso voters in 1962. The little town, unincorporated and at the end of its bonding powers, waited for the next annexationist attempt, which came in 1968. Previous to the election a private development association was organized by some wealthy property owners of Alviso, with which the city council of San Jose negotiated a contract guaranteeing the residents of Alviso civic improvements of various kinds. Copies of this contract, in English and Spanish, were distributed to every householder.

Exploiting the propaganda value of the contract, San Jose city hall agents and local partisans of annexation waged an intense campaign. Petitions were circulated, jobs were offered, modest payolas were tendered, confidential negotiations were conducted and the voters were courted as they never had been before. On election day residents who had moved away years before showed up at the polls, and other techniques of winning an election were applied. The annexationists won, 189 to 180.

On appeal, the validity of the election was upheld by the Superior Court of Santa Clara County. However, in September, 1970, the California Supreme Court reversed the decision and invalidated the election on the ground that 11 voters were ineligible. (*Jesus Canales et al. v. City of Alviso and City of San Jose*). While the election has been overturned, it has left the Mexican *colonia* divided by the issue of annexation. If it had been upheld, Alviso as a name would have disappeared from the political map of Santa Clara County, and the deteriorated houses in which the Mexicans live would have been marked for destruction by real estate developers. The residents would have had to move to San Jose and pay two or three times their present rent, or to "south county," a pocket of poverty resulting from the demolition of other *colonias*. As there is no guarantee that the proponents of annexation will cease their efforts, the residents of Alviso may yet suffer this fate.

As it is with Alviso[,] so it is with Union City, Guadalupe, and many other *colonias* throughout the Southwest caught in the tide of progress. Anthropologists may well ask as the *barrios* and the *colonias* go down: where will Mexican culture in the United States find a land base in the next 50 years?

THE PAST 70 YEARS: A RECAPITULATION

Here, I will stop for a flashback, to sharpen the outline of Mexican cultural evolution in the Southwest since 1900.

It has been, and largely continues to be, a culture of immigrant poor people coming from a society in convulsion and radical transition. The civil war that lasted more than 20 years obscured the other revolutions that were taking place in Mexico—in transportation, in the agricultural economy, in the process of industrialization, and in class structure. Except as its victims, those who fled into exile had had no part in the old regime; except as its casualties, they had none in the new.

Propelled across the border, again they found a society in the midst of radical change—a revolution of transportation fully under way, a massive drift from country to city picking up momentum, vertical and horizontal integrations of the economy (including agriculture), mobility of residence to match mobility of jobs. In a half century the Mexican immigration spread itself well beyond the Southwest, into the Northwest and Middle West. Scattered and thinned out, its efforts to drop anchors have failed. What were some of these?

The Failure to Gain a Land Base

As a small farmer, as a husbandman, as a yeoman, the Mexican failed. Even though he was unquestionably a dedicated and industrious worker of the land, he acquired none of it for his own in the United States. And this was not because of a prejudice in American society working notoriously and exclusively against him. It was because even small-family farming—the only kind accessible to the landworking Mexican—was beyond his means, and because family farming was proving no competitor for agribusiness. Because he came, typically, from rural Mexico he fitted appropriately into rural America in the role of an agrarian proletarian, not in that of a brown yeoman on the Jeffersonian model.

The *colonias* became the residential base of this proletariat and remained such for many years. In the way in which a people have of dealing with their fate, the *colonias* were a rough shaping of the Mexican culture in exile. But their livelihood depended upon their being used, their survival upon not being noticed. But their usefulness declined; the *bracero* and the wetback competed even with their miserable living levels, and machines took over many jobs as well. The lands on which they squatted became noticeably more valuable to the Anglo entrepreneur. The *colonia* was condemned. Alviso and Pascua Village in Tucson both illustrate the process.

The Fate of the Labor Contractor and the Work Crew

Let us now see what took place in the process of agricultural production itself. I want to mention two things: the labor contractor system and the crew system.

The Mexican farm labor contractor early became something of a polarizer among the Mexican farm migrants. Aside from unusual abilities and initiative, his assets were a system of contacts with Anglo employers of seasonal labor, transportation facilities, a camp, a store where food could be bought on credit, and often a bar where job leads could be obtained free and hiring deals closed. These were the more respectable functions of the labor contractor as a cultural agent. He had others, such as wine, women, song, and marihuana.

But the contractor had a brittle lease on his role among rural Mexicans. That role was a parasitic one, transparently dependent on the Anglo's economic dispositions, and in the 1940's those dispositions called for the bracero program, a system of managed migratory labor and administered wages into which the contractor did not fit. As an anthropological situation it was intriguing; the farm labor contractor was displaced as a cultural agent by the Anglo's farm labor associations, if by any stretch of the sociological imagination it can be said that such an association has been or could ever be a cultural agent. Many contractors survived, but on condition that they assume the more menial tasks of managing the brown manpower for agribusiness.

The same fate overtook a form of organization around which Mexican rural life, dimly and gropingly, tried to arrange itself, namely, the crew system. The work crews were teams of seasonal laborers that put themselves together spontaneously in the *colonias*. They were based upon neighborhood acquaintance, kinship, and a common experience that sorted out the industrious workers from the lazy. Crew leaders emerged; they were not appointed. Crews tended to develop ties of confidence over the years. They became incipient bargaining units operating on a rough democratic basis. Their membership was voluntary.

It is possible to imagine how, in the long run, the rural work crews could have themselves become polarizing agents in the Mexican society. But there was to be no long run. The crew system was destroyed. How this was done I have described in *Merchants of Labor* (1964), where you can read how the farm labor association combined forces with the U.S. Department of Labor to bring about that destruction. Considering how short-lived the crew system was and how small the number of workers it reached in proportion to the farm labor force, one can appreciate how feeble, how incipient, this Mexican cultural process was when it was crushed.

The Impact of Urbanization

With no roots in rural America of their own, the Mexicans were ready to join the exodus to the cities. Beginning in the 1940's, Mexican society again experienced a severe wrench. Its demographic location moved drastically.

From a predominantly agrarian subculture, it became a predominantly urban infraculture. By 1970 close to 90 percent of the Mexicans in California were city dwellers and workers. I have indicated above how they have distributed themselves regionally and compacted themselves in the tracts of city poverty.

In the cities the cracking of the social fabric has continued. The family no longer works together, as it did picking and harvesting. The cohesion that the authority of the male head imposed, however arbitrary, is gone. Fathers and mothers both work to make ends meet in moonlighting families and consequently their young are out of sight and out of hand.

Does the *barrio* offer a last resort for the culture of the Southwest Mexican? I do not think so, the way matters stand and the way they are moving. The *barrios* are physically marked for destruction. From one end of the Southwest to the other they, like the *colonias*, stand in the path of Anglo progress, political requirements, suburbanism, planning, and primitivism in sociological perception. I have cited the case of Alviso. Multiply the Alvisos many times as to land area and population, and you will understand how Mexican neighborhoods in San Jose, Oakland, San Antonio, Albuquerque, Phoenix, or El Paso, have been abolished.

I am not speaking here of points of friction between two cultures, but of points of attrition, at which the destructive power of the dominant society is at work. If contemporary social science were inclined to study these effects it would meet with two difficulties. First, the evidence is quickly removed from the site; the Mexican residents scatter as a kind of human debris that is as quickly removed as that of the smashed and splintered homes. Second, federal programs of various sorts are already busy with remedial acculturation. The list of their lenitives is long: subsidized housing, cross-town busing, urban remodeling, brown minicapitalism, perpetual training, occupational prosthesis, a modicum of community participation, headstarts up short alleys. After all this, what is left to the Mexican minority are its cultural residues. Where, among them, will Mexican culture find a base?

THE CULTURAL REACTIVITY OF MEXICANS

I have called this part of my essay "cultural reactivity" to imply at once that the Mexican type and its varieties are beginning to act in response to containment by the Anglo. I will mention some of these manifestations, well aware that I am not so much looking at minority Mexican culture in isolation as I am at its interactions at many points with the contemporary society of the majority. The responses include the student movement, the news media, economic security, the search for identity and history. We can regard these as areas of cultural protest that appear at the same time to want in and to want out of the larger, encompassing society. No one individual or group or organization is planning this protest. There is not one national, coordinated Raza Unida but a hundred or more.

The Search for Identity

Basic to all the other expressions of the protest culture which I am going to try to outline is the reassertion of a self-image worthy, as the Mexicans see it, of themselves. First of all this requires the destruction of offensive stereotypes. These have been the products of Anglo literature, of motion pictures, and of advertising. At least it has been the ads and the movies which have flaunted these caricatures on a mass scale. The effects have been highly visible. A character type that historically belonged to the Mexican because he created it—the *vaquero*—was rustled and retouched as a *gringo* hero, the "good guy" cowboy. Another character type that grew out of the Mexican's typical economic roles of farm and section hand was perverted into a picture of the peasant dozing by a cactus. Comic strips and cartoons picked up this distortion, adding to it a gallery of *bandidos*, comic opera generals, paunchy bar tenders, and brown-skinned lackeys. Stereotypes of a more subtle kind have pervaded novels and textbooks by Anglo authors.

All of these are under heavy fire, and no matter from what sector of the Mexican minority it comes, its object is the same: to destroy the caricature. For example, Mexican social scientists are busy taking apart certain lists of alleged ethnic traits supposedly characteristic of Mexicans. As the caricatures are demolished the goal becomes clearer, and it is simply the return of self-confidence. How firmly this self-security will stand up in those who are asserting it presently, and how soon it can spread as an experience rather than as a slogan in the mass of the Mexican population, remains to be seen.

The remaking of the image amounts to an assertion that inferior status is no longer to be accepted as a means of survival. As I have suggested it is taking place in many quarters of the Mexican culture. It can be heard loudest and seen most dramatically in the Chicano sector—that is, the young avant garde. Its stress is on Mexican Me, not on the American Me of 20 years ago. In this sector the keynote is impassioned defiance, the determination is to "show them." It is an emotional drive of reckless courage and jubilation that for the time being occupies most of the front stage. If there is a moment when passionate self-expression is the only spur that can set events in motion, the Chicanos are providing it. It is from them that new pejoratives are being flung: *Tío Tomás* [Uncle Tom], *vendido* [sellout], *coyote*, *placa* [police]. Chicanos rehearse these, mixed with the traditional obscenities, with great delight. They declare that "our blood is our power," that they are the deliverers of "the land of our birth," "the destroyers of precision, profit, and conformity." All this, too, is part of the return of self-confidence, perplexing as it may seem to some.

However grandiloquent the Chicanos may sound when they identify themselves with their Indian ancestors, the Empire of Aztlán, they are in this respect moving with a significant effort at historical reinterpretation. No one writer has yet put all its pieces together, but several are beginning to try. It will be the work of scholars and therefore painstaking and slow in coming. In the meantime, the effort to achieve a sense of common history, as part of the recovery of image and self-confidence, exalts traditional heroes and forms of political address. Emiliano Zapata is now worshipped by the grandchildren of men who fought with him. The *plan*, as a form of public address, is the historic version of the manifesto, and there have been published in California a Plan de Delano and a Plan de Santa Barbara. A Mexican journal of social criticism is called *El Grito*, of which there has been only one in Mexican history—the call to revolt by the Reverend Miguel Hidalgo y Costilla a century and a half ago. And on the marches of militant farm workers, banners of the Virgin of Guadalupe are raised again.

In this great leap backward to recover the common historical identity, the Mexicans of the Southwest have unconsciously jumped over a void in their chronicles. They have practically nothing in print that tells them what happened to the immigrant *La Raza* after 1910. The efforts to fill this void have been mainly those of Anglos. During 40 of these 70 years, the Mexican experience was largely that of an agrarian culture in transition and in conflict. It is this most recent period of the Mexican evolution that holds important lessons that will not be learned until they are written down.

Matching this gap, there is another, namely, the lack of critical understanding, especially among the youthful Mexicans of the Southwest, of the drift of the Mexican Revolution. The young Chicanos want to go home again, but if they do, they will find that Mexico, too, is on the way to becoming a land of precision, profit, and conformity. Its model is the complex industrial civilization of the United States. Their joint product is the formless society of the Border Belt wetback, their common goal the partition of common markets.

I must say, in the light of these comments, that the search for historical identity is still pretty much in the fiesta stage. Or, to change the metaphor, the worship of Zapata has become more the end of a pilgrimage than the beginning of a search for the historical forces that lie behind tragic symbols like his.

Language and the Schools

More immediate results can be expected in the area of bilingualism. There is a very broad base for this revival in the persistence of Spanish in everyday life. University courses are being designed "to develop confidence in its use, to combat negative attitudes toward it and to improve the ability to understand and speak it." If printed Spanish does not yet go much beyond the headlines of the militant press, or the occasional article translated into Spanish but written in English, all the same the Spanish language is no longer on the defensive. I have already said that the formal bilingual programs in the public schools have a long way to go, but they are going in the right direction because they too reflect a cultural reassertion of the Mexican community.

This suggests an additional comment or two on the educational involvement of the community. There is no level of public instruction to which the Mexican is not giving vigorous attention. The stimulus of the Headstart program, and the increasing awareness of dropouts, retardation, the miscarriage of testing, and the devious malfeasance of tracking systems have given the Mexicans new causes around which to protest, if not yet to organize. It is a zig-zag progression through issues that have not been sorted out. Characteristically, there has been more controversy over busing than over the philosophical issues of a Mexican concept of education. The closer we come to the university level, the more likely we are to find persistent pressure on the curriculum, the instructional budget, the recruiting practices, the content of courses, and the ethnic color of the instructional staff.

Confrontation with the Media

As with the schools, with the press, radio, and television media the Mexicans are showing their positive discontent. One form of it is the local Chicano publication, ephemeral but stinging. A press association of these papers has been formed[,] and when one member vanishes another appears promptly to take its place. The point is that here, also, on the cultural spectrum the young Mexicans are determined to have their own devices for communication, since the commercial newspapers will not carry their news or their denunciations.

A more conventional approach is also being tried on the media. This consists of demanding more staff jobs for Mexican reporters, script writers, and various kinds of technicians. It is contended that this not only opens more job opportunities but also guarantees that a Mexican interest, if not a Mexican point of view, will be reflected in the news. Already one national conference on the subject has been held, in which the Mexican participants declared that their purpose was to bring about more articulation of their minority through the mass media.

The other way of accomplishing such articulation—by creating an independent press—has not succeeded to date. The Spanish language dailies that are published in a few of the metropolitan areas do not link the mass of the Mexican population. There is no provincial press to create this network. Publication is a capitalist enterprise which has needed half a century to establish a Negro press of even a million circulation. Whatever the approaches, all pose the same question: why has the Mexican been thus far screened out of the dissemination of information and opinion in the affluent society?

The Mood in the Universities

In the universities the critique of education is under way. It is now almost entirely in the hands of students and professors who are clear about what they want and why. First of all they want larger numbers of Mexican students on the campus. They want proportionately more of the resources of the university for increased enrollments. They want, not always but often, parallel institutions controlled financially, administratively, and academically by them. Once a piece of the educational establishment is in their hands, they candidly state that they want to parlay it into a liberation movement, a cultural home for the rediscovery of self, and a means to reconquer a sense of community for all Mexicans. The Plan de Santa Barbara, through which some of these ideas run, is worth reading.

The first result of this critique has been the establishment of ethnic departments within which Mexican studies are offered. I do not have an exact count but I am sure there are nearly 100 universities and colleges in the Southwest where this is occurring. What once was supposed to take decades to develop—graduate studies, postgraduate degrees, advanced research, and full complements of ethnic staffs—is taking place in the span of a few semesters.

The upcoming Mexican scholarship is announcing its purposes with gusto. It will, it says, begin by slaughtering the sacred cows of academic scholarship in general. It intends to lay the myth of the conquering Spaniard. It will expose the Anglo as a cultural sneak thief. It will create its own scholarly journals on which Anglo editors will not sit in editorial judgment. This is iconoclasm with a program. It already has a fairly critical edge. Mexican intellectuals, activists, organizers, critics, and students compiled a volume of documented indictments for the Cabinet Committee Hearings on Mexican-American Affairs, El Paso, Texas, 1967 ([and] 1968).

Political Action

As to politics, the Mexican today is in a secessionist mood. Over the past 20 years a small segment of the minority was learning and applying the techniques of vote delivery. The meteor-like course of the Kennedy Clubs may well have been the brightest and briefest moment of the Mexican partisan apprenticeship. The Democrats had previously asked not what they could do for the Mexicans, but rather what the Mexicans could do for them the next time around. They gerrymandered no "safe" districts for *barrio* loyalists, who point out that there is not a state with a Mexican governor, nor a large city with a Mexican mayor.

So, if we are to cite expressions of the current mood, they would be those of one political organization that has announced it will no longer be a kept woman, or of another which has adopted the slogan, "*Huelga*" (strike), vis-a-vis both Democrats and Republicans.

Political dissent thus far has the ring of disgruntlement more often than that of social criticism. But it could move in that direction. The way is being prepared by others who do not aspire to public office, directing their talents and their energies to economic issues.

In this sector, again, there is no concert of plans or of action. The criticism comes from many angles and is aimed at many targets. In the last year or two the statistics have been gathered and published which at last document how far down the job ladder the Mexican blue- and white-collar workers really stand. Brown pressure is responsible for statistics of this kind, as it has compelled negotiations to establish at least a minimum quota system in trade-unions. It persistently asks why the barrios have rates of unemployment double or more the national rate, in good times and bad. Much talent has been coopted by federal programs, with the consequent short-run loss of brains for the critical examination of the economy. As this talent multiplies, it is not likely that such programs will absorb the whole or necessarily the best of it.

Without any doubt the two most dramatic thrusts in the economic area during the past decade have been the insurgence of the villagers of New Mexico and the strike of farm workers of California. The New Mexican *Aliancistas* [members of Alianza Federal de Mercedes, Federal Alliance of Land Grants] have been crushed, but their defeat has been a timely reminder to Southwestern Mexicans how far the Anglo is from returning to them even a token portion of the land base necessary for an autonomous culture and a genuine identity.

With the farm laborers[,] the frame of reference, as the sociologists say, is somewhat different, but it is still an Anglo frame of reference. Fundamentally this is a movement which accepts dispossession from the land as final and the conversion of husbandmen into an agrarian proletariat as irreversible. The movement leans heavily on a coalition of sympathizers to protect the recognition which Mexican farm workers are gaining; the boycott, a belated stirring of organized labor's conscience; a deep sympathy for the lowest of the underdogs which has been stirred by the struggles of 30 years; the tarnishing image of agribusiness; and money in sufficient amounts, for the first time, to organize, propagandize, mobilize and publicize on an adequate scale.

I have not said anything about many matters that deserve not merely mention but attention. But I am running out of space and I can only list what I have omitted: the *Teatro Campesino*, now rapidly becoming also the *Teatro del Barrio*; the construction of urban *mercados* (markets), which could go either in the direction of a rash of Olvera Streets or in that of a community-centered life; the urban-wide coalitions and unity councils; the Southwest Council of La Raza; a potential pattern for regional direction of all the *Razas Unidas* now milling about; the new literature by Mexicans about themselves; the storefront reading centers and libraries; the tutorial programs through which thousands of students are sharing knowledge and companionship with younger ones who have had little of either.

I cannot say whether these fragments of culture are moving toward an inward consistency, a polarization, a configuration, or [are] drifting past us on the surface of a tide that will sweep them into a turbulent pothole somewhere. Any of these are possible, and that is why I want to conclude with some fragments of my own concerning the minority and the majority cultures, face to face.

ANGLO AND MEXICAN: SOME FINAL QUESTIONS

We should not overlook this fact: whatever the Mexican cultural process may be at the moment, and wherever it may be moving or drifting, the Anglo will continue to look at it through his own eyes, particularly through the eyes of his own anthropology. By "his own" I mean that discipline which has been rigorous enough in its scientific method, but which has gathered its classic materials at best by participant-observation or merely by observation. This is not, however, the relationship of Anglo to Mexican culture in the Southwest today. It is a relationship of container and contained—of two cultural processes enormously unequal in all those components which a genuine culture, integral and whole, commands, blends, and diffuses among the men it holds together.

I do not say that American anthropology, in looking at the Mexican Southwest, has allowed itself to be biased by the culture from which it springs. I just want to make sure that it is not. This anthropology began with the detailed study of primitive isolates. They were regarded as laboratories which stayed fairly fixed while being observed. It was an early conditioning to a primitivistic outlook. During this time anthropological work was principally devoted to the identification and analysis of cultural traits, rather than to the study of cultures as articulated wholes. I suspect that this infirmity continues today.

Moreover, when we look at the Mexican minority, we are not distinguishing between cultures that have at hand all the elements for autonomy and cultures that have been deprived, deliberately, of some of these elements—land, for instance. It has been said that history cannot be reconstructed from the ruins of a decaying memory. Nor can a culture be reconstructed from the fragments of a dismembered society.

For that is what happens when two social groups [that are] palpably unequal in technology or some other vital factor intersect each other. Those who are overcome, if they are not annihilated, are left with the residues of culture, those resources and institutions which are least useful or threatening to the winner—indeed, which might even be amusing to him. Thus cultural pluralism can conceal paraplegic subcultures that were not born that way. Mexican Southwestern culture has been crippled; that is the essence of its history.

But we must look further. Within the minority culture what I would call a militant penetration is constantly going on. Inflation does not stop at the edge of the barrio; if anything it causes more havoc inside of it than out. The economics of land speculation have decided the fate of *colonias* and *barrios*. The electronic teaching machine, displacing the human teacher, is making its way into classrooms of Mexican children. This militancy is not being checked by vigorous counter values armed with appropriate institutions, and there is no future for a culture in this condition.

Still more important to take into account, in case it is lurking somewhere among our assumptions, is the proposition that integral cultures can exist as plural members within a complex industrial society of the current American type. And by integral, may I say again, I mean cultures that have access to those nutrients that satisfy all of the basic biologic and social needs of men. Therefore when we say that cultural pluralism is possible—indeed, is extant in this society—we ought to discuss whether the minority plurals are not much more than residues, surviving by sufferance.

I suspect that this has not been clarified, because the Anglo culture has not talked as much about its own minorities as it has about other peoples'. Let me get at this in a roundabout way. The industrial society on the scale of the American is complex by definition. Complexity is a cultural process which is unique to industrialism on this scale. It is an arrangement of complicated working parts necessary to maintain its far-flung balance—an arrangement that tends to enlarge beyond the ability of its human attendants to cope with. With this exception: professionals do emerge who can manage the complexity by a division of labor of their own. These managers are few relative to the whole society and they tend to become fewer. They function in the locus of power, which becomes more and more remote from the many who cannot cope. Those who specialize in that power are the most important minority in America today. With regard to this power, American society is not culturally pluralistic.

This is the criterion which must guide the Mexican in the allotment of his efforts. Some of them will have to be applied to preserve of his culture what the Anglo, for whatever reasons, has allowed him to keep. Some will have to be directed to extending the pluralistic principle to those essentials which an Anglo minority has reserved for its singular possession.

But Mexican ethnic policy will not be able to hew to this line easily. Mexicans must take care that theirs does not become a culture of protest only. As such it is unified mainly from without; its strategies must depend on alien decisions; it is constantly forced to be where the reaction and not the action is; its anger is constantly liable to turn inward under frustration; it forgets that some protests can be cooled into grievances and these into settlements, while others should not be quieted by anything less than basic transformations. Protest will eventually lose its appeal for larger numbers of the minority if it continues to lament that "we are a conquered people." The Aztecs fell, but the Mexican youth that I see today are not acting like a subservient lot. Something in them will sound increasingly hollow if they make this the burden of their complaint.

Separatism is another course many Mexicans are seriously considering—separation by stages, with total separatism as the goal. The separatism of the Blacks of the early 20th century, of the Mormons, and of the Zionists are hardly needed as historical case studies by the Mexican separatist. His drive is immediate and self-fulfilling. It does not take into account two things: that separatism, if achieved by all the ethnic minorities, must cut them off from the possibilities of mutual aid; and that ultimate separatism, economic and political, lost its last battle in the western hemisphere with the American Civil War. Even if the Mexican separatists could imagine, in the distant future, their own Zion, undoubtedly it would be one that would hang on decisions made in foreign capitals.

Separatism, fashioned on strictly ethnic lines as a tactic of protest[,] carries an insidious danger of the very racism the Mexicans are combating. For the present, separatism must continue to demand its share of the national charity fund, for which other minorities compete, principally the Blacks. To justify this demand by an appeal to skin color is a temptation to which the Mexicans, too, are exposed.

To achieve ethnic solidarity by the route of a common historical experience presents another difficult task. Such an experience, to be shared, must first be written and then widely diffused. This indispensable historiography must fill with facts and interpretation the gap in the Southwestern Mexican record between 1900 and 1970. To this end Mexican scholars must determine their own strategy.

Politically, it remains to be seen how the Mexican sums up his frustrations. He could be lured back into the party folds, or he could learn the lesson and make his own political behaviour a faithful response to the needs of brown people.

There is also the practical problem of communication between the dispersed efforts of *La Raza Unida*. These efforts are taking place in every corner of the Southwest, itself a vast territory. But more, they are clamoring for attention and support in a dozen other states, from Oregon to Illinois. To link these widely separated efforts is an urgent order of business for *La Raza*.

It is not so much a case of approaching an ideal definition of a culture (for example, Malinowski 1944)—a functioning, active, efficient, well-organized unity—as it is of compensating for the disunities that are at work. There are a dozen ideologies striving for influence, from the sayings of Netzahualcoyotl to the sayings of Chairman Mao. The Mexicans who are "making it" are doing so unevenly, and many are not making it at all. The class cleavage is beginning to show.

With all this and more to ponder, the Mexicans of the Southwest waited for the end of 1970, which has been declared somewhere to be the Year of the Chicano. The year ended as it had begun, pretty much, for the minority. Perhaps it was the beginning of the decade of the Chicano, or his century. The longer the stretch, the better the chances for his culture.

THE MEXICAN-AMERICAN MIGRANT WORKER— CULTURE AND POWERLESSNESS

Excerpt from Galarza's testimony before the Subcommittee on Migratory Labor of the Senate Committee on Labor and Public Welfare on July 28, 1969, in *Migrant Seasonal Farmworker Powerlessness, Hearings before the Subcommittee on Migratory Labor of the Committee on Labor and Public Welfare, United States Senate, Ninety-First Congress, First and Second Sessions on the Migrant Subculture, July 28, 1969* (Washington, D.C.: Government Printing Office, 1970–1971), 460–465.

Galarza was called upon for service by public and private organizations, elected officials, community leaders, and media outlets because of his unique personal background and his expertise in international labor migration and Mexican American community development.

The following is an excerpt of testimony Galarza gave before the Subcommittee on Migratory Labor of the Senate Committee on Labor and Public Welfare on July 28, 1969. This committee had previously called on Galarza in 1952 to testify on labor and management relations with regard to migratory labor. By 1969 Galarza had published multiple books and studies exposing how agribusiness was abusing and exploiting labor; these writings helped end the Bracero Program. Galarza had also helped build the structures necessary for farm workers to organize. By 1969, he was transitioning out of trade unionism and into economic development and educational reform work.

Notable life event during this era:

- 1969: Galarza, with Herman Gallegos and Julian Samora, publishes *Mexican-Americans in the Southwest*, which provides a demographic profile and a detailed account of the living and working conditions of the Mexican American community.

My name is Ernesto Galarza. . . . I suppose the reason for my being invited here is that my experience in and with farm labor goes back some 40 to 45 years. I spent my early life in California between sessions of school work in the fields and canneries and from 1948 until 1960 I was field organizer and educational director for the National Farm Labor Union.

In this connection my assignments took me to the Southern States, Florida, Louisiana, Texas, but for the most part to California and Arizona. So that I have worked with Mexican farmworkers who are residents, with locals, with wetbacks, with Appalachian farmworkers or farm workers from the Appalachian region, and with Negroes. . . .

Right off, let me stress that we are concerned mainly with workers who hire out to very large private agricultural enterprises in which they own no equities and from which they have no contractual guarantees or other social securities based on custom and tradition. As a class with these basic characteristics, they have been around, if we stretch a point, barely a hundred years. Considering the time that a genuine culture needs to mature into a pattern of life for a given society, a century is hardly enough for a peculiar and recognizable culture of farm labor to develop.

The span has been even shorter for farmworkers of Mexican ancestry who have migrated to the United States. This migration dates roughly from the 1910's. Even under the optimum conditions for the birth and maturity of a culture, in these past 60 years Mexican farm laborers could not have developed a peculiar and recognizable culture that did not exist before in the Southwest.

Within these scant 60 years, moreover, the Mexican farm laboring class has experienced the worst of all disasters that can overtake a culture—instability. These people have had no permanent and secure habitat. Indeed, cyclical dispossession has been their lot. The land that was theirs before 1848 became an alien land after the Treaty of Guadalupe. Since then they have been dispossessed of the value of their labor by a wage system designed for that purpose. They have been displaced by the advance of technology. They are being dislodged again from rural communities in which they had found refuge by the steady advance of freeways and the lowering upon their heads of the real estate boom.

This has not been all. A culture can be transmitted only in one way. It passes from generation to generation more rather than less intact, more rather than less integral. But among Mexican farm laboring families what has been happening is clear: the sons of the original migrants begin to suspect that laboring for American agribusiness is for their parents. Their sons in turn become convinced that it is "for the birds." The third generation leaves the land for the city. Rural cultural transmission comes to a dead stop when they migrate to the cities. We may speak of this as an escalator routine, in which the young and discouraged are continuously leaving at the top and new migrants from Mexico are continuously getting on at the bottom. And I may add that what I call the top of the escalator is only the threshold of some teeming, poverty-ridden *barrio*.

NO CULTURE OF THEIR OWN

I repeat that under these historic conditions the Mexican farm laborers, as a group, have not and could not have developed a culture or their own. They could not and have not acculturated their young in the way that all societies acculturate them and thus survive. They have rather been subject to the special mode of acculturation that takes place when one culture is plumped into the midst of another on unequal terms. To make a living, the members of the culture-away-from-home must accept terms and conditions that enable them to survive and little more. With this type of acculturation there is relegation, of which discrimination and segregation are merely psychological and administrative techniques. We now have a superculture and a subculture.

What distinguishes this kind of acculturation from the original and genuine article is that the former is nearly always compulsory. To be sure, "they" can always "go back where they came from." And if they don't, they ought to make the best of it and not complain. The proof that they consider it better here than where they came from is that they do not, in fact, go back.

But I am not concerned with looking into the minds of persons who are ready to offer this easiest of all choices—the choice between two distresses[,] neither of which touches them. I am concerned with pointing out that the Mexican farm laborers, as a class, have been acculturated by extrusion. What comes through the mold are those ways of doing things that are practically useful to the superculture. What is permitted to remain unmolested is the quaint, the harmless or the amusingly exotic. To the supercultured it can be fun eating tacos or listening to mariachis. But the ancient attitudes and the old values that are as to tacos as dawn is to a flickering match, have no currency anymore.

It is of course quite true that down the ages the people of one ethnic group have indeed adopted the culture of another. Whether this adoption takes place with hostility or with mutual sympathy, it takes place. I only want to express my opinion that migrancy between cultures is far more damaging than migrancy between jobs.

FARMERWORKERS OF MANY KINDS

There is something else I would like to point out in this connection. We can speak of farmworkers in this country as a class but we cannot speak of them as a homogeneous cultural group. Among farm laborers there are Mexicans, Filipinos, Negroes, Indians and Appalachian whites. But there is more than this. Within the Mexican farm labor component there are cultural variations. The self-styled *locales* are workers who have spent most of their lives in this country and on the land, undergoing the accultural extrusion of which I have spoken. There are the "green card commuters" who, if they are border professionals, have begun to mingle in their attitudes and behavior the Mexican and the American. There are the outcast wetbacks, an underground society drawn from the poorest of the poor in interior Mexico. All of these persons have common cultural origins, if we take them back far enough. But it is important to note that they have very different survival tactics. They are all competing with one another for farm jobs, and when I say "tactics of survival" I mean that *locales*, wetbacks, and greencarders are more separated from one another by such competition than they are bound by common cultural traits.

The foregoing are some of the aspects of the question of culture in relation to farm laborers, especially Mexican, which are raised in this hearing. There is also raised the question of the powerlessness of this group. . . . I do, however, want to take note of the fact that in raising the question of powerlessness of farm laborers in our society, the question of power is necessarily raised also. If we speak of the powerless we must, it appears to me[,] talk of the powerful. . . .

A culture is a multitude of items or the ethnic group behavior and the countless ways of manipulating the environment. If it is an integrated culture, behavior and manipulation fall under the sway of dominant attitudes and values that give the whole a unique pattern.

A culture is a human invention, it is transmitted only by social experience, it lives only by perpetuating itself in its original form, it must assimilate change in sympathy with that form, and it must express the collective anxieties of the society. All members of the ethnic group must be evenly exposed to the unique pattern[,] and their acceptance of it must become the personal way of life.

If a culture evolves it may become a civilization. When skills have been sufficiently refined, techniques developed, the machinery of public administration invented, and material resources hoarded and concentrated, a culture is on the way to becoming a civilization. Its launching pad is the city.

In a culture the decisive element—that which makes the difference between tone and decay—is vitality. In a civilization the decisive element is power. A culture is such because it responds vitally to the organic demands of nature upon man and of man upon nature. A civilization is such because it provides a practical organization for society to get things done. The management of the organization is power.

In these perspectives we can now look more closely at farm laborers as a group. What are they, culturally speaking? Because I know them better, I will discuss the Mexican land workers as a component of this group.

It is my belief, based on a lifetime of work and study among them, that the Mexican agricultural workers of the South and Middle West exhibit cultural characteristics that may be called Mexican. These characteristics affect in many ways the manner in which they deal with American society and the manner in which it deals with them. These traits are probably in decline as acculturation proceeds, but they are still sufficiently real to demand our attention.

A MEXICAN LIFE STYLE

These traits are the Spanish language, intercessory religion, family cohesion, family labor, a patron system, a pretechnological view of production and work, a reluctance to act publicly and to act organizationally, education as nonutilitarian, an ethics of *vergüenza* [dignity], and moral obligation as a function of *palabra* [one's word as a promise]. . . .

Within their own group Mexican farm laborers communicate in Spanish. This is undoubtedly the strongest bond between *locales*, *braceros*, wetbacks, and greencard commuters. The Spanish speech brought to the New World by soldiers and priests has been stamped, in the course of more than three centuries, with unmistakable Mexican word forms, meanings, and intonations. Until this mark is rubbed out by acculturation, these forms, meanings, and intonations provide an instant key to ethnic identity. In many unnoticed *colonias* Spanish speech still flows in the sensitive style of true conversation, the *platica*. One can still hear the *platica* seasoned with traditional proverbs and folk sayings that convey something even deeper than identity. . . .

However vital this ancestral speech may be, it is of little use in dealing with the alien culture that surrounds and engulfs the farmworkers. Everyday activities for which there are no inherited words but which are identified in English stimulate the invention of half-and-half expressions. We have *locales* for "local laborers," *chanza* for "job," *jale* for "deal," *ganga* for "crew," *raite* for the "day haul," *bonos* for "bonus," *cleme* for the "claim," or allotted work in a field, and so on.

These are, one might say, in-house adaptations of language to deal with the ordinary items of work experience. They are not a vocabulary through which the Mexicans can deal with the outside agencies that determine production, investment, allocation of various sorts of wealth created by the industrial operation as a whole. I know of no common and widely understood equivalents in Spanish or quasi-Spanish for "congressional hearing" wage determination, "Farm Placement Service," or "referral." In short, the Spanish of the Mexican farm laborers does not have the conceptual tools to deal on equal terms with economic reality in its broadest scope.

Mexican farmworkers are overwhelmingly Roman Catholic. Not that they are overwhelmingly pious, but that the sacraments of the Church still ritualize the high moments of their lives—baptism, communion, matrimony, death. Between these high points there are innumerable crises in which ritual does not intervene. They are on-the-spot clutches in which there is an eyeball-to-eyeball confrontation between the believer and his guardian saint. What is demanded of the saint is instant and efficacious intercession to ward off the harm.

This intercessory role is the cultural answer which the Mexican farmworker invokes in his economic relations with agribusiness, especially if the worker is a wetback or a *bracero*. I have attended prayer meetings of *braceros* in which the help of the Virgin of Guadalupe was fervently invoked to obtain the renewal of work contracts, the removal of a brutal crew boss or to implore a raise in wages of five cents an hour. There can be no doubt that these men believed that the Virgin was listening to them. But it was a question whether their employers were listening to the Virgin. I have never found any evidence that they were.

The family is still the principal bond of the Mexican farm laborer to society. The extended family is in his Mexican tradition and he clings to it even though it is becoming more and more the extenuated family. There is a hierarchy within the family and one of its functions is to see to it that the family confronts the world as a unit. To say that in the year 1968 the Lopez family worked for XYZ Corporation picking tomatoes is in a sense to juxtapose 16th-century Mexico with 20th-century America. As the Mexican farm labor family moves from crop to crop it is abiding by an ancestral custom. It is also abiding to an ancestral need—the need to wring from each and every member a share of productivity to keep the family alive.

HOW THE ANGLO
MANIPULATES THE
MEXICAN-AMERICAN

Speech presented at the Mexican-American Leadership Conference, Camp Max Strauss, Los Angeles, California, May 15, 1965, in *Proceedings of the Mexican-American Adult Leadership Conference, May 14–16, 1965, Camp Max Strauss, Glendale, California,* edited by L. M. López (San Jose, Calif.: Mexican-American Community Services Project, 1965).

Galarza was asked to provide the keynote speech at many conferences during his active career and after retirement. He took these opportunities to address ills that plagued working communities and to set action agendas.

In this speech, Galarza argued that mass manipulation of the Mexican American community had occurred and would continue unfettered unless the community took self-interested action. He advocated for the creation of a Mexican-American institution that would conduct self-research, communicate its findings to the general population, offer leadership training to activists and elected officials, and maintain a core of trained staff to carry out these responsibilities. This is how Galarza felt the Mexican American community could combat mass manipulation.

Notable life events during this era:

- 1965: Ernesto Galarza, Julian Samora, and Herman Gallegos
  serve as urban affairs consultants with the Ford Foundation. Their
  purpose is to assess issues affecting the Mexican American community and make recommendations about how best the foundation
  could award grants to help address these issues. Their work and
  recommendations led the foundation to grant significant funds that
  initiated the National Council of La Raza and the Mexican America
  Legal Defense and Education Fund in 1968.

Some months ago Lino Lopez asked me if I would talk at this meeting, and I said I would be glad to. We agreed on a topic that ran something like "The Sociological Involvement of Mexican-Americans in the Political and Cultural Life of California." When I received the program, it said "How the Anglo Manipulates the Mexican-American." Since I got the program day before yesterday, I have had to do some thinking about manipulation. What I have to say this evening begins with the fact that since I didn't know what I was going to talk about and didn't have time to prepare, I will have to speak honestly and frankly on the subject.

I don't think I would have agreed to speak on this subject as it is entitled, because manipulation in my judgment is something that has no ethnic peculiarities. Manipulation of individuals and groups is not necessarily an Anglo trait.

I recall a statement by George Bernard Shaw which I think is appropriate to this topic. It was something to the effect that there is nothing more repulsive in human experience than to be used by someone else for someone else's purposes. I believe that is about as good a definition as we could find for the subject of manipulation.

Manipulation, in order to be clearly used in this discussion, can refer to individuals as well as to masses. The manipulation of one individual by another takes certain forms. Usually this is a private kind of manipulation—it is my use of another individual through the devices of hypocrisy or dissembling or downright misrepresentation—but it is not the same thing as manipulation of large numbers of people.

The manipulation of masses of people, of groups of people, requires techniques. I don't believe the Anglo has a monopoly on it. The techniques of mass manipulation have become commonplace. One of the most common forms of it is commercial advertising. That is why at the outset I want to distinguish between these two forms of manipulation, the manipulation of one individual by another and the manipulation of masses of people by individuals.

I also want to make it clear that this distinction is of particular importance to those of Mexican ancestry, because if I ask myself, "Is the Mexican as an individual very subject to manipulation? Is he a man or a woman who submits easily to manipulation?" I think the answer is a very obvious no. I know very few ethnic types who are less easily subject to individual manipulation than the Mexican. The Mexican is rebellious. He's sensitive. He has *malicia* [malice]. I can't think of a time in my life when I did not resent and rebel against attempted manipulation of myself. So who am I to be speaking to you about how the Anglo manipulates us, when I know that no Anglo has ever manipulated me. I don't think you are manipulatable people, as Mexicans. This is one premise that I am laying down, that the Mexican-American of California as I know him is not easily manipulated by the Anglo as an individual. This is a temperamental matter and a cultural matter, and I think a very healthy characteristic that we have as an ethnic group.

When we come however to the question of manipulating Mexicans in groups, or as masses, my answer would be yes, it is possible to manipulate the Mexican-Americans as a group. My own experience, which is largely in the field of labor, has taught me that this is possible, the manipulation of people who are poorly educated, of people who have come from poor environments and continue to live in such environments in California. I have seen these people manipulated, used by others for other people's purposes. I have also seen these people become aware of the fact that they have been manipulated and revolt. When suddenly the Mexican, who is an impetuous, temperamental individual for the most part, finds out that he has been taken, he doesn't just write a letter to the governor, he takes action. I have been involved myself in many scenes in California where I saw this beautifully illustrated.

In 1954 when I organized the cotton pickers' strike in Kern County we had several thousand people out on strike, most of them Mexicans, many Negroes. I remember a Mexican contractor who was tagging along to see what was going on. A little Mexican cotton picker came up behind me and we heard the remarks that this contractor was making, ridiculing the strike and yelling to the pickers who were in the field to stay on the job, that we didn't amount to anything. An Anglo who was next to me said, "Let's report this guy to the Labor Commissioner." The little Mexican came up with a tire iron from his car and he said to the contractor, "Look, you see this in my hand? I brought this to change a tire; I'm going to use it to change your mind." That was all it took to make the contractor get into his car and leave us alone. The realization in the mind of this cotton picker that all these years he had been misled and exploited by this contractor didn't lead to an intellectual reaction, it led to action. This is a typical response to manipulation when we discover it. But there are cases when this isn't true. The manipulated Mexican usually never finds out that he is being manipulated, and when that happens we see situations go on year after year, and we are struck by the apathy, indifference, humility and submissiveness of the Mexican who is being manipulated. There are many of us who have had the good luck to be awakened to manipulation and its evils, and we don't submit to it. But those of our ethnic group who have not had these opportunities can still be manipulated and still are.

This discussion probably should draw another distinction, and that is that we are mainly talking about political manipulation. Frankly, I think that is why this subject was placed on the agenda. Economic manipulation we are used to. California agriculture has been built upon the manipulation of a labor force composed mostly of Mexicans and Mexican-Americans.

We find manipulation in various forms, but the one which I think interests us most tonight is political manipulation, because it is here that we come face to face with the fact that the Anglo-American is the top man in politics. No matter how we dress the political organizations of California, the Democratic and the Republican Party, they are operating political machines that are in the hands of the Anglo. It is in relationship to this political apparatus that I think most of you have thought of manipulation. The question now becomes, "Does the Anglo-American manipulate the Mexican in politics?" My answer to that is not a very direct one, it is not a simple one, because I don't think the answer can be a simple one.

I feel that there are three considerations with respect to political manipulation which have to be borne in mind. One is that whether we are speaking of the Democratic Party or the Republican Party, the most important item in political life in America, which is money, dollars, campaign funds, is in the hands of the Anglo-American. The Mexican-American who wants to participate, who wants to be recognized, who wants to start going up the political ladder, must first recognize that the thing that makes American politics turn is money. The party funds are spent by people who know what they want, and you know what the pattern is in every campaign. The state committees of the Democratic Party and the Republican Party set up a minority section. The money then flows out and seeks the leadership of the particular minority community. The allotment of that money is a decision which the minority group does not make.

This brings me to another obvious fact, the manipulation of the political position of the Mexican-Americans in California requires mediators, people like ourselves, who become Republicans or Democrats and who are in touch with the Anglo politicians. It is us they talk to, not to the masses. They depend upon us to interpret situations and to tell them what to do. I am convinced that in this relationship, there is no manipulation, but I am also convinced that it is the unspoken intention of the Anglo politicians to secure the manipulation of the Mexican-American group as a whole through the mediators, who are ourselves. Herein I think lies the first and most important temptation to the Mexican leadership. When two cultures meet such as they do here, our own and that of the Anglo, it is impossible to avoid this kind of mediating role. There is no other way for the two ethnic groups to begin to understand each other. But if this is a necessity, it lays a tremendous burden upon the mediator because he is in the peculiar position of knowing what each of the parties brings to the relationship when neither of the two parties knows what the other party really is up to. The bridge between the two parties becomes then a very crucial one, and it is here where manipulation can be encouraged or where it can be stopped.

The next observation I would like to make in connection with political manipulation is that party appointments are not in the hands of the Mexican, not even the Mexican leader. They are not decided here among us; they are decided in Washington and in Sacramento. The basis of this decision is a very interesting one. There are many meritorious people I know in California who should have gone up the ladder of recognition and who haven't. This tells me that the Anglo politician is sensitive to the kind of Mexicans that he wants and the kind he doesn't want. In observing this distinction we can learn a great deal about what mediators are supposed to do and what they should do. I say this because so much of our political indignation and political aspiration is based upon the idea that the Governor of the State of California and the President of the United States and the Mayor of Los Angeles simply have got to appoint more Mexican-Americans to important offices. I don't think the Anglo is really acknowledging the importance of the Mexicans in California by appointing X, Y, or Z to public office. These are very carefully calculated appointments, and the fact that so many men of such obvious worth and merit have been appointed has been an incidental quality rather than a central quality. The reason I make this distinction between the significance of an appointment of a Mexican-American to public office and his individual merit is that the man who receives such an appointment has to then play a double role. He becomes a public servant but he cannot shake off his role of mediator between the Mexican-American and the Anglo, because we expect this of him.

To summarize this part of my remarks, what I am trying to say is that if we are talking about manipulation, we are really talking of the responsibility that rests upon those of us who have moved up into that very thin layer of leadership, and no matter what we do professionally we cannot avoid the position of mediator between the Anglo and the people who we are a part of ethnically.

I want to stress the fact that we are a very thin layer in California. Not long ago I drew up a list of those whom I consider the Mexican-American leaders of California and came up with about 115 or 130 men and women—out of a population of a million and a half. Because of the many demands on them, this handful of people is spreading itself so thin that it has become more of a symbolic leadership than anything else. The million and a half Mexican-Americans of California are not getting leadership, they are getting token leadership. Because we must also work for a living, it is all that we can provide.

Let me generalize further about the Mexican-Americans who represent the Mexicans of this state. I am going to try to give you my opinion of the role that we have drifted into and that we now play.

First, I think the thing that characterizes us most of all is that we are very forthright in protesting. We always have a grievance. We have been forced to play the role of men whose function it is to present the grievances of the inarticulate Mexicans, people who have no way of getting their grievances to the powers. I suggest to you that one of the reasons that the Negro is on the march today is that he has had this kind of traumatic experience for many generations more than we have, and I can understand why he is on the march. My feeling is that he should not stop marching until he gets where he wants to go. In a way we stand in danger of having the same public image of the Negro leader, of that of a man who is very expert at protesting and complaining, but that's all he knows how to do. As long as the bulk of the Mexicans in California remain in poverty and out of touch with authority, we must play this role.

Another point is that we base much of our social strategy on ethnic pride. Very often in going into the office of a political leader, we bring two things with us: we bring a concrete grievance but we also bring an injured pride. We are not saying, "You're doing this to us because we are poor and disenfranchised and unemployed," but instead we are saying, "You're doing it to us because we are Mexicans." I think there's a danger in this. While our ethnic identity is important to us, it is important for us to distinguish between those things that we are doing because our self-esteem as Mexicans has been hurt and what we are doing because certain social conditions should be changed. We can be much more useful without losing our identity if we base our social protest upon the facts of the case. We must make our case upon the facts rather than upon injured ethnic pride. It is a caution that we must observe.

Another comment I would like to make: In numbers we are so few that if we succeed in persuading an Anglo politician to appoint one of our number to an important political office, we are deprived of that particular individual's leadership. I feel this very keenly now. For the first time in my life I am a bureaucrat. I work in a bureaucracy and I see it from the inside. I have a profound aversion for bureaucracies. I think they are a necessary evil—you can't run a big country without bureaucracies—but I still don't like them. And yet I'm part of it now, and every day I see this conflict, and I watch myself. There are things to be done in East Los Angeles which have been crying to be done for fifty years, and here we have a law, the Economic Opportunities Act, that is based upon a tremendous concept. They tell us to go out and organize the poor in the neighborhoods, teach them, help them to elect their representatives, and lead them up to the point where they can run their own program and get out of poverty by the bootstraps. But I wish I could tell you how difficult this is inside the bureaucracy. I don't know how long I'm going to last. I won't last beyond that point where I am convinced that either the bureaucracy cannot be moved or that I am expected not to try to move it because now I am a bureaucrat. This will not do. But it represents in my personal experience this fact, that until California has instead of 125 competent men and women who have dedicated their lives to this role, until there are 1,250 of them or 12,500, a million and a half Mexicans are not going to move very far. Those of us who accept positions of political distinction must face the fact that we become less useful to the Mexican community than when we were out there in the sticks battling without money, without political support, but always also without manipulation.

I have one more comment to make. Here again I am trying to speak in an analytical frame of mind, not a critical one. I have been very much impressed in the last ten years with our inability as a group to grasp and to take advantage of the important crises that offer us an opportunity for real leadership. I want to give you two examples of this. You all remember the Chualar accident near Salinas. The reaction to that was an international reaction—a tremendous wave of indignation and horror. For several days I thought: how can we get over to the Mexican-Americans in this state who for years have been battling on this front, who have been protesting the killing of farm workers in these needless accidents, how can we get together and see that here we have a tremendous opportunity. So I printed a leaflet and I made phone calls for three days, and I had individual reactions of tremendous indignation from many of my friends, and I called two meetings in my home hoping that we could tie this together and go to Sacramento and talk to Governor Brown and see to it that fundamental changes were made and that some responsibilities were pinned on the people who were responsible for those thirty-two deaths. I'm sorry to tell you that the Chualar accident has become a disgusting memory. We missed an opportunity. Before that there was a crisis in the Department of Employment. Again I saw not apathy, not indifference, not lack of will, but just inability, sheer technical inability to pull together and form a team and call certain manipulators to task and to terms and to make this system change. But we didn't. I must confess to you frankly that the way we are set up now—the way we overwork ourselves, the lack of staff, the lack of continuity between meetings of this kind—means that we are not taking advantage of a great opportunity for us to make an impression on the Anglo politician, to impress upon him the fact that we mean business. The Economic Opportunities Act has legally instructed us to organize the poor, and we are not organizing them. Unless we grasp these opportunities and develop them and lead them where they ought to go, I think that we will remain what we have always been, energetic and sincere and very vociferous and articulate protestors, and not much more.

I've got some suggestions to make concerning the future. I'm going to suggest that you as individuals and as a group, and those that you represent, consider the possibility of creating an institution in California that shall be our institution, that we shall run and manage and direct and administer ourselves, an institution in which four things would happen.

First, we with the skill and demonstrable experience and ability lay out for ourselves a task of doing our own research on our own problems. When any academician sets out to study the Mexican-American he has got to do it through mediators, and he is using the Mexicans for the purpose of writing a term paper or a Ph.D. dissertation. But we find that the poor Mexicans resist this; it is a violation of their privacy, and they will yield information and give facts only to those of us who have lived our lives with them. In the future an institution might exist in which the kind of research that is done on housing, on education, on a multitude of other problems that afflict the Mexican people, is done by us, in collaboration with the universities to be sure, but that we add something new, the confidence of the people, for they know that we are there to solicit their help in getting information because we intend to make a difference with that information, a difference to them, not to us.

The second function of this institution would be information, based upon facts and objective study and honest analysis to create in California the devices and the means of communicating with the Mexican people. One of our problems is that we have not set our minds and energies and resources to create a communication system by means of the printed word, perhaps even by radio or television, that will speak to the Mexican people about the things which matter to them and keep them informed on what is going on.

The third function of the institution would be leadership training. The human material is there but it doesn't know where it is going. The community leaders are not trained people, they are not skilled in knowing what steps to take above their own little neighborhood vision. From that level up to results they have to go through a labyrinth of agencies, government officials, bureaucracies and so forth. It is this process which they must be helped with, and we have a responsibility to teach them how to get through this maze. There are over one hundred communities in this county that would require one organizer in each community to do the job, and it is not being done.

Finally, we must consider the matter of staff. Such an institution should provide you and your organizations with continuity, with staff work.

And finally, to conclude, if we have our own research, our own information system, our own leadership trained to our own needs, and a staff to tie it together, we can then go into action, and I think the time has come. We have the Economic Opportunities Act, a law which in my judgment should rank as one of the most important pieces of federal legislation in the history of the United States. But I'm asking myself whether we are going to be able to take advantage of it. I hope that we can. And if what I have said tonight is of any help in that direction, I think that I will feel that I have not wasted your time.

PART 5

ORGANIZING AGAINST CAPITAL

LABOR ORGANIZING STRATEGIES, 1930–1970

[Notes on a Talk at United Farm Workers Boycott Office, San Jose], in Ernesto Galarza, *The Burning Light: Action and Organizing in the Mexican Community in California*, interviews conducted by Gabrielle Morris and Timothy Beard in 1977, 1978, and 1981 (Regional Oral History Office, The Bancroft Libraries, University of California, 1982), 13–16. Date of recording: May 7, 1974.

In this interview Galarza contextualizes the farm workers' labor movement and its struggle to build a union. His candid remarks and critiques are as insightful as they are direct. He delivers a message that unions can be built during hostile times if the workers choose to organize themselves. Unfortunately, hostile environments were often shaped by representatives of organized labor itself, including leaders of the AFL-CIO, labor activists, and other trade unions.

The principal challenge to the farm worker union was the Bracero Program, which the agriculture industry used for nearly twenty-two years to break organizing drives. Galarza and his allies estimated that they needed a ten-year public campaign to kill this program, and they were right. Only by ending the Bracero Program could the workers retake power at the point of production and organize. The campaign to end the program exposed to the general public how growers and the state consistently violated temporary work contracts, housed *braceros* in substandard dwelling, and often denied medical care to *braceros* when they were hurt on the job. The Bracero Program was brought to a halt in 1964 because of this campaign based on action research.

Notable life events during this era:

- 1983: The Occidental College Alumni Association awards Galarza Alumni Seal Award, the highest honor presented to Occidental College alumni for outstanding work in the academy and in the community at large.
- 1983: Galarza's *Kodachromes in Rhyme: Poems* is published. In the foreword of this book, Mae Galarza describes his poetry with the following statement, "By using the imagery of poetry to relieve the strife and hostility of seeking undisclosed facts to explain and prevent injustice, these themes appeared to the author: nature's refreshing beauty, personalities reflected, and philosophy woven from childhood days into experiences of the workday of men."

QUESTION: Do you think the political scene now is conducive to a better understanding of what the Mexican community is trying to do?

GALARZA: I'm having a hard time knowing just where it stands; that goes for the Mexicans and for the farm workers. I think if you look at the situation from the standpoint of where the Delano union is now, I'm very concerned over the possibility that Nixon may be able to weather this storm and a reaction may set in in the country between now and '76 that would strengthen those [opposed to farm worker organizing]. I don't think it's likely to happen but I'm not sure that it won't happen. [discusses Watergate situation with Nixon and tapes] I am watching the American people to see what they do. I met Nixon in Bakersfield at hearings in November 1949 of a subcommittee of the House of Representatives to investigate the DiGiorgio strike. One of three representatives was Richard Nixon. He was there two full days and a half day and cross-examined six or seven of us who appeared as witnesses. My personal recollection was him sitting across the table as inquisitor and the witnesses were sitting on this side. The thing I remember about Richard Nixon was the way in which he played to his audience. That room in the Bakersfield Inn was filled to capacity with growers from all over the state who came to see the union raked over the coals, and Nixon was in glory. I remember his face. Every time he made a point, like scoring the union for bloodshed or subversion or whatever point he made, he would look up at his audience to see how he was doing.

And this happened so continuously that I began to wonder whether his mind was on the witness or on the crowd. I couldn't tell. That committee went back to Washington. Incidentally, the chairman of that committee was a Democrat, because as you remember it was a Democratic Congress. The second member was a Democrat and ranking member for the Republicans was Nixon. That committee went back to Washington. There was an enormous amount of heat placed on the chairman to issue a report hostile to the union or to the effect that the union officers, which included myself, had embezzled strike funds in the hundreds of thousands of dollars, and that we had published a motion picture film, which was a pack of lies. But the chairman wouldn't yield, and, as you know, in the House of Representatives the chairman of the subcommittee is the top dog. Nothing happens on that subcommittee that he doesn't approve of. And so this chairman refused to issue a report hostile to the union. He killed it. But the DiGiorgios—Mr. DiGiorgio and his corporation—absolutely had to have a report. That was what the whole thing was about. That was why they had the committee come in. So what they did was this—Congressman Werdel, who was not on the subcommittee but who was congressman from that district, on the 9th of May 1950 got permission from the House to print a report of the committee's visit to Bakersfield. That report appeared in the *Congressional Record* and the next day it was on the wires all over the country. A statement was issued by the DiGiorgio Corporation in San Francisco that the subcommittee had filed a report, that it was an official report and it said all these things about the union, that officers were a bunch of crooks, that they had embezzled thousands of dollars, that they had published this libelous film and so on and so on. It was a very vicious statement. I never read a denunciation of a union like that one. Everybody believed it. Our friends in the labor movement believed it. And that was the beginning of the end of the strike. We had to call it off two weeks after that. We had very little support financially from the labor movement, but what little was coming in was cut off and our president, Mr. Mitchell, decided we had to call off the pickets. And there were several hundred former employees of the DiGiorgio farms that had been fired. They had to leave Arvin and Lamont.

Now, the union didn't fold until 1960, but the beginning of the end was in May 1950. That report was of very great interest to me because I was at the hearings. I was one of the organizers of the union and on the picket line every day, and when the committee left Bakersfield[,] myself and my union friends were convinced that was the end of it. There would be no report because we had talked to the chairman and he said, "All this is nonsense."

But there was a report and I didn't know how it got there, but I started checking, and from 1950 to 1965 I tracked down the history of that report. To make a long story short, what I found out was that that report had been typed in the offices of DiGiorgio, San Francisco, had been sent to Werdel in Washington who took it to Nixon and to Steed and to Thruston Morton and asked them to sign it. Nixon read it and signed it as a genuine report.

QUESTION: Did the chairman sign it?

GALARZA: No, no, the chairman had nothing to do with it. It got in as an official statement in the *Record*. You know what the rule of the House is: a representative can ask unanimous consent to put in a recipe for blueberry pie, so it's printed. . . . Congressmen get into habit of getting up and saying, "I ask unanimous consent to extend my remarks." Nobody protests; they all do it. So it goes into the *Record*. And then when it's reprinted, as this report was, on the single sheet with the letterhead of the Congress, the seal of the United States of America, you hand it out to newspapermen and to them it's official. So the next time somebody hands you an official report of the House of Representatives, look on the back side.

So the chairman did not have to—he was surprised. The first thing we did the day after it appeared, we telephoned him from Bakersfield. Cleveland Bailey, his name was. He said, "I am shocked. There is no report. There was no meeting. We didn't even discuss it in committee." Consequently, that led to the break-up of the strike.

QUESTION: Could you explain the *bracero* program and the effect it had on your union?

GALARZA: It was very simple. The state was flooded with *braceros* while we were on strike, and before the strike and after the strike. So everywhere we went we had to contend with these workers who were isolated, they were really in camps, we couldn't get to them. I lost track of the number of times I was thrown out of camp talking with *braceros*. Once I remember I was near Corcoran, the camp located about ten miles west of Corcoran. I went out to talk to the *braceros*; there were about three hundred in the camp. We were getting ready for a cotton strike. And it was my job to explain to people what we were doing. Because we didn't have any money even for bulletins, we couldn't publish pieces of paper. So I had to go personally.

When I got to this camp I had to walk clear around the camp to find the gate in the barbed wire fence. I waited till evening and walked in, contacted some of the men and told them the strike was coming and please don't pick cotton. That was about all the time I had till the camp director, the cop, came and told me to leave. Of course, I left.

So everywhere we went during those years there was more than enough manpower to do the work, particularly during those strikes. From 1948 to 1959 I participated in probably twenty strikes and always that was the problem. And if there were not enough *braceros* in the area to satisfy the growers that they had replacements, they would bring them in from Mexico. After the strike started, with permission from the Department of Labor, they had no trouble getting permits for *braceros*.

So my answer to your question is that all during those years, the thirteen years that I was in the fields, the first thing we had to face was the presence of *braceros*. They were inaccessible, kept in the camps. The men were afraid to talk to you. If they were seen talking with you in town they were spotted and changed either to another part of the state or sent home to Mexico. So the survival of the union for ten years under those circumstances is something I've never been able to understand.

BRACEROS AND WETBACKS; U.S.-MEXICAN RELATIONS

QUESTION: What was responsible for the *bracero* program being stopped?

GALARZA: It was a long campaign. The whole strategy of our union was based upon three concepts. One, we had to bring about the termination of the *bracero* program. We figured it would take us ten years, and it did. Our view was that when that was accomplished that we next would have to undertake a similar campaign to bring to the attention of the country and to bring about legislation concerning the wetbacks. Our view was not to exclude the wetbacks. Our view was that the so-called wetback is a product of the political and social conditions of Mexico; and consequently we favored a campaign of publicity, confrontation, documentation, protest and so on that would zero in not on the wetback as a person, but on the Mexican government and its policy in Mexico that created such terrible poverty conditions that the wetback was a natural product of this burgeoning Mexican capitalism. That was our pitch.

Maybe that would take us ten years and at the end of that ten-year stretch we then thought we could begin organizing farm workers. Maybe fortunately or unfortunately, I don't know, the strategy of the union was cut off halfway. We never got to the wetback issue, not really. That brings us to 1960 and the union went down the drain.

I still believe that the way the wetback—the illegal—problem is handled in this country, particularly in this state, completely fails to focus on where the trouble really is. There are probably today 75,000 or 80,000 people who are here illegally working here; and they are here because Mexico is worse off today than in 1917, the year of the revolution. That's what produces poverty and that's what brings poor people here. So to close the border or to denounce the illegal or to continuously talk about the horrible conditions that he works under takes our mind off the main track.

QUESTION: Poverty in Mexico and burgeoning capitalism; Mexico and U.S. related in their economies. Could you carry that thought through farther? Is it because of corporations in the U.S.?

GALARZA: Not entirely. Let me go back a little ways. In 1952 I wrote a resolution for our union that was approved at our convention in New Orleans in which I proposed that our union enlist the support of the labor movement with appropriate lobbying and political pressure to create an international zone extending one hundred miles south of the border and one hundred miles north of the border and that in this zone both countries join to bring about changes, particularly in the matter of land tenure, so that these peasants and small town people in Mexico who were constantly trying to jump over the border could be stabilized. They would have employment and some kind of equity in the land and technical assistance too. We never got anywhere. The national unions, the AFL-CIO paid no attention.

The reason we worded the resolution is that I felt that the way things were going in 1950 in due course the Mexican economy would be so much like the American economy in terms of its control, ownerships, etc., that unless we started way back twenty-five years ago to build a different model to stabilize people in their communities and assure them the right to live on the land and give them the means and the instruction to be able to make a living in the land—the resources are there—that the trend that I could see in Mexican affairs would reach the point where there would be such a vast number of Mexicans for rent, for hire, that it would be impossible for farm workers of this country, of this state, to make a living as farm workers. That's what happened, and the Mexican economy has gone from a somewhat primitive capitalism to a full-blown capitalism.

Today if you look at the Mexican economy very closely, you find the usual characteristics. I would say that today not more than 35 percent of the industrial plant is in use. Three or four banks in Monterrey and another three or four in Mexico City control 90 percent of the bank business. What does that mean? It means that since the Mexican economy is so dependent on United States favors, nothing will happen in the way of labor policy in Mexico that will turn the country around and spread the wealth. Today there is more concentration of wealth in Mexico than there is in this country, and more than there was in 1910 when the revolution broke out. And looking into the immediate future I see no change.

The Mexican dollar will depend entirely on the U.S. dollar. The Mexican dollar is stable because the American government is more than glad to pour credits into Mexico. Tracking these conditions in a wide circle, you always get back to the fact that the level of living in Mexico is so low that possibly three out of five Mexican adults are looking for opportunities to come to work in California.

QUESTION: Is there any labor union movement in Mexico?

GALARZA: As you look at the Mexican scene from the outside you can right away see . . . there are craft unions, industrial unions, agricultural workers unions. The movement as it is today, though, is not at all what it was in 1916, 1917. You see, the labor movement in Mexico emerged as a part of the revolutionary struggle. It didn't emerge, as it did in this country, as a part of civil resistance—the emergence of trade unions—as a long, hard battle for collective bargaining. In Mexico it was the emergence of armed workers who participated in the armed struggle of the revolution and out of that came the trade unions. But in the last ten years the union has become part of the political machinery of the state; and so you see secretaries, presidents of unions are rewarded by seats in congress. They have these two heads, politicians and labor officials. To my knowledge the Mexican labor movement has *never* taken a straight trade-union stand on the problems of farm-workers who were migrating to this country. Never. They have made certain motions, but it has not been an effective position. So you go to Mexico and talk to these officials, as I did, in the hope that they would see that the Mexican working man was being pushed out of the country by extreme poverty; and that the trouble was in Mexico, but the trade union leaders didn't see it that way; so today there is not a definitive trade union movement in Mexico, but part of the official machinery of the state.

ORGANIZED LABOR AND THE POWER STRUCTURE

QUESTION: What, who, cut off your organizing strategy?

GALARZA: We had been in it, the union was out here since '46. The big strike was the DiGiorgio strike which started in October of '47 and the efforts to organize continued to the end of 1959. During those thirteen or fourteen years (to make a long story short), those ten years, '50 to '60, were years in which there was no hope we could organize farm workers.

All we could do was to build our own knowledge of the *bracero* system and keep hitting at it till we could reach a stage where public opinion was so convinced that the arguments of growers was a fraud. And when that climate had been created we could then move into the lobbying stage in Washington and gain enough support from friends of the union and those who were seeing the truth and that only then could we hope to repeal the *bracero* law. That we did in '63 but our union was out of business in 1960; and we had to disband because we were not, from the point of view of the labor leadership in the U.S., an orthodox union. We were constantly stepping on the toes of growers and bankers and others who had their own understanding with certain other portions of the labor movement.

So we were a threat to the way in which power was put together in this state. And I never made any bones about it. I always said to our members and to whoever would listen to me that if our union lasted thirty years we would change the power structure of California. That was our goal. And this was by no means a part of the philosophy of organized labor in California. So we lost ground until 1960, and then we were faced with this dilemma. The State Federation of Labor had long cut off any financial support. I think at the top of our record the State Federation of Labor was giving us $2,500 a year.

We started out with four organizers in California. We each had areas of the state. And by 1955 we were down to one and that was myself. Now obviously with one organizer servicing seventeen locals from Mexicali to the Oregon border that's no labor movement. So part of the answer is that the growers wore us out. I was hospitalized for three months in 1959. I couldn't move. Just fatigue. The other reason was that by 1960 the leadership of the labor movement had made up its mind that we weren't a good bet. And so the word got around that we were inefficient. Here we'd been in the fields fifteen years and we had no contracts. We hadn't reduced any grower to terms. What kind of nonsense is this?

All during those ten years I doubt that we were getting more than $300 or $400 a month from organized labor, but even so we had proved to be incompetent; and by 1959 the suggestion came down from Walter Reuther to us that the best thing for us to do was to turn in our charter and give it to the Packinghouse Workers. And I told Walter to go to hell.

My advice to our president was, give the charter back to me; and he can do what he wants with it but we're not going to be ordered by anybody. So by 1959 we were in the worst possible shape: no money, no organizers, no support and all these suggestions coming to us to get lost quick. So from September of '59 to May of 1960 the liquidation process just went *fast*.

The only thing that saved a smidgeon of the union was the offer the Butchers' Union made. They wanted our charter. It happened that the president of our union, H. L. Mitchell, had been a lifelong friend of the secretary-treasurer of the Butchers' Union, Pat Gorman, so on that basis Gorman offered to salvage what little there was left of the union, and the charter was transferred by Mitchell to the Butchers, and they've held it ever since. But just as soon as they got it, they invited me to go to Louisiana as an organizer because Mr. Meany didn't want me in California. And Mr. Gorman was not about to incur the anger of George Meany by keeping me here. So by the spring of 1960 I was in Louisiana.

QUESTION: [inaudible]

GALARZA: It's hard for me to say, for in the years I was talking about, it was part of my duty to shuttle; and the working time I spent in California I was on the road, and weekends and spare time I was in the East talking to the top people in the labor movement trying to enlist their support. So in those years I could give you a reasonably close answer as to what calculations those guys were making. I can't now.

I can only guess that probably—there is still something about the situation that was very clear to me in the 1950s and that was that to the extent the American labor movement and its leadership was becoming stuffed-shirt, straight business trade-unionism, that all the more they needed someone to be good to. And we were the favorite Christian charity of organized labor. Whenever the leaders in those days were hard-pressed to explain jurisdictional strikes and exorbitant wage demands and the tremendous differences in wage scales in California between, say, the engineers' union and the farm workers, they could always point to these donations and they could always make speeches about us poor farm workers who went around with wrinkled bellies. "We've been good to these people so we can't be that bad."

And as a public relations asset, it was tremendous. We were the last remaining working joes to whom one could be kind.

QUESTION: Teamsters?

GALARZA: I can just refer you to what the Teamsters have said. Dan Tobin said it. Hoffa said it. Fitzsimmons has said it. Einar Mohn has said it through the years. It's a very simple answer. Our power rests with our contracts with the canneries, with the packing sheds. We're haulers, primarily, and we cannot let an independent union control the source of the produce we haul. It's that simple. I remember 1950 (we were working in Salinas). I asked that question. At that time it wasn't quite so clear. The Teamsters hadn't said this often enough for people to have really heard it. But when my union asked me to analyze the situation, that's what I said.

I said, "You don't have to speculate or theorize, all you have to do is look at the economic picture. The growers have contracts with the Teamsters to haul the produce; the workers are not organized; we're trying to organize them. As soon as we do you can just bet we're going to run into Teamster opposition because from their point of view they cannot let us control the farm workers."

From 1949 to 1958, a long stretch, in spite of the weaknesses of our effort, we were able to stop production on a large scale by economic action in cotton, peaches, tomatoes, cantaloupes, lettuce, grapes. The stuff just didn't come out of the fields. That's economic action. And every time it happened we were sure to have a Teamster business agent on the spot to shoo in the drivers, to get them across our picket line. The Teamsters in 1949 and in 1974 cannot afford to let an independent union control conditions of production. And they're saying so. They're covering their [flanks?], that's all. And to the extent that they can persuade the growers that it's in their best interests to let them control the farm workers, to that extent you will have sweetheart contracts.

FUTURE OF THE UNITED FARM WORKERS UNION

QUESTION: Can you venture a guess as to what lies in the future for the UFW?

GALARZA: You know, I found out that every time I thought I was looking into a crystal ball, I was looking at the eight ball, and so my prophecies are not very useful. But I would say that, short of a very drastic political upheaval in this country and also short of a genuine and massive support from labor for these efforts, that the present farm labor union is a long way from consolidating its efforts. Mainly what is lacking is the committed support of labor. Be careful you don't measure that support in terms of dollars.

When I was a lobbyist in Washington, I discovered that the money the unions were giving the farm workers was not the important thing: it was the lack of support in Washington. The labor movement for thirty years to my knowledge has had a very powerful lobby in Washington, very skilled guys. You should see them in action. They know how to work the Hill. There must be twenty-five or thirty of them on the payroll today and they know their oats. These people could swing votes in favor of farm labor legislation, but they won't do it. These are not their instructions. And until you see the AFL-CIO lobby operating in Washington, right on the spot, lining up votes for [inaudible]. And clearly Chavez can't afford to maintain a lobby in Washington, to be on the spot the way the AFL-CIO is on the spot 360 days a year. An individual union can't do that, particularly the Farmworkers. They're lucky to have one lobbyist in Sacramento once in a while.

If the American labor movement were other than what it is, its commitment would be financial, it would be political, it would be legislative, it would be propagandistic. On all those levels labor would have to be active to turn the political machinery around so that farm workers would get legislation. The labor movement isn't doing that.

For years Walter Reuther was the lady bountiful of our union. In the middle of a strike we could always count on him for two or three dozen bucks for soup kitchens. But this is not the labor movement as a whole.

QUESTION: AFL-CIO support? Tainted with CIA connections?

GALARZA: Chavez would not be asked to commit himself to such shenanigans. Taking money would not mean endorsement. . . . I would caution you against looking too deeply for motives in George Meany because he's not a deep man. All you have to do is to look at the labor leadership and how they operate and how you can predict what they will do in a given situation and that will give you a key to the man. So I would suspect that he is under pressure from some of these internationals. "Come on, George, fork over a couple of million for these poor farm workers." And then at the next meeting of the executive council, he'll make a little speech about "Farmworkers Forever."

QUESTION: Was AFL support responsible for contracts farm workers won back in 1970? How much did the AFL have to do with that? If the support wasn't there, how were they able to win those contracts?

GALARZA: Oh, I can't answer that question. I'd have to be much better informed in detail about what happened from 1967 to 1971. But I can guess that, for one thing, the novelty of the boycott had a lot to do with it. You see, one thing you have to remember about power, whether it's trade union or power of the growers in California, if you are fighting that power you have a tendency to be overawed by the way it looks from the outside.

I remember in the cotton strike of 1952, there were three of us who organized that strike in Kern County, Tulare, Fresno, and Stanislaus. We were fighting a wage cut. I was at the northern end and I was able to see from day to day how it was going. During the first fifteen days or so, it was great. We were pulling workers out of the fields by the hundreds. We were caravanning. We were stopping the delivery of cotton to the gins. But I was partly responsible for financing that strike, so I had to watch all kinds of angles. I had to listen to the workers to see how their morale was going. And about two weeks into the strike I began to have a sense that this thing better be settled *fast*, because our pickets were running out of food. Some were pulling their families out of the area and moving off to Oregon, to Arizona. And as I was trying to weigh the chances of sweating it out (I had almost come to the conclusion that in two or three more days that strike would have to be called off), one grower down in the southern part of the Valley put the wage back where it was and as soon as the word got around, the contractors and growers started to settle. So technically we won the strike. But it was too damn close for comfort. And the reason that we won that is that the growers were looking at what you might euphemistically call human power. We had these workers out and I imagine that the big shots, the cotton growers, said, "Well, my golly, we really underestimated these guys. They've been out for twenty days. They still look strong. The cotton isn't getting picked. Our contracts are in jeopardy. We better settle. We better restore the old wage."

That's the way we looked to them and I also recall situations in which we had the same feelings about the growers. We'd look at the DiGiorgio Corporation, "My God, who would ever think of attacking this *monster*? They will *never* break." But we had them on the ropes for thirty months. And we broke for reasons that were completely unforeseen. One of them was Richard Nixon.

So when you look at power from the outside, remember that you're not looking at it from the back side. My guess would be that that original victory, the biggest that Chavez' union has had, partly was due to the fact that the growers, looking at the power of the union as outsiders, overestimated the economic strength of the union. And they settled because they had this boycott working very effectively. And I would guess they feared that if they challenged the union another year on this front that people would become so used to the idea of boycott, they'd be boycotting potatoes. They'd be starving in order to support the farm workers. That was a risk they wouldn't take. Now this is all speculation . . . based on experience we had.

EARLIER LABOR GAINS

QUESTION: Changes with Brown administration on farm labor interests?

GALARZA: I had a lot to do with that situation and I can tell you that Pat Brown never gave us any such support. What happened was this. I took over the union in California right around 1953 or 1954. One of my goals was to destroy the Farm Placement Service. I used to say this at public meetings. So we made our preparations to destroy it and one of the things I had to do was to keep tabs on the deals that Ed Hayes and his crew made with the growers. It took us five years to accumulate the evidence, and when we had it there was nothing Pat Brown could do about it except to move in and cleanse the house before we cleaned it for him.

My goal was not to have Mr. Ed Hayes removed, that was the least of my concerns. My goal was to have the Farm Placement Service abolished. Pat saved the Farm Placement Service by firing Ed Hayes and disciplining a few of the farm placement guys who had been so indiscreet as to accept a crate of asparagus and take it home to the wife. This kind of stuff. Governor Brown had no choice. He couldn't condone these kinds of practices. And my view has always been that the dismissal of Ed Hayes and his lieutenants was a failure of the union. And the Farm Placement Service is in place today. It's still right there.

QUESTION: Change of attitudes as far as [the] union is concerned between those years and today?

GALARZA: Oh, yes. The difference is as night is from day. To point out the contrast, during the melon strike, the second melon strike in the Imperial Valley which I helped to organize in 1952 or 1953: at the height of the strike we wanted public support in L.A. in order to stop authorization of *bracero* replacements. So it was my task to leave the strike and go to

L.A. looking for an audience, looking for some people to talk to to tell them the story. Didn't find any. I telephoned friends, said, "Get to the newspapers. Do something." But an audience, ten people? Now today you have meetings like this all over the state. There's a *big* difference. The time wasn't ripe for these kind of groups to become aware of their role in the social struggle; it was twenty years too soon.

During the tomato strike, I had to organize that myself in Tracy in 1953: we had about eighteen hundred tomato pickers and their families out on strike and about fifteen days in the strike, I needed market information, went to Giannini Foundation in Berkeley. Found a tomato specialist and asked for marketing reports on tomatoes and [the] day's ticker report. "I don't know what you're talking about," [he replied,] and all he had to do was to reach over and pick up some pieces of paper in his files. Today your farm labor union knows where to get this information. You have people who are doing market research for Chavez, and there are no mysteries that he can't solve by telephone. This is a big difference. And I could go on showing you by contrast how much more capable farm workers are to do battle on all of these fronts. And I don't think that is going to diminish.

QUESTION: Role of volunteers?

GALARZA: We had just begun to get volunteers when we folded. In the late fifties people were just beginning to hear about conditions in the fields. This is beginning to sound like a hard luck story, isn't it?

Let me back up ten years before we came in, and those were the days when it wasn't a question of knowing somebody at the University of California, or talking to some people in Los Angeles; those were the days when the big question was, can I as an organizer go into Fresno and come out alive? Talking with Pat Chambers, he was doubtful about what the hell good he did. He was a farm-labor organizer back in the thirties. He spent three years in the penitentiary, convicted under criminal syndicalism laws. So I thought Pat was a little depressed about what had his life meant, anyway. And I told Pat, "If you hadn't been in the Imperial Valley ten years before I was, I wouldn't have been in the Imperial Valley at all."

So you have to keep these things in mind. This present turn in farm labor organizing is a very long link in a much longer chain. And that's the way you have to look at it. To me one of the great men in farm labor history is Pat Chambers. He doesn't think so, but I do.

And so we move in after these—for fifteen years Pat Chambers and

Caroline Decker and those people took the rap and went to jail and were under continuous assault and so on. It was those ten years that from one point of view could be regarded as a total loss, because when they were incarcerated and did time there weren't any contracts in the fields, there were no locals, there were no unions, there were no sympathizers of unions, there were no boycotts—so that if you look at their careers in labor organizing from the standpoint of product, they were a total and dismal failure. But what did they do? For ten long years their struggle brought to the attention of the country the fact that rural California was a place in which there was no free speech: there were no civil liberties in rural California and the main victims were Okies, the Mexicans, and the Blacks. That's *all* they did. So when we came on the scene in the late forties, the growers' associations were by no means the ferocious things that they had been ten years before.

We could hold meetings in Fresno, where Pat had had to sneak around alleys to get a few guys together. So, as our work was made possible by Chambers, my feeling is that Cesar's work is made possible by the apparently insipid record that we accumulated during those fifteen years. The question is, what will be the legacy of the Delano movement, looking forward into the future of our country? Answer: Victory!

POVERTY IN THE VALLEY OF PLENTY

A REPORT ON THE DI GIORGIO STRIKE

Ernesto Galarza, "Poverty in the Valley of Plenty: A Report on the Di Giorgio Strike," May 14, 1948, unpublished report. Courtesy of Department of Special Collections and University Archives, Stanford University Libraries.

This is the original report Galarza wrote to document the eight-month strike of Local 218 of the National Farm Labor Union against the DiGiorgio Fruit Corporation. It was later published in his book *Spiders in the House & Workers in the Field.*

Galarza and his organizing team built worker committees who recruited more than 500 DiGiorgio workers to the union within the first month of organizing in February 1947. In October of that year, more than 1,100 DiGiorgio workers marched and demanded that their union be recognized. This organizing drive was in itself impressive, but the fact it was achieved with minimal state and federal labor protections makes it a remarkable accomplishment.

Agriculture corporate interests feared that this labor movement would spread throughout the Southwest, and they exercised their power over elected officials and public institutions and flooded California's Central Valley with *braceros*—effectively killing the NFLU's organizing efforts.

Notable life events during this era:

- 1946: Galarza earns a Ph.D. in History and Public Law from Columbia University.
- 1947: Galarza resigns as the head of the Division of Labor and Social Information of the Pan-American Union, an international organization that promoted cooperation in trade, agriculture, travel, and finance among North and South American nations.
- 1947: Galarza takes the position of director of research and education in California for the Southern Tenant Farmers' Union (STFU).
- 1947: Galarza begins organizing farmworkers at the DiGiorgio Fruit Corporation. This agribusiness giant owned much of California's Central Valley farmland and had the largest fruit-packing plant in the nation. The organized workers sustained a thirty-month strike and boycott in an attempt to pressure the company to recognize their labor union.

A REPORT ON THE DI GIORGIO STRIKE

The Di Giorgio Fruit Corporation's 12,000-acre ranch in Kern County, located 18 miles from Bakersfield, California, is one of the largest enterprises of its kind in the United States. It is the backbone of $20,000,000 business owned by Joseph Di Giorgio's family corporation.

Di Giorgio requires some 1,200 employees to operate this ranch. At the peak of the season he hires additional field hands and packers. Many of these full time workers live in the towns of Arvin and Lamont, a short distance from the Di Giorgio corporation's fields and packing sheds. Other workers live in Bakersfield. Still others drift with the tide of migratory labor that rises and falls with every change of the California seasons.

The majority of Di Giorgio's employees were once small farmers and share-croppers [who were] blown out of Arkansas and Oklahoma by the dust storms of a decade ago. They are of self-reliant American stock, used to hard work, with large families and good credit at the grocery store. Among them is a sprinkling of Mexicans, many of whom have long records of service with Di Giorgio.

On October 1, 1947, over 1,100 of these workers called a strike. They had organized a union and had voted to strike for union recognition, collective bargaining and better pay.

The strike, now in its eighth month, has lifted the curtain on the next act of the "Grapes of Wrath." In California's central valley, the homesteader and the family farm are yielding to the assembly line methods of corporations like Di Giorgio's. The man with the hoe is being pushed out by the mechanical cotton picker and the potato digger. Farming in Kern County has become a complicated operation involving heavy investments and expensive machinery; financial connections with the big money pools of San Francisco, Los Angeles and New York; national and international marketing; advertising, public relations; contacts in the state legislature and in Congress; and many other elements that the little man of the soil cannot afford and barely understands.

The Di Giorgio field and packing shed "hands" are the by-products of this process. At the low point of the agricultural year in California (March 30th in 1946) major seasonal crop operations required only 69,000 workers. At the high point (September 7th) requirements rose to 244,000.

Between these peaks lies the valley of insecurity in which the Di Giorgio strikers and hundreds of thousands like them are forced to spend what the California Welfare Code euphemistically calls "seasons of repose." These figures, and the rural slums that pock the central valley, help to explain the Di Giorgio strike.

The four freedoms have given way to the four fears—fear of competition for the job; fear of inadequate wage; fear of unemployment; and fear of destitution.

These fears are harder to endure because the Di Giorgio workers are not entitled to compensation for unemployment, social security or accident benefits. Di Giorgio and the other corporations in his class have seen to that. Their powerful lobbies, representing finance farming, have obtained exemptions from Congress and from the state legislature on the pretense that they are "little fellows" struggling along on 40 acres and a mule.

These are the issues that the Di Giorgio strikers have brought to the attention of the entire country.

Joseph Di Giorgio keeps a silent watch on the picket line from a vantage point [of] 3,000 miles away at his headquarters, 66 Harrison St., New York City. He contends, through his lawyers, that "There is no strike. There are no issues."

But the determination of the men and women who have kept vigil on a 20 mile picket line for more than seven months has forced Di Giorgio to recognize that there is a strike, a problem and an issue.

Di Giorgio has recognized the facts of the situation in deeds, if not in words. The Corporation has hired hundreds of strike breakers.

It has used Mexican contract workers, imported from Mexico under the auspices of the Mexican and United States governments, to work behind the picket line.

It has harbored a mob that set upon and beat peaceful union pickets.

It has presented misleading sworn statements by foremen and field bosses posing as ordinary day laborers, happy with conditions as they are.

It has employed illegal Mexican workers smuggled into this country in violation of the law.

It has refused to sit down with state and federal conciliators.

It has tried to prejudice citizens of good will against the union by distributing a statement entitled, "A Community Aroused."

It has attacked the strikers before Congress and before the nation through the Congressional Record.

It has organized hostile public demonstrations against relief caravans sent by organized labor to aid the strikers.

It has caused to be published full page newspaper advertisements stating its side of the case.

It has persuaded the state legislature to investigate the union for alleged communist activities.

It has sent agents to Texas to enlist and employ strike breakers.

These are characteristic signs of industrial conflict. They represent management's resistance to organized economic pressure from the workers. On the record they show that Di Giorgio's key position against the union—"there is no strike"—has been made untenable.

There is a strike. The corporation can no longer blink at this fact. But the case of the corporation has rested not only on this refusal to face the immediate, obvious issue. The corporation has counted heavily on several behind-the-scenes factors which it hopes will eventually crush the union. These factors are: the reservoir of strike breakers; the use of violence; the backlog of unemployment in the central valley; the reserve of unemployed workers outside the state; the specter of relief; the use of illegal Mexican workers; the legal importation of Mexican contract workers; the use of local Mexican labor; mechanization; the elimination of government management of the labor supply camps; congressional investigation: the provocation of community sentiment against the union; and the oblique use of race prejudice to separate the workers and divide them into mutually hostile groups.

Some of these elements are within the power of the corporation to direct and control. Others arise out of economic and social conditions which can be exploited to the disadvantage of the strikers. Taken together they throw light not only on the strike but also on the fundamental problems out of which it arose.

Use Of Strike Breakers. The corporation has now in its employ hundreds of "scabs." They pass through the picket lines in the presence of a heavy police guard that is on duty at all times. The sheriff's supply of reserve arms and strike breaking equipment is kept in a trailer just inside the corporation yard.

The strike breakers are a mix lot. They include Anglo-Americans from Arkansas and Oklahoma, Filipinos, illegal Mexicans and Mexicans who had worked in the area many years.

Di Giorgio has drawn his strike breaking crews from the "skid rows" of the valley towns and from Texas. Signed statements are on record showing that many of these men were hired without knowledge of the strike.

Violence. As long as the corporation can successfully cross hundreds of strike breakers through the picket line it will probably refrain from using violence. It has not always been so considerate. On one occasion a mob of forty persons ran out of the corporation yard armed with tire irons and clubs and severely beat three pickets. The day before this incident took place, Di Giorgio had organized a motorized column against the relief caravan sent by California trade unions. As the caravan passed the main gates of the Di Giorgio ranch, a hostile line of trucks and cars moved in the opposite direction on the same road. The demonstration was apparently intended to provoke mass violence, which was avoided by the presence of mind of the caravan leaders.

While the strikers are determined to keep the peace on the picket line, they have been forewarned that violence may be used again.

Unemployment throws its shadow over the men and women who are holding the Di Giorgio picket line.

On March 5, an official of the state employment department stated that there were 50,000 unemployed in seven valley counties. This figure included all types of labor. Other authoritative sources placed the figure of unemployed agricultural workers at around 40,000.

Rough breakdowns by counties gave the following estimates of idle farm workers: Fresno 10,000; Kings 5,000; Kern 10,000; and Tulare 10,000.

It would not be far off to say that on the basis of all available estimates, there were in California during the first week of March over 40,000 unemployed farm workers whose demand for a job was registered at some point. "Registered at some point" are words intended to point out that the figure of 40,000 does not cover certain groups which form an important part of the labor supply of the state. These groups are: Mexican nationals who have "skipped" their contract and remain illegally in this country; Mexican illegal workers who have been smuggled across the border; and thousands of men and women of all groups who are in transit on trains, in buses and in their own dilapidated cars at any given moment of the slack season.

It is not improbable that this group in transit during the last week of March of this year numbered not less than 12,000 to 15,000. The illegal Mexicans and the "lost" nationals in California probably do not number less than an additional 20,000.

The foregoing groups, taken together, represent the pool of unemployment that the large agricultural corporation regards as desirable for profitable operations. They represent a reservoir of some 75,000 men and women [Di Giorgio] can draw [upon for] fresh supplies for his strike breaking crews.

Relief. For the finance of farmers like Di Giorgio, another sign of a favorable labor market is the increasing demand for public assistance by workers. Relief is the device by which responsibility for indigent workers, caught in the valley of destitution between the peaks of employment, is spread [to] the whole community.

On March 21, more than 1,600 penniless families were reported in the Coalinga-Huron area of Fresno County. Service clubs, the Red Cross and the Salvation Army were supplying food, fuel and clothing to these families on that date.

In Merced County 300 families were reported stranded and without means of subsistence. A drive was being conducted by the Elks Club of the county seat to provide clothing for children who could not otherwise attend school.

"Struck between harvests without food, clothing or funds" is the way the situation was described in Bakersfield on March 26 by a local newspaper. Relief workers in that area reported that in the vicinity of Di Giorgio's operations, families had been found who had not eaten for two or three days. Mexican families in Shafter were keeping their young children at home because they could not feed or clothe them adequately.

California's prolonged drought has been blamed by many for these appalling conditions. However, it is also widely recognized that an unprecedented immigration has taken place coincidentally with the drought. Many of those recent comers, according to the San Francisco Examiner of March 29, "were lured into the valley by false reports of free rooming and plenty of work."

Unemployed sailors in the Bay area have been urged to tide themselves over by seeking jobs in the central valley. Wondering Navajo Indians were to be found in Bakersfield early in April, trudging the migrant trails from New Mexico through Riverside as far north as Stockton.

With county relief budgets near exhaustion and with the state government reluctant to declare a relief emergency, which it had the power to do under the law, it can be understood why the Di Giorgio Corporation is complacent about a plentiful labor supply on its own terms.

Illegal Workers. Throughout the strike Di Giorgio has also resorted to the use of workers smuggled from Mexico.

On February 20, federal immigration officers raided the ranch and picked up 45 illegals for deportation. In another raid, carried out on April 1, another 30 of these men who had been working behind the picket line with Di Giorgio's knowledge and consent were arrested.

It is a commonly accepted view in California that these raids are not effective in eliminating the employment of illegal Mexican labor. Di Giorgio is a good illustration. Mexican residents in Arvin and Lamont report that a few days after the illegals are arrested they re-appear at the ranch, perhaps under another name, and are again hired. There can be no question as to the status of such workers. The corporation knows who they are. It does not voluntarily report them to the federal authorities.

The advantages to Di Giorgio in the employment of illegals are obvious. The Mexicans are in no position to bargain for wages with the corporation. They do not speak English. They are completely ignorant of any legal obligations that the employer may have with respect to them. They cannot file claims of any kind because of their illegal status. They cannot invoke the protection of the Mexican consul. They are, in short, perfect strike breakers.

Mexican Contract Workers. Di Giorgio, like all the finance farmers of whom he is an outstanding example, can still play another formidable card against the union. He can hold over its head the threat of importation of legal admitted Mexican contract workers, commonly called Nationals.

During the war hundreds of thousands of Nationals were brought to the United State. This migration was carried out under a limited term agreement between the governments of the United States and Mexico.

At the close of 1947, there were 6,000 Nationals in California being held over after the termination of their contracts.

Big growers, including Di Giorgio, found that this type of labor has advantages for them not unlike those presented by the illegals. It is docile, tractable manpower whose rights under the agreement are but dimly enforced by the United States agencies or the Mexican officials charged with their supervision. The record of this particular type of labor transaction during the war clearly bears out this assertion.

Before the wartime agreement expired last year, the agricultural corporations began to request large consignments of Nationals. Between August and November of 1947, twenty four such requests totaled 19,000 men.

Under this pressure a new agreement has been negotiated between the two governments. This agreement became effective on February 21 of this year. According to statements which have appeared in the press and attributed to officials of the Department of Agriculture and the Department of Labor, it is expected that over 60,000 Mexican laborers will be imported this year. The agreement, among other things, lays down the one-way principle that work contracts may be terminated only at the request of the employer. The effect of this provision appears to be that the Mexican National who is dissatisfied with his employment either has to work out the six months term of the contract or break it and thus lose all rights he may have under it.

Di Giorgio used Mexican Nationals during the war. He had 130 of them on his ranch when the strike broke out on October 1, 1947. The Nationals refused to work the first day of the strike but they did not join the picket line. Following visits to the ranch by representatives of the Department of Agriculture and the Mexican consulate at Fresno, the Nationals returned to work. What kind of persuasion was used by the corporation and government officials is not known. Experience shows, however, that in similar circumstance in the past, the Mexican Nationals have been told to go back to work "or else."

Pressure by the National Farm Labor Union eventually brought about the removal of the Nationals from the Di Giorgio ranch.

A possible backlog of 60,000 imported Nationals is not an unpleasant prospect for Di Giorgio. Even if the union should succeed in preventing certification of such workers to this particular operation [Di Giorgio], the effect on the overall labor market in California would be to make more native workers available on terms set by the cooperation.

Mexican Resident Labor. The labor power of the Mexican farm workers who have resided for many years in California is still another resource that Di Giorgio has used.

In Arvin, Lamont, Bakersfield, Shafter and other neighboring communities there are sizeable concentrations of families of Mexican ancestry who have worked in the crops for years. Many of those workers are citizens of the United States by birth. Usually they live in segregated slums called "*colonias.*" The economic status of these people is, if anything, lower than that of their Anglo-American fellow workers. In addition, they face serious disabilities arising out of the inferior racial and social status to which they have been traditionally assigned.

Under these circumstances, the Mexican colonies make ideal hunting grounds for contractors and agents of the large corporation farms. Di Giorgio has taken advantage of the need of these Mexican workers to supply his strike breaking crews.

Mechanization. Not the least of the forces that work with Di Giorgio is the process of mechanization that finance farming is introducing in the central valley.

Corporation ranches like Di Giorgio's foster the use of machinery wherever it can be profitably substituted from human hands. The potato digger and the cotton picker have appeared in the valley. The characteristic objects on the endless horizons of Kern County are the bulldozer, the tractor and the high tension power lines. Together they spell rationalization of production, displaced workers, [an] increasing differential between costs of [the] little farmer and the big one[,] and more competition for jobs.

Housing. No one who observes the California agricultural scene can fail to be impressed by the problem of housing that the seasonal workers and their families face. Within sight of Di Giorgio's huge new winery[,] tent colonies, dilapidated trailer camps, ditch bank settlements and full blown vineyard ghettoes dot the landscape. They stand out like ugly rips in the smooth green baize of crops that cover the valley, flat as a billiard table. Kern County's prize exhibit is Cottonwood, where Mexicans and Negroes spend their "seasons of repose."

During the past decade, a notable improvement in housing facilities took place under the leadership of the Federal Government. Farm labor supply centers, as the migratory camps are called, were set up in various parts of the nation. As of March of this year there were 24 such camps in California.

At present Di Giorgio and the finance farmers with who he is associated are engaged in an all-out offensive against the public ownership and management of these camps. The reasons are clear. The camps represent a great improvement in migrant housing standards. They foster the community spirit. They are inter-racial. They harbor union members who cannot be summarily evicted. They are public property where men and women may freely assemble and talk. They are a step away from the traditional company town and a step toward the town meeting.

Hence the determined opposition of corporation agriculture and finance farming to the labor camps. Di Giorgio is represented on the committee of Kern County farmers who are battling to eliminate them.

Congressional Investigation. Di Giorgio has sought to place the label of communism on the strikers. Already the state legislature, through the Tenney Committee, has held hearings to investigate alleged communist financing of the union. The hearings of the Committee, held in Los Angles on February 18, 1948, were a disappointment to Di Giorgio. The union got a clean bill of health. Its officers answered all questions. The case of the corporation was so weak that Di Giorgio himself failed to appear.

More recently, the suggestion has been advanced[,] in the nature of a veiled threat, that the investigation be continued by Congress. Union officials have welcomed this proposal.

Di Giorgio has also asserted through Congressman Elliott that the pickets are outsiders imported into Kern County expressly for the purpose of agitating and provoking violence. A check on the picket line made on April 1, 1948, showed that 42 pickets stationed in front of the main gates of the packinghouse yard had been employed by Di Giorgio for periods varying from one to sixteen years. Service records of five, six and eleven years were not unusual. The Executive Committee of Local 218 of the National Farm Labor Union was composed on that date of nine workers who had been employed by the corporation for periods varying from five to twelve years. Jim Price, strike committee chairman, work[ed] for Di Giorgio for over ten years as shed foreman.

Community Prejudice. Thus far the only answer that Di Giorgio has given to the strikers['] demands has been in the form of a pamphlet entitled, "A Community Aroused." This booklet has been widely distributed directly by the corporation. It was prepared and published, however, by a committee of citizens among whom Di Giorgio's name does not appear.

The main object of the pamphlet was to give the impression that the citizens of Bakersfield and surrounding communities had come to the defense of the corporation with an unbiased voluntary study of working and living conditions on the ranch. The illustrations in the pamphlet give a totally misleading impression of such conditions. They purport to show housing and recreation facilities which are in actual fact not used by the workers. Neat bungalows surrounded by pleasant lawns are supposed to be the quarters of contented field hands. The union has offered a reward for any field worker who has ever been seen playing on the tennis courts which the corporation maintains for its foremen and other high-bracket employees.

Even though the effort to make it appear that the entire community is hostile to the strikers has failed, the corporation continues to distribute "A Community Aroused" throughout the country.

Race Tensions. Finally, and not the least important of the factors which operate in favor of the corporation's contests with the union, is the problem of racial tension between the various groups which compose Di Giorgio's present and potential labor force.

The Di Giorgio strikers have a sober and rational view of race relations in the valley. Practically all of the strikers are white workers from Arkansas and Oklahoma. There are a few Mexican among them. In the past the white has been pitted against the Negro, the Negro against the Mexican resident, the Nationals against the Filipinos, the Filipinos against the Japanese. The "Okies" and the "Arkies" look back upon their own mistakes in their relations with workers of other nationalities and races and generally take the view that union membership, equality of opportunity for jobs based on competence[,] and joint sharing of privileges and responsibilities should not be affected by racial differences.

This small beginning toward racial sanity, however, at present does not by any means have the power of an informed, solid and articulate public opinion. It may not stand the strain of real economic pressure in the months to come. Several damaging trends work against it.

Segregation on the job is practiced by the Di Giorgio corporation. Mexican and other non Anglo-American employees are organized in separate field crews. They work at separate stalls in the packing shed. Di Giorgio employs no Negroes. Housing is separate.

The resident Mexicans are bitter toward the illegals and toward the Nationals. They remember past incidents of non-cooperation with the "Okies" and feel apprehensive about their own security.

Rumors have been circulated around Bakersfield and Shafter that neither Negroes nor Mexicans can join unions. The Anglo-American workers have heard from vague sources that Mexican illegals have come voluntarily to break the strike. They look with alarm upon the increasing number of Mexican[s] who pass the picket line along with their own kinsmen.

Behind each of these groups is a story of indigence, unemployment and insecurity. Ignorance of the conditions which prevail in Mexico and which force the Nationals and illegals to seek employment in the United States, and eventually show up on the Di Giorgio scab line, will make it easier for race prejudice to stir among the "Oakies." Ignorance on the part of the Mexicans of the conditions from which their Negro competitors have fled in other parts of the United States will strain their tradition of racial tolerance. In this brew of potential racial strife, Di Giorgio continues to fish for replacements for his strike breaking crews.

This is a brief summary of the forces behind which finance farming and corporation agriculture are moving to crush unionism in the central valley of California. It measures the gallantry of the men and women who are risking all to bring a greater measure of economic security and social dignity to the migrants of the Pacific coast.

They have held out for seven months already, and they show every indication of holding out until Di Giorgio is willing to break his stony silence and negotiate.

Against formidable opposition the strikers have reason to be confident. Twice since the strike began the A.F. of L. unions of the state have sent relief caravans carrying food, clothes and funds to the strikers and their families.

The California American Federation of Labor, through its president, Jack Shelly, has declared that the distance between industrial and agricultural workers is being bridged by this demonstration of solidarity.

The Hollywood Film Council of A.F. of L. motion picture crafts has made a documentary film on the strike and [the] issues involved. This film is being shown throughout the nation.

Union organization is making headway in the San Joaquin Valley.

One attempt at wage cutting has been stopped.

The profits of the Di Giorgio Fruit Corporation have fallen from a net after taxes in 1946 of $2,404,289 to a net after taxes in 1947 of $419,512. Operating expenses have increased from 55.7 in 1946 to 78.8 in 1947.

Local 218 of the NFLU is proceeding with the construction of a union hall on land donated by a friendly farmer.

A state legislature investigation has been successfully faced and a congressional investigation has been publicly welcomed by union officials.

The strikers have shown that they can conduct a peaceful campaign in the face of violent provocation. The attempt to arouse community feeling against the strikers has failed. Chamber of Commerce officials in Kern County have met in conference with the president of the union and expressed a willingness to support extension of unemployment insurance to agricultural workers in the state.

The corporation has been compelled to admit by its deeds that it recognizes the existence of a striker.

The strikers have focused public attention not merely on their own plight, but beyond that on the basic issues that face millions of American citizens whose labor raises the crops that feed the nation and a starving world.

PLANTATION WORKERS IN LOUISIANA

Excerpt from Ernesto Galarza, *Plantation Workers in Louisiana*
(Washington, D.C.: Inter-American Education Association, 1955), 43–72.

Galarza was part of the progressive democratic left wing of the labor movement that believed that social problems were labor problems. This guiding principle challenged organized labor to reflect on its agenda and note whether it had the interests of all workers in mind regardless of industry of employment and or the ethnicity, race, gender, or immigration status of individual workers. Galarza believed worker solidarity could bring pressure to bear that would address social inequalities created by political structures that benefited industrial elites.

This excerpt describes the living and working conditions of African Americans laboring in the sugar-cane industry of Louisiana. Galarza worked alongside H. L. Mitchell of the Southern Tenant Farmers' Union and other labor organizers during this campaign, and in this report offers a firsthand account of the massive strike sugar-cane workers waged against this industry. It was the first strike of its kind in the Deep South since the Civil War.

The Inter-American Association published a larger version of Galarza's report titled *The Louisiana Sugar Cane Plantation Workers vs. The Sugar Corporations, the U.S. Department of Agriculture, et. al.: An Account of Human Relations on Corporation-Owned Plantations, 1937–1953* in 1954.

Notable life events during this era:

- 1954: Galarza becomes vice president, director of research, and field organizer for the National Agricultural Workers Union.
- 1955: Galarza receives a grant from the Fund for the Republic to study the Bracero Program and its impacts on worker and civil rights and society.
- 1956: Galarza publishes his first book, *Strangers in Our Fields*.
- 1959: Galarza leaves organized labor when he is passed over by George Meany, president of the AFL-CIO, to head the Agricultural Workers Organizing Committee (AWOC).

THE 1953 STRIKE OF SUGARCANE
PLANTATION WORKERS

The National Agricultural Workers Union–AFL began organizing plantation workers in southern Louisiana in the spring of 1952. Shortly after [that,] it established Local 317, with headquarters in Reserve. District affiliates of Local 317 represented every important cane producing parish in the Lafourche, central River and eastern Teche areas. The membership of the union, including men and women, Negroes and whites, represented the field work force of every one of the largest corporations and a majority of the commercial farms in the Sugar Bowl.

The union immediately undertook to represent cane field workers in the hearings held once a year under the provisions of the Sugar Act. Participation by the workers in these hearings had been discouraged by the corporation planters, though never formally or on the record. The cane belt grapevine simply carried the rumor that any worker seen at the hearings would be in trouble. Moreover, the Negro agricultural workers were very much aware of the distaste with which their white employers viewed any common participation in public meetings of any description. There was also the obvious handicap that the field workers, unassisted, were not able to prepare and present reasoned arguments, supported by evidence of an order that would compel the attention of both the government examiners and the employers. Union representatives appeared at the 1952 hearings held in Thibodaux, Louisiana, raising for the first time not only the issue of wages but also other long-simmering problems relating to hours and working conditions.

Following the 1952 hearings, the union prepared a joint wage claim involving several hundred of its members and amounting to more than $32,000. The claim was based upon the custom of requiring tractor drivers and other employees to work more than the 9 hours a day, stipulated in the wage determinations. Tractor drivers, for example, were called by the plantation bell fifteen minutes before going to the fields to grease and warm up their machines. At noon, the men were called from their lunch fifteen minutes before the start of their paid working time.

Workers other than those employed in the operation of machinery were also involved in the claim. The stableman of one corporation farm, for example, rang the first bell at 4:30 a.m. He was given half an hour for lunch and worked to the last bell at 5:00 p.m. He worked 12 hours and received pay for 9.

The 392 individual claims were submitted jointly to the sugar branch of the Department of Agriculture on November 14, 1952. It was the first real test of the grievance procedure created under the Sugar Act and administrative determinations issued under it since 1937. The union asked that the claims be made retroactive for two years. It was estimated that 15,000 plantation workers had similar claims amounting to more than $500,000.

At the same time that the union submitted the claims for unpaid labor time during the preceding two years, it asked the Department of Agriculture to rule against a charge which had been made by the plantations against wages of field hands for raincoats. The union contended that raincoats were essential in the equipment of the harvest worker and that the cost should be borne by the employer.

In spite of assertions by Department of Agriculture officials that wages and living standards on the cane plantations had risen to satisfactory levels and the contention of the corporation planters that they could not pay more without going bankrupt, the union prepared to raise the fundamental issue of collective bargaining and the improvement of other conditions of employment.

Direct negotiations between the union and the sugarcane companies were out of the question from the outset. Although the union offered to submit its membership lists and other evidence of its right to represent the workers, the growers, taking their cue from the American Sugar Cane League, whose policy was in turn laid down by Godchaux Sugars and other members of the inner circle, took the position that the union did not exist and that their employees were already adequately protected.

The union letter requesting direct negotiations was dated July 29, 1953, and was sent to the following corporation planters: Godchaux, Southdown, Southcoast, Savoie Farms, Armelise Planting Corporation, E. G. Robichaux, Dugas and LeBlanc, Uncle Sam-Mt. Airy, and Milliken and Farwell. The union's proposal was turned down unequivocally. Godchaux's answer was typical: "We are not aware of the existence of any valid claims of our employees under the Sugar Act," wrote Mr. Richard McCarthy, Jr., adding that Godchaux Sugars, Inc. "takes great pains to be sure that our company complies with said Act in every particular. . . . Any individual employee who has any doubt in his mind will discuss the matter with his overseer, or field manager . . ." The rejection notices of the other companies were similar. Some did not bother to reply.

The union then turned on August 12 to the conciliation service of the Louisiana State Department of Labor. Membership and application lists were submitted to officials of the Department on August 14. The state Conciliator accepted these records as bona fide proof of the union's claim that it represented the field workers. The Department thereupon invited representatives of the planters to meet and negotiate with the union.

The corporation planters unanimously turned down the invitation given them by Mr. L. H. Simmons, State Conciliator. Speaking for them, Mr. William

McCollam, of Southdown Sugars, wrote: "We consider it our obligation to protect our workers, the largest percentage of whom do not wish to belong to any union. As you know, the public policy of the State of Louisiana prohibits anyone from taking any action whatever which would have the result of coercing an employee to become a member of a union organization. Under these circumstances, we feel that it would be grossly unfair to the workers of our plantations for us to meet and discuss with you their representation by a union, when, in fact, they desire not to be represented by a union. . . . We regret that we are unable to accept your request to attend the proposed meeting." This rejection was dated August 23, 1953.

Early in September the union began preparations for a strike vote, which was completed on September 27. With only 8 votes cast against, 1,808 votes were cast in favor of stopping work. During the poll, union officers continued their efforts to reach the corporation planters to discuss an amicable settlement, but to no avail. The position announced by Mr. Durbin of the American Sugar Cane League that "the government has already set the worker's wages and working conditions" was maintained throughout. "The sugar industry," said Mr. Durbin, "can't live with all of the workers organized. . . . Unscrupulous people can destroy the industry by striking or threatening a strike" (*Times-Picayune*, October 20, 1953).

On October 2, the union made a last effort to avoid strike action. In an open letter addressed to the most important cane producers, the union pointed out that the strike vote authorized its officers to call the people out. The corporation planters were convinced that the union had only a handful of members in the cane belt; that the mass of the resident plantation workers were too intimidated to challenge their bosses; [and] that in the event of a showdown, the union would be overwhelmed in a few days.

Not since the 1880's had the planters faced such a situation. It was to be expected that they would approach it with a mixture of contempt and self-confidence. After all, it had been nearly three-quarters of a century since any voice had been heard in the "quarters" other than that of the bell. The planters had what they thought was an iron clad understanding with the Federal Government not to change the "historic relationship" between employers and workers which determined wages and other conditions of employment. Outwardly, then, the political and economic machinery of the cane belt was wired in such fashion as to assure beforehand a prompt and smashing victory over the union.

The planters, however, were not reading the signs aright.

When the cane corporations had offered a voluntary five percent wage increase at the Thibodaux hearings in July, the union had rejected the offer and asked for a more equitable wage scale. The increase of ½ to 1 cent an hour approved by the

Secretary of Agriculture in his 1953 wage determination did not impress union officials or members.

Moreover, the planters had already lost a major skirmish with the union before the strike vote was announced. For several months they had been attempting to complete arrangements for the importation of alien contract workers from Jamaica. This request had been made on the usual grounds of an alleged shortage of labor for the forthcoming harvest. It was generally known that approval of Jamaican workers would have led to similar requests for Mexican Nationals, whose role in breaking strikes and cutting wages had already been tested by the corporation farmers of the Southwest, notably in California.

When efforts by the growers to import alien labor into the cane belt had begun in April 1953, the union had promptly made known its objections to state and federal officials. The Louisiana State Department of Labor did not hesitate to invite union officials to express their views on the supply and demand of farm workers in the state. It was officially recognized by Louisiana officials that the need for Jamaicans or other alien harvest hands was "insignificant." The use of displaced European refugees on some plantations had left unhappy memories. Previous experiments with Jamaicans in Louisiana had aroused the hostility of resident workers, especially in Terrebonne Parish.

On October 7, Mr. Robert Goodwin, [a] Department of Labor official, announced that the Department did not recognize any difference between the planters and the field workers of Louisiana in a labor dispute, "in a technical sense of the term." This was the ground on which Mr. Goodwin had proceeded to certify that the amount of domestic labor available for the 1953 harvest of cane was insufficient. This, in turn, was the basis for authorization of the employment of British West Indians in accordance with the demands of the sugarcane corporations (*Times-Picayune*, October 8, 1953).

It appears from the record that Mr. Goodwin was taking a bold step to reverse a field that was running strongly against the corporation planters. On September 28, the Acting Secretary of Labor, Mr. Lloyd Mashburn, had informed the union that information as of that date was inadequate to permit a decision on the certification of Jamaicans. And on September 30, the British Embassy had made known its decision not to approve the use of British subjects in the 1953 cane harvest, regardless of certification by the Department of Labor. The drive to mobilize a reserve of alien workers and have them ready to replace striking American citizens was stopped in its tracks.

The progress of organization and the success of the union in the Jamaican incident made the planters hesitate between a policy of bold and immediate reprisal and one of enlightened self-interest. During August and September on the plantations the air softened and the money hardened. Overseers spoke affably to their men. Personal loans were not only easier to negotiate, they were extended with a smile. Better still, wages rose. Mechanics on one plantation received three wage increases between September 1 and October 5—from 70 to 95 cents an hour. Another increase on October 8 brought their pay to $1.00 an hour. Tractor drivers in the Lafourche district who had been making $4.13 a day in June drew paychecks of $6.30 a day on October 10—a readjustment violently out of line with the wage escalator provisions of the 1953 determination. In the Vacherie area[,] tractor drivers received increases varying from 15 to 25 percent. A few days after the union sent its letter to the big planters asking for direct negotiations, the Big Three raised their wage rates voluntarily. Godchaux went from a base rate of $4.05 for tractor drivers to $5.04 a day. Southdown took a flier from $4.05 to $5.04 and Southcoast followed suit. All planters complied with the government order of a 5% raise, but some added another 10% for good measure.

These concessions, however, failed to stop the union drive. To the workers they were simple proof that collective action was the only way to secure and maintain improvements in wages and other conditions. The voluntary increases unexpectedly confirmed the union's argument to the Department of Agriculture that the corporation planters were able to afford more than a 9 cents-per-day increase in wage rates.

The "carrot" policy was maintained by some employers up to the eve of the strike; but the majority, principally the large operators, soon gave it up in favor of the "stick" alternative. The president of the Montegut district of Local 317 was fired by Southcoast Sugar Corporation. Dugas and LeBlanc fired a leading union member. Godchaux fired four men who took an active lead in the organizational drive in the Napoleonville area. Local union officials in Donaldsonville were thrown out. Key union men were spotted and given strong intimations of trouble if they did not quit the union.

The answer of the workers was a series of quick stoppages that in some cases brought about the immediate reinstatement of the dismissed members. There were enough of these "quickies" in August and September to indicate the temper of the organized plantation work force.

Months of conciliatory efforts by the union having failed, strike orders were issued late Sunday night, October 11. Public notice of the walkout was posted before dawn on the plantations operated by Godchaux, Southcoast, Southdown, and Milliken and Farwell. On these plantations nearly 1,200 men and women notified their overseers that they were going to union meetings instead of to the fields. At 6 a.m. on Monday, October 12, Hank Hasiwar, strike leader, issued the following statement:

> The issue is the right, guaranteed under our Constitution, of agricultural workers to have an organization that will represent their interests. The employers, who themselves exercise this right, have gone so far as to state that this right can be enjoyed only by them but not by the plantation workers.
>
> All members of the union have been instructed against violence of any kind, or against the use of threats of violence. As a precaution the union will not place pickets on the struck plantations for the present. The union has requested the co-operation of the sheriffs in the affected areas to insure the maintenance of law and order.
>
> We are ready to sit down and discuss in a friendly manner the differences now existing between the union and these corporations. The biggest obstacle is their denial of our constitutional, God-given right to organize for peaceful purposes. It's up to them to remove the barrier.

The original intention of the union to limit the movement to the plantations of the four largest corporations was abandoned when they began to organize transfer relief crews from plantations that had not been called out on the 12th. Since these relief crews were made up mainly of union members and since their function was that of strike-breaking, the union extended the walkout as rapidly as the employers chose to spread it. By the end of the first week 87 plantations were wholly or seriously affected by the strike.

In Terrebonne Parish about 60 percent of the harvest workers answered the strike call. On the larger operations, such as Godchaux's, the walkout was better than 90% effective. Planters who had expected the movement to collapse quickly saw it spread until it included over 3,000 men and women who represented the core of the labor force on the principal plantations in nine parishes. Throughout the strike union members attended meetings off the plantation, cramming into a course of four weeks the training and education in collective action that had been denied them since the collapse of the slave system. Holding their ranks in a way that impressed even their opponents, the plantation workers overcame the difficulties of illiteracy, distance, poverty, fear, and racial segregation. White men shared with Negroes the positions of responsibility in the strike. Together they talked out the problems of relief, discipline and employer strategy, knowing well that they were testing a way of life in which they were second class citizens or less.

The strike moved quickly from the limited, non-picketing stage into that of an industry strike affecting plantations 150 miles apart. Eventually it was decided to picket the mills and refineries in Raceland and Reserve. A steady current of information in the form of press releases and statements was maintained by the union, whose objective was to make the cane belt the focus of national attention, breaking once and for all the smoke curtain of ignorance and indifference behind which the corporation planters held their authoritarian control.

In this the corporation planters were the unwilling but inevitable partners of a major research project laid out by the union in advance of the strike. The sugar program of the United States, installed in 1937, had presumably set up a system of protection for sharecroppers, tenants, small farmers and wage earners. The effectiveness of this protection had never been questioned. During the four weeks of the strike the corporation planters revealed, by their strategy and their publicity, all that was essential to understanding of the true condition of their employees, the nature of federal paternalism, and the character of corporation sugarcane planting.

Realizing that the plantation workers were in earnest, and having failed in their efforts to recruit alien strike-breakers, the large plantations fell back on the small farmers as their first line of defense. "The small farmers will save our crop," said an official of Southdown sugars. Delivery quotas, which normally hold the small tributary grower in check and force him to carry a large part of the risks of the harvest, were brushed aside. In doing so, the large mills hoped to maintain their grinding schedules during the early part of the strike, thus demonstrating its ineffectiveness. The small farmers not only thus reaped directly the benefits of union action, but also received the unusually high wages with which the corporation planters were hoping to lure back the strikers. For nearly a month[,] harvesting in the Sugar Bowl was badly crippled; but by these and other devices the large plantations managed to meet the challenge of the union until they could bring to bear their decisive weapons—firings, force, evictions and injunctions.

Once the planters had decided that they could not entice the workers away from the union by voluntary and unusual wage increases, they began a systematic campaign of dismissals. Some district officers of Local 317 were fired as early as September 10. The tempo of firings increased as the strike deadline neared. On October 7, 8, and 9, new firings were reported from widely separated plantations. All of them followed the same pattern—orders not to wear union buttons on the job; prohibitions against attending union meetings; extra work with no overtime pay on union meeting days; cross-examinations at midnight in the "quarters" by deputized overseers. Resistance or protests over these and other forms of provocation were met with immediate notice of dismissal.

Firings continued throughout the strike and even after it had ended. Practically every one of the 150 stewards who were the backbone of the movement was made the target of this type of intimidation. When the planters were ready to throw their eviction policy into high gear, dismissals increased. Under the theory of tenancy by accommodation invoked by the growers and sustained by the courts, it was necessary to fire a man before the planter could legally proceed to evict him. Over 250 dismissal notices were served on union members between October 7 and November 5. All of them were "effective at once" or "immediately."

Typical comments of overseers who were handing out such notices even after November 10 were: "We have orders not to use union members." . . . "Can't use you because you are a union man." . . . "We're going to lease the land to tenants so we won't need union people around anymore."

Wage holdbacks were used by the growers to break the morale of the plantation workers. Threats of such holdbacks preceded the strike. They were put into practice immediately following the first wave of plantation shutdowns. To a worker carrying a heavy debt for groceries, medical services and other necessities, the prospect of having his entire pay check withheld while at the same time he was presented with a demand to pay on sight all his accumulated obligations was no slight test of his loyalty to the union. Yet it was a test that scores of union stewards passed successfully, if bitterly.

Overseers made it plain that their employers would exact full settlement at once of all those who had stopped work and that all sums earned would be withheld if they amounted to less than sums owed to the employers.

Pay envelopes received by union members after October 10 show that the corporation planters were not bluffing. Will——, [a] tractor operator, had $45.85 coming; his envelope showed a balance of "0". Jesse—— had earned $93.75 in two weeks; his employer, the Mt. Airy-Uncle Sam Planting Company, withheld the entire check and presented him with a bill showing a "net balance due the company" of $130.45. Fourteen other employe[e]s of the same company received similar statements, all of them showing net balances due the employer and none of them allowing for any cash take-home pay. Fifteen employees went home without a cent in their pockets and with over $700.00 in debts, due at once, staring them in the face.

Throughout the cane belt on the first pay day after the strike began, it was the same story. C. J. Tucker Company, for example, handed out empty pay envelopes with statements attached showing cash wages and balances due from 12 cents to $38.00. Alex Boardman read on his pay envelope: "Your account—$149.00; time worked—$59.01; balance due me—$99.99." Apart from the fact that the arithmetic showed an error of $10.00 in favor of the employer, Boardman at least had the satisfaction of a man who has paid his entire wages to meet a small part of an honest debt. Gregg Peters of Caldwell Sugars worked 87 hours, at 60 cents an hour, and earned $52.50. His pay slip had two small pencil lines in the square marke[d] "net pay." The lines were equivalent to zero. Peters still owed the company $85.58. Arthur——, had $54.11 coming and received the amount marked on his pay envelope—two zeros to the left and two zeros to the right of a decimal point. Other envelopes carried not two pencil lines or a blank but the cryptic word "Void." Thus Warren——and Elston—— had their total wages for the period ending October 14 "voided" because they were on strike and in the union. Their balances due the company, however, were not similarly voided. They were warned that they would have to pay such balances "or the company's lawyer will get our money from you."

Many a worker of the Milliken and Farwell plantation, Little Texas, returned home from the paymaster's office that first grim strike Saturday with envelopes marked in red pencil showing debits of various amounts. Where [a] debit was not marked in red, two lines indicated that the worker need not look in the envelope for the "balance due—cash enclosed."

Godchaux Sugars field workers fared no better. Pay slips for the period ending October 14, 1953, set forth with meticulous detail the hours worked, the rate of pay, wages earned—and the familiar "void" in the column second from the right of the statement. Godchaux employees who had small grocery balances or other obligations were lucky to squeeze through with take-home pay of $4.95 or $7.12 for the two-week period.

There is serious doubt that the planters had the legal right to withhold the entire earnings of the workers in this arbitrary manner. Of some 200 complaints received by the union in this connection not one worker had authorized the employer to deduct all his earnings. These deductions were never tabulated, but it is certain that they amounted to many thousand badly needed dollars. The time and manner in which the planters foreclosed the obligations of their workers showed clearly how calculated and self-serving the paternalism of the sugarcane plantation is. The lesson they intended to teach the field workers was clear, immediate and relentless—to give up their freedom to organize or starve.

Faced with an unprecedented labor crisis, the corporation planters swiftly played their entire repertoire of economic pressures. These devices, compressed into a union-busting campaign of a few weeks, made a pattern of habits, attitudes and practices that had obviously been practiced at leisure for generations.

Blacklisting followed on the heels of wholesale firings. Men who had lived and worked a lifetime on a corporation farm and were fired on joining the union walked from plantation to plantation looking for work, only to be told that word had been passed not to hire them. Sometimes the excuse was given that the plantations had a gentleman's agreement not to hire employees who already "belonged" to one of them. Union members who were fired early in the strike made the rounds of their districts, tried finding a job at distant points of the cane belt and ended by going to New Orleans or Baton Rouge.

Growers who might be tempted to break the rules of the game as it is played in the bayou cane country also found themselves in difficulties. A leading union member who had been evicted from a Lafourche plantation was hired by a small farmer to harvest a 20-acre stand of cane. A house was provided for the man and his family. The day he moved his few belongings from the plantation to his new home he was stopped on the highway and questioned personally by one of the wealthiest men in the sugar country. The next day the small farmer was informed that the mill which had contracted for his cane would not receive it if the new hired man cut the cane. "We don't want that —— working here," the farmer was told. Rather than cause the certain loss of his employer's cane, the union man voluntarily quit.

Another tack used by the planters was the notice circulated during the strike that at the end of the harvest administration lands would be leased to tenants who would automatically displace year-round wage workers. The day after grinding was finished some plantations actually served notice to vacate.

Grocery stores began cutting out credit altogether or restricting it to certain days of the week—usually those on which the workers found it less convenient to do their shopping. Some stores "ran out" of staple foods usually sold on credit. Sharp hints were dropped that accounts would be due for immediate settlement by any man who entered the store wearing a union button. "The only thing we've done," said a company official to the *State Times* of Baton Rouge, "is to cut off the credit of those who failed to come to work" (October 16, 1953).

Drugstores showed a sudden reluctance to fill prescriptions on credit. Telephone calls to the company office indicated that the guarantee of payment usually given against deduction from future paychecks had been withdrawn from certain individuals. Automobile notes were called in for full and immediate payment. Insurance policies, the premiums of which were deducted from wages, lapsed. These policies seemed to have been written with practical considerations in view. They terminated automatically "when employment with the employer terminates . . . or if (the worker) fails to make when due, agreed contribution toward payment of the premium. . . . Termination of employment will be deemed to occur upon cessation of active work." One union member and his wife were advised that the delivery of an expected child would not be covered by insurance since the policy had lapsed upon "cessation of employment" of the husband because of union activities. On one plantation the small daughter of a union man [who was] injured seriously while playing on the front porch of her home was refused medical attention by the local doctor. The child had to be taken some sixty miles to New Orleans by ambulance for emergency treatment.

But these were only variations on a more ominous theme that was sounded even before the strike was called. This was the theme of violence.

It was clearly the hope of the corporation planters that the union would allow the strike to degenerate into a wild, uncontrolled rebellion that would justify an open counter-attack with overwhelming force by guardians of the law and order of the cane belt. That the union disappointed them in this regard did not prevent the planters from deploying a bristling front of arms to show who commanded the police power of the community.

In the publicity issued by the American Sugar Cane League, frequent reference was made to the threat of violence from the union's side (*Sugar Bulletin*, November 1, 1953, p. 36). Visions of men "marching up and down the levee, armed with cane knives and clubs, intimidating quiet and well disposed workmen," as Sitterson described the strikes of the 1880's, were revived. The private homes of millionaire sugar men were ostentatiously guarded by state highway patrolmen, allegedly to prevent kidnapping and other criminal plottings of the union. Against the union's appeal to reason, the American Sugar Cane League immediately sounded its appeal to force. "The Sheriffs and the people you work for will protect you," the League said in a leaflet distributed on the plantations.

A month before the strike Godchaux Sugars requested that an impressive number of its supervisory employees be deputized. Similar preparations were made by corporation planters throughout the cane country. A day before the strike started, highway patrolmen were riding the plantation roads as well as the highways. Special police escorted scabs to the fields singly and in groups. State troopers were quartered on some plantations for duty around the clock, apparently on the theory that the armed overseers were too few to resist the expected insurrection of the farm field workers. On October 20 a union check showed that in the Lafourche district alone over 100 state, local and special police were on duty at the entrances to plantations, in the quarters, at the grinding mills and along the routes travelled by caged wagons. At the height of the strike over 300 armed regular and special police were on duty.

The show of force, liable to explode into tragedy at any time, had a touch of corny dramatics. One well-known plantation operator in the river district regularly met his cane trucks at the Mississippi ferry, his deputy's badge gleaming and his sidearms ready and willing. A bus load of scabs imported from Alabama sped into [the] town of Reserve late one afternoon, its occupants bulge-eyed with fear, the driver searching the road ahead for union roadblocks. At an intersection outside of the town the scab bus went one way and the escorting car filled with armed police went another. A union man smilingly offered to put the police car back on the right road.

But the humor, what little there was of it, was grim. A plantation near Baton Rouge clamped a curfew on the quarters, and shots were fired after sundown at shadows moving on the guarded lanes. Godchaux placed its armed pick-up trucks at strategic intersections on the busy airline highway to escort scabs going to and from work. Seasonal workers [who were] brought in under cover of night from Alabama and Mississippi were confined to their barracks. Scab drivers of tractors, cane loaders and harvesters were sent to the fields armed with rifles and pistols.

From the general atmosphere of intimidation to the specific acts of violence it was but a short step. A plantation manager a few miles from Baton Rouge, the state capital, assembled his striking employees and threatened a house to house search for arms. Midnight calls by deputized overseers kept the people in the "quarters" in a state of anxiety and fear. This was the softening up approach of the back-to-work movement, of which deputized employees of the plantations were the backbone. Some houses were broken into and searched. Others were padlocked while their occupants were at strike meetings or at church. One striker who was on parole was called in and told his liberty would be cut short on request of his employer unless he turned in his union book. The union was denied [the] use of [the] public school where meetings had been held much to the irritation of the neighboring planters. Strikers were forbidden to visit relatives living on other plantations. Lights blazed all night in the quarters and machinery assembly points. Armed deputies on one plantation stood guard as the paymaster handed out his "void" wage envelopes. The wife of one union member wrote on October 16: "AFL. Dear Union: The overseer came about 11 o'clock and ask about my husband. He say that that the people are going to shoot them if they don come back to work because he is not studying about the union he is got the people to save his crop." A negro preacher appeared on one plantation with a message for all strikers. "If there were any more shootings, they would arm all the strike breakers and shoot every damn—— on the place."

In Assumption Parish two union members were arrested for threatening a scab. They were held until they promised to return to work. Another union man was held without charges, bail being refused, until he, too, agreed to go back to the fields. In Houma a union member was held on suspicion and struck several times by a deputy. On October 29 two men were held for questioning and received "physical blows" at the hands of police. In Thibodaux a young union member was pistol whipped by a deputy on the morning [of] November 7; the victim's brother had previously been jailed on a trumped-up traffic charge. The pistol whipping, carried out while the worker was held at gun point, was intended to be a show, as the deputy himself stated, "Who is the king of the N—— around here?" The beaten man, who had worked on the same plantation all his life, was ordered to "get the hell out of the parish." He and his family of seventeen men, women and children were moved by the union to another community.

A few days before the Thibodaux incident a sixteen-year-old worker had been beaten with a chain by an armed overseer on a plantation near Napoleonville. The boy's father was known as an active union worker.

Throughout the strike union members were picked up on the streets, in their homes and after union meetings, questioned and given to understand how displeased their bosses were with their conduct. The workers took this deliberate punishment without once giving way to violent retaliation. They quickly understood from their leadership that the strike was not a desperate and blind adventure in arson and murder but a deliberate challenge to a system of economic power that had too long remained concealed behind the Sugar act.

Undoubtedly the corporation planters were able to terrorize the workers on the plantations, but they could not as easily stampede every law enforcement officer to do their bidding. Godchaux Sugars was restricted to three additional deputies by the sheriff of St. John the Baptist Parish. The sheriff, in commissioning the deputies, advised the company that "their police power will be restricted to the property of Godchaux Sugars, Inc.["] The sheriff also made his position clear on the strike. "We have never taken a stand against labor organizations nor against management because of the fact that we firmly believe in collective bargaining."

In this chapter of the sugar story, several points become clear. The rumors of impending violence on life and property that were supposed to accompany the strike were the work of the corporation planters. That the workers failed to be incited to such violence, even by repeated provocation including bloodshed, was perhaps the most important single failure of the American Sugar Cane League during the strike. It showed the extraordinary understanding of the workers, developed during an extremely brief organizing period. Instead of emerging victorious over a shambles of discredited unionism, the league was forced to play its cards to the end of the deck. By resorting to mass evictions and injunctions, the corporation sugar cane planters of Louisiana unveiled the picture of dominant irresponsible power over the plantation workers [that had] built up in [the] shadow of federal paternalism.

Some measure of the courage it took for plantation workers to join a union and support a strike is given by the fact that with few exceptions, more than 3,000 union members and their families lived on plantation property and were therefore subject to summary eviction.

This was regarded by the planters as a trump card that would surely break the morale of the strongest union member. During the two weeks preceding the strike overseers and company officials let it be known that in the event of a walkout the workers would be compelled to pay rent. Housing is a so-called perquisite, required under the wage determinations of the Secretary of Agriculture. Through the last week of September and in the early days of October a co-ordinated whispering campaign swept the cane country by which the planters let it be known that rents would be charged and occupancy permits would be terminated on short notice. The planters were evidently not ready to make good their threats immediately following the calling of the strike. While making preparations, under the guidance of the American Sugar Cane League, to use this weapon to the limit, they resorted to practical measures such as cutting off the water entirely on some plantations, restricting the use of water to scabs and others. Some union families were supplied by union trucks. Others fell back on abandoned wells or dipped their pails in the bayous.

By October 17 the planters had been sufficiently briefed to proceed. A mimeographed sheet of instructions on the legal and tactical problems of evictions had been circulated by the American Sugar Cane League. On October 15 dismissal notices began to appear. Eviction notices followed immediately; as the pressure increased both dismissal and vacating notices were handed to the strikers simultaneously.

Typical cases show how the system worked. Edward——, father of six children who had worked on the same plantation for 33 years, received notice to get out within five days. Alfred——, who had spent 33 years of his 43 years working for the same planter, was served papers to move on the day he was told he was fired. John——, after 29 years of faithful and silent service on one corporation farm, received his papers on October 17. The management of Little Texas plantation handed the following letter to striking employees:

> In view under your satisfactory services and relations with Little Texas Plantation for some years, we have patiently waited for you to return to your job. Your failure to do so convinces us you do not care to continue working for us.
>
> Under the circumstances we must replace you, and require the house you now occupy for your replacement.
>
> If you have not reported for work by 6 a.m. October 30th, you are officially discharged from our employment, and eviction proceedings will be started at once. Pending the time you are legally evicted from our premises, your heat and light will be disconnected.

The combined operation of turning off the water and the lights added up to turning on the heat, in which long years of satisfactory service counted for nothing. Clarence——, for example, had been born on the plantation on which his father before him had served fifty years. A brother of the old servitor had been killed in World War I. Another son was serving in the armed forces. But Clarence was called off his tractor to receive his papers, returnable within five days. One planter took the additional precaution of renting the few available vacant shacks in a nearby town to make sure that his evictees would not find shelter in the neighborhood.

The plantation of Seeley and Lagarde, of Bayou Lafourche, led the way. On October 9—one day before the strike—two union men were fired and given notice to vacate. Southdown Sugars came next, followed promptly by Godchaux, Southcoast, and Milliken and Farwell. From Terrebonne to Baton Rouge[,] eviction notices were handed out in generous batches.

Up to October 17 exactly 136 union members had received peremptory orders to pack up and get out. Including family members, this group represented more than 700 people faced with the loss of their homes. The average length of service and residence of these workers on the same plantation was 13 years. The reasons given by overseers privately to the strikers included: carrying a union button; refusal to work; attendance at union meetings; refusal to accept transfer to other work, usually a demotion from tractor driving to common labor; transporting friends to union meetings; talking back to an overseer. By November 3 nearly 200 eviction notices had been served, affecting some 1,500 persons on 30 corporation plantations in five parishes. The potential number of families under the threat of eviction was close to 2,000 with a total approximately 10,000 persons affected, among them children, and men and women too old to work.

A survey of 100 cases of eviction made by the union showed that 6 percent involved adults who had spent 30 years or more working on the same plantation; 16 percent had satisfactory service records of 20 years or more; and 30 percent had been employed on the same farm for ten years or more. Some families had as many as 11 members; others as few as two; the average size of family was 5 members.

Typical eviction notices contained the following statements: "On October 17 you were discharged and therefore, the purpose of your occupancy and possession of said house has ceased and terminated". . . . "This notice is given you pursuant to Revised Statutes 13:4911 et.seq." . . . "It is proposed to eject you through summary procedure established by such Statute and to hold you responsible for all costs of Court.". . . "In connection with such employment you were permitted to occupy a house and premises on said Plantation described as follows". . . "plaintiff has heretofore employed——as an agricultural worker, and in connection with such employment, and only because of such employment, furnished the said defendant, without any lease, either written or oral, and free of charge, a house and promises described as follows" . . . "Since you have failed to report to work, you are therefore occupying a dwelling on my premises illegally."

In these phrases the legal theory of the evictions was clearly set forth. Mr. Lawrence Myers, director of the Production and Marketing Branch of the Department of Agriculture, promptly agreed with that theory. In response to a telegram from the union protesting the evictions en masse, Mr. Myers stated: "Perquisites provided for in the Secretary's determination are a part of the wage and are required to be furnished only to the extent that work is performed" (Telegram dated October 19, 1953).

Hundreds of plantation workers and thousands of members of their families would have been ejected from the plantations had it not been for the opposition offered by counsel for the union, the firm of Dodd, Hirsch and Barker of New Orleans and Baton Rouge. That any legal defense of the workers should have been offered at all was a surprise to the planters. In one of the first test cases, counsel for the planters appeared in court with judgment already drawn indicating that defendants had failed to appear and were unrepresented.

Union counsel succeeded in transferring the eviction trials from the jurisdiction of the justices of the peace to that of the district courts. Throughout the month of October and up to the day the strike was called off, the American Sugar Cane League, brandishing R.S.13:4911 et. seq., was held at bay. Mass evictions were stopped but not before it had been shown how precarious indeed is the tenure of plantation workers living under the nominal protection of the Secretary of Agriculture. As a weapon to destroy morale and smash the strike, they had failed. As a lever to pry men loose from their jobs and their freedom, they were confirmed in a theory of law upheld by the Secretary of Agriculture.

The final and decisive weapon used by the corporation planters was the injunction. As sympathy for the strikers increased among the mill and refinery workers and as evictions and more violent forms of intimidation failed to break the movement, it became clear that the showdown would come only with the shutdown of the raw sugar processing plants. The field workers placed pickets at the gates of the Godchaux and Southcoast plants in Reserve and Raceland. Previously a large group of Southdown mill workers affiliated with the C.I.O. had walked out, bringing the issue to a head.

On October 21, Southdown Sugars petitioned for a temporary restraining order in the court of Judge Watkins, of Houma. On the 22nd Godchaux Sugars and Southcoast filed a similar action anticipating picketing of their Raceland and Mathews mills and refineries. On the 24th Godchaux prayed for an injunction in St. John Parish. Restraining orders and injunctions were granted and subsequently the Louisiana Supreme Court denied a writ of prohibition, requested by the union, to dissolve the sweeping, blanket orders of the lower courts.

All the petitions were drafted in practically identical language and developed the same legal arguments. Undoubtedly they represented the best that the American Sugar Cane League could do in a battle which had already lasted much too long. The nature of those arguments, the basic philosophy of industrial relations of the corporation planters, and the view they take of the position of plantation workers in the sugar economy is clearly expressed in the language of the petitions and reflected in the final orders of the courts (Temporary Restraining Order, Southdown Sugars Inc., vs. Robert Dabney, Jr., State of Louisiana, Number 15417; Godchaux Sugars, Inc., vs. Paul Chaisson, No. 10672; Southcoast Corporation vs. Paul Chaisson, No. 10673; Godchaux Sugars, Inc., vs. Frank Lapeyrolerie, No. 304; Southdown Sugars, Inc., vs. Irving Picou, No 15432; and Order for Preliminary Injunction, Southdown Sugars, Inc., vs. Irving Picou).

Petitions for restraining orders and injunctions were based by corporation counsel on a premise which recalled the legal reasoning of their forebears in the 19th century. "Defendants," alleged Southdown Sugars, Inc., "have combined and joined together in a conspiracy against petitioner contrary to the public policy and the laws of the State of Louisiana . . ." That the organization of plantation workers was also a conspiracy against the public policy of the United States was set forth in an extraordinary argument. Counsel for Southdown said:

> That the Labor Management Relations Act of 1947 specifically excludes agricultural workers from coverage under the Act of the National Labor Relations Act of 1935, which was enacted by Congress specifically for the purpose of fostering and encouraging organizational activities of workers in other industries . . . that the foregoing exclusions are based upon sound reasons of public policy and were specifically made to hamper and prevent individual agricultural workers from organizing and acting in concert for the purpose of obtaining recognition as a union . . . that the organization of agricultural workers into labor unions for the purposes of bargaining . . . could cause irreparable damage in said agricultural industries. . . .

In the same brief it was then argued that since the Labor Management Relations Act declares strikes or boycotts unlawful by a labor organization seeking recognition unless it has been certified as the representative of the employee, and since the petitioner was engaged in interstate commerce, the activities of Local No. 317 of the National Agricultural Workers Union were patently illegal. Further, it was stated that inasmuch as "agricultural workers are specifically excluded from the National

Labor Relations Act" and other Federal legislation, their actions were unlawful under that legislation and contrary to the public policy of the United States.

For good measure, counsel from Southdown, Godchaux and Southcoast prayed that "if this court should deem that . . . the Norris-LaGuardia Act . . . for any reason, operates as a bar to the issuance of an injunction herein, then petitioner specifically pleads that any provisions of said Act so constructed as to restrict the right of this court to issue an injunction in aid of its injunction is null and void and unconstitutional . . ."

It was also argued that individual workers would lose their sacred right of choosing their representatives if the union were recognized; that small, independent farmers were vitally affected by activities of the union; and that the very nature of harvesting operations creates an emergency during which collective action by agricultural workers cannot be tolerated.

It was therefore clear that agricultural workers were to be denied the protection of federal laws but were nevertheless to suffer the penalties imposed by those laws. The exclusion, as contrary to the public welfare, of agricultural laborers from the exercise of rights held by all other classes of workingmen had been very lucidly expounded in 1950 by Mr. Richard Nixon, then congressman from California and later elected to the vice-presidency of the United States. In a document frequently cited by the American Sugar Cane League, Mr. Nixon had outlined the essentials of a policy which had now been brought to bear, with great judicial weight, against the sugarcane plantation workers.

In sustaining the pleas of the big three, the 17th District Court restrained members of the union from "picketing . . . disseminating printed cards containing information which is damaging or erroneous, that is, those cards containing statements to the effect that petitioner is denying its employees the right to organize . . . or from taking any other action which would have the result or effect of interfering with the operations" of the petitioners' business. Included in the orders were "all defendants named herein, and all other agents, officers, attorneys and employees of the aforesaid union."

In the Reasons for Preliminary Injunction, the Court emphasized its former status as the son of an employee of Southdown and as an actual employee for brief periods. The court scolded counsel for the corporation for haphazardly sketching "a bare outline of the alleged irreparable injury purporting to form the basis of the demand for relief." The Court explained that it found itself in "the awkward, unhappy and extremely difficult position of attempting to draw a line of demarcation between the testimony in the record and our own personal knowledge." At a point the Court was "uncertain of the facts in the record as distinguished from those within our own knowledge."

Upon this line of judicial reasoning, the conclusion was reached that "it is primarily the rights of plaintiff that are at issue here." In view of the fact that sugarcane is an "annual emergency[,]" the avoidance of delay "as preventative to serious property losses transcends for the moment any right the defendants might have to impress upon plaintiff their demand for recognition as a bargaining agent other than by persuasion." The court recognized the right to organize and to strike but refused to recognize picketing as a necessary incident to those rights.

On November 9, when over 1,100 members of the union were still holding out, it was clear that the injunctions could not be immediately appealed. The union advised all its members to return to work. The majority of these workers were reinstated; in some instances key leaders were fired and blacklisted. Others had already left the plantations to seek employment in industry.

The union failed to obtain recognition, but the effectiveness of the strike in other respects was undeniable. At its high point, the walkout affected more than half of the cane production in all the organized districts and as much as 90% of production in a few strategic areas controlled by the large corporations. The majority of the skilled and experienced year-round workers supported the union, either by joining its ranks or by staying away from the fields. For a time grinding mills in the struck areas were slowed down below the worry point of the seemingly confident planters. In its statement calling off the strike, the union stated; "For the first time in 200 years the overlordship of the sugar planters has been effectively challenged. There is a new spirit of freedom among the workers and the little people on the farms and in the towns of the sugar country."

The challenge had also reached one of the definite objectives of the union; to put the Sugar Act and its theoretical system of protection for little people to a thoroughgoing test. Before the strike it was possible for the corporation planters to take cover behind the wage determinations issued by the Secretary of Agriculture which in turn were based on a series of assumptions that could now be shown to be completely out of line with the facts.

As a test of skill in handling public relations, the strike also showed that the American Sugar Cane League had met its match in the union. During the strike the League hired the services of a Negro preacher, the Rev. E. J. Poindexter, who regularly broadcast from New Orleans appeals to the strikers to go back to work. In full page advertisements published in the metropolitan and rural press the league made personal attacks against the union's organizers.

The general manager of the League tried to pin the communist label on the union, alleging that it was the tool of a communist front organization. Mr. Durbin, who made the charge, never retracted it, and he never proved it. Pink circulars were distributed by the league throughout the cane belt in which it was stated that "the union bosses force you to do things you don't want to do if you join the union."

The League's campaign of personal defamation and political sideswiping was singularly ineffective. It merely helped to call to the attention of the entire country a situation to which Americans would not normally point with pride. The press of the nation for once had a close look at the sugarcane industry. The newspapers of New York, Detroit, St. Louis, Chicago, and the West Coast carried the story of humble bands of field hands joined in prayer and in unions to demand a better deal.

In the cane belt itself, many Catholic priests opened their parish halls to the union. The pastor of Our Lady of Grace welcomed the organization of the plantation people. A well-known labor priest from Loyola University pointedly reminded the planters that "Every employer is bound in conscience before Almighty God to pay wages and provide working conditions that will allow a decent human life." On October 15, in the heat of the strike, the Catholic Committee of the South issued a forthright statement in support of the strikers. "Stripped of beclouding issues," the Committee said, "this strike was called because plantation owners and growers refused, 1). To accept the existence and meditation of a union of employees and, 2). To admit the right of agricultural workers to organize on the basis of the owners' interpretation of Federal and State regulations."

Moreover, the strike, though lost on the immediate issue of recognition, brought the underpaid, long-silent workers on Louisiana's secluded cane plantations into the stream of American trade-unionism. Recognition and collective bargaining were not achieved, but the existence of a large group of exploited workers was called dramatically to the attention of America's labor movement. Unions affiliated with both the American Federation of Labor and the Congress of Industrial Organizations contributed to the relief fund of Local No. 317. The C.I.O. members of the refinery workers union refuted the charges of communist influence made by the American Sugar Cane League as "totally false" and pledged their unqualified support to the AFL union. And through trade union channels, the organized workers of Central America, Chile, Puerto Rico, Cuba, Mexico, and Western Europe sent messages of sympathy and support.

In the aftermath of the strike, however, the crucial question was whether the sugar program of the government of the United States, committed on the human side to the protection "of all those engaged in the domestic production of sugar[,]" had met the test of experience. The mass protest of the plantation workers of October 12–November 9, emphatically showed that it had not. The facts on wages, income, hours, perquisites, determination of working conditions, living levels, education and the condition of the small farmers bear this out.

THE FARM LABORER
HIS ECONOMIC AND SOCIAL OUTLOOK

Presentation to the Western Region Migrant Health Conference, UCLA, June 1967, co-sponsored by Migrant Health Branch, U.S. Public Health Services, Washington D.C., and the School of Public Health, UCLA.. Original transcribed from tape recording. Courtesy of Department of Special Collections and University Archives, Stanford University Libraries.

Galarza delivered this speech at the Western Regional Migrant Health Conference, June 26–28, 1967, which was cosponsored by the Migrant Health Branch of the U.S. Public Health Services and L. S. Goerke, dean of the School of Public Health at the University of California at Los Angeles. Galarza's intention was to challenge social services professionals to think beyond their customary client-servicing model. He argued that using alternative methods to deliver services that focused on developing community empowerment would foster an atmosphere of self-determination and promote social, political, and economic development.

Another interesting topic in this speech is Galarza's discussion of the use of low-wage workers in industries other than agriculture. He notes that the agriculture industry's pattern of creating pooled labor was reflective of the tactics manufacturing and electronics industries used in the eastern United States as a response to globalization. He argued that they too had reorganized themselves then laid off workers in order to create a reserve army of labor.

Notable life events during this era:

- 1967–1968: Galarza, Herman Gallegos, and Julian Samora receive large grants from the Ford Foundation. They use these funds to create two advocacy organizations, the Mexican American Legal Defense and Educational Fund (MALDEF) and the Southwest Council of La Raza (now the National Council of La Raza, NCLR).

The topic assigned to me was the economic and social outlook of the migrant farm worker. I pondered about this assignment for a good bit because I could see two ways of approaching it. One was for us to assume that we suspect, or we believe, what the social and economic outlook of the migrant ought to be or might be. The other would be to try to collect from my experience, current and past, the evidence which has come to me of the conversation, the reactions, the views, and the opinions of the workers themselves which, taken together, would enable us to get an impression of what their outlook is as migrant workers. So what I am going to try to do is very briefly convey some of the impressions I have received through the years on this subject, namely, what the economic and social outlook of the migrant worker is.

I should say there are many areas and factors in the experience of a farm worker of which he is not aware, and consequently he expresses no opinions about them. There are other kinds of which he is truly aware—for instance, a migrant farm worker knows instantly upon arriving in a community what the housing situation is like. He has advance reports. He has gathered this through [the] grapevine; he's been there before, perhaps. So when you talk to him about housing his reactions are precise and his information is concrete. If, by contrast, you try to elicit from him his outlook on social assistance or welfare services, you run into difficulties. He has had personal experience with agencies, but beyond a certain horizon he is not able to understand or to see what is going on. Therefore, I think we have to be very careful at any point when distinguishing between what a farm worker knows from his experience to be true and how he is reacting to that experience and other factors of which he is only dimly aware.

First of all let me try to set some factual basis for discussion by calling attention to some figures on farm labor in general in the United States, particularly in the Southwest. As of the week of May 21st of this year, there were 1,391,000 hired farm laborers in the United States. Of this number, about 225,000 were hired in two states—California, with approximately 145,000; and Texas, with approximately 80,000, representing about 25% of the hired labor force on the job during this period—the month of May.

The situation in California I want to sharpen a bit because of the obvious importance of the state in the total agricultural picture and also because in California, perhaps next to Texas, we have had the most experience and the most trials with the migrant worker. As of two weeks ago, there were in California about 120,000 farm workers employed. They were engaged in harvesting, land preparation and various maintenance operations on a total acreage of 3,750,000 in the state. To repeat, that is 120,000 workers engaged in agricultural activities on 3,750,000 acres, which represents a total of some 225 different crop operations—probably without any doubt the greatest variety of crop production of any state in the union. From this table, I also want to point out that in these 225 crop operations covering the entire state, only 20 of them reported that there was housing available for families—only 20 out of all the counties were providing, advertising and/or offering housing to families. I have occasion to refer to these very brief figures in the course of my outline. These figures, of course, are minimal; they do not give any idea of the number of dependents that these hired workers represent. If I were to make a very loose guess, I would say we would have to multiply the figures given for total employment of 1,300,000 more or less, for the entire country by about three. That is to say we would have to bring 3½ million people who were economically dependent on the wage earners who were on the job. Now we have to narrow these figures down in another way, since we are not talking of migrant workers but of the farm labor force, which by no means is the migrant labor force. So far as California is concerned, the tendency in the last 20 years has been for the migrant sector of the agricultural economy to diminish very, very steadily. About five years ago a spot check of the percentage of migrant labor in the principal agricultural counties of California was made. It was found that in some counties like San Diego, San Bernardino, Fresno and Santa Clara, where migration had been notable in the 1930's and 1940's, the ratio of migrants (state workers) was below 5%—less than 5% of the workers were out-of-state migrants. The proportion of in-state migrants was higher, but I say this to caution you about projecting a stereotype of the migrant worker, which comes from Steinbeck's writings and from very large amounts of literature dealing with the migrant worker.

Nevertheless, the migrant worker, as a matter of fact, is a very small minority within the farm labor working class, although he is present in large numbers in certain parts of the Southwest and creates continuing crises in social services. We see this in California if we notice what is happening to the distribution of population. When I worked on the farm as a boy in California many, many years ago between the First World War and say 1930, over 85% of the Mexicans residing in the state were farm workers. Today over 85% reside in the cities, and by 1980 I dare say that in California better than 90% living in the state will be permanent residents. This is significant because in great part, the influx into the cities can close down opportunities for employment in the rural areas.

So we narrow our subject down to what would be called the vestiges of the agricultural and social systems existing in the Southwest in the 1920s—a system which moved enormous numbers of people from one state to another; e.g., Texas being one of the big labor pools; California being another; and the southern part of the Atlantic coast being the third.

From 1920 to 1935, or thereabouts, this was the pattern, but it has changed drastically, and what we now have is a number of very acute sore spots—areas in which the flux, change and variations in demographic distribution are very acute. Population rises during the slack season and it thins out very drastically when people are out on the road. This is true in areas like San Antonio, e.g., the lower Rio Grande Valley, the Central Valley of California, and the Salt River

Valley of Texas. Now I am not suggesting that because the number of migrants has been reduced, this is not an important problem—on the contrary, numbers have nothing to do with the case, as far as I am concerned—the needs are there, the tensions are very high and the deprivation is very, very marked. I am only trying to set the social and the statistical framework within which I hope to focus this discussion.

Now, of the most representative areas where the old order has changed but has left behind some pockets of very intense misery and deprivation, I just want to name two or three. One of them is northwestern New Mexico. I have reason to call attention to this because in the last three weeks, there has been an uprising of Mexican-Americans in New Mexico as a result of a long process of dispossession and being cut off from economic opportunity. These people have reached a stage where a very drastic gesture, because that's all that it was, seemed to them to be the only way to call the attention of the country to their plight. Make no mistake about it, even though the people in New Mexico who have risen in arms are few in number, and the odds against them are overwhelming, there is no reason why we should turn our attention away from their plight and think this is just a faint echo of a storm that is fast disappearing, or a part of our social system which we will be completely rid of in the next decade. On the contrary, the uprising in New Mexico and what's happening in the Central Valley of California today are symptoms of something which I think should demand or require our very serious attention because they reveal problems that are not peculiar to the migrant farm worker, but peculiar indeed to the characteristic of our society as a whole. The disappearance, therefore, of the change, the shifting and the distribution of farm labor from the country to the cities is, to my judgment, a most dramatic, the most significant shift of the last 30 years.

I want to call your attention to some other aspects of this matter. One is that as changes have been taking place within Texas and California, particularly with respect to conditions in each industry which I will mention in a minute that have made life harder for the migrant worker, there are some very important changes occurring which are not obvious to the migrant worker himself but which are of very great importance to us. One of them is that if you take the history of the last 50 years and the economic history of the Southwest as a whole, one sees that from about 1920 to the present time there has been a massive drift—a kind of magnetic attraction—for industry in the United States by the availability of the low cost, low wage manpower of the southwestern states. The transplanting of industry from the New England States, from the Eastern Seaboard to the Middle West and now more recently to Texas and California is a long-term drift which is so slow that it is hard to discern, but it is there; and this drift, of course, ties in with what's been happening in the Southwest demographically during the last 50 years. The enormous increase in the Mexican-American population of some 5 million that we have in the 5 southwestern states, and by 1980 I would so project the figure to be somewhere in the neighborhood of 6 or 6½ million, is essentially a vast reservoir of low-cost, low-wage labor. American industry, American enterprise, agriculture, electronics, transportation and services have been moving in this direction. To join hands, to dip into this vast labor pool, has made a basic change in the economic opportunities for the Mexican-Americans, and along with it has gone another trend which is also not easy to discern but which is of very great significance; namely, that in Mexico the same thing has been happening except in reverse. The demographic population drift in our country has been from northeast to southwest, generally speaking. In Mexico it has been from south to north, and in the last 20 years this has been accelerating to the point where the border cities of Mexico, like Tijuana, Mexicali, and others such as Laredo and Matamoros have become a dramatic example of what can happen in the general area of migratory shifts in population.

Today the City of Mexicali has a population of approximately 300,000. I remember Mexicali 30 years ago when it was a village of 6,000. What's happening? The opportunities in rural Mexico are so low, so negative that people are drifting to the north, and the only thing that keeps a merging, coalescing of a vast reservoir of very cheap manpower that has been drifting up against the border for 25 or 30 years from becoming a part of the labor force of American industry, which is moving southwestward, is the international boundary. A purely political division, which has many facets, of which I am going to try to point out a few.

At least two basic general drifts of capital and industry moving to the Southwest and manpower moving up from Mexico northward set the stage, in my judgment, basically for everything for the major problems in social assistance—such as public health. Having said this much, I want now to pinpoint attention to some of the things that have been happening within agriculture itself that have affected the farm worker as a worker and as a social human being. Let us look at, for instance, the agricultural industry internally, particularly the point of view of technology. The progress in substitution of machinery for manpower in California and Texas has been phenomenal. The example that first comes to mind, of course, is cotton picking; but there are many, many other areas in which mechanism has taken over. Within the last 4 years, something like 75% of the labor force in tomato picking, for example, has been displaced; and when you consider that in California alone the amount of manpower required to move the harvest of tomatoes in some years is as high as 60,000 people and the number of people against whom mechanism or into which mechanism has moved, you realize when I give the figure of the displacement ratio of 75% by machinery, you are talking of something like 35 or 40 thousand adult workers with their dependents.

It is not only in picking that this has been happening, but in other branches of agriculture. For instance, in irrigating one can drive up and down the state of California and see a totally different system of irrigation than that which has prevailed during the last 30 years. The old-time irrigating crews are going, going fast; and today you have farms which are gridironed by pipes, and these pipes are controlled at a central spot where the farmer can come by in his pickup truck twice a day and push certain buttons and regulate the flow of water for over an area of two or three thousand acres. You have to ask yourself what happened to the irrigators who used to manage this part of the operation. Well, they are gone; they are gone to the cities.

Let's look at hiring. In the last 30 years the system of labor has changed very dramatically, very drastically. There was a time when hiring was mostly the function of labor contractors. That isn't so any longer. It is now a function of very well coordinated associations of growers; and these associations don't like to deal with individuals. They must, in fact, in order to be economical, deal with masses of workers who are put at their disposal; and the most dramatic, of course, the most impressive example of this is the Mexican *bracero*—the Mexican National hiring system which prevailed in this country for some 20 years. This kind of hiring system has led to the displacement of the domestic farm worker, who always came as an individual or, at most, with his family to the farm placement office for a job. This is too inefficient. This is too trivial. The farm labor associations in the Southwest like to deal with situations in which they can contract for thousands upon thousands of people and have them delivered on schedule in large numbers.

Today we have in the Southwest the combination of feeder systems into the agriculture labor market; we have the farm placement service, which operates more or less on the fringes of things—although we like to think it is the big tent in the circus. There is the wetback system, which still prevails. There are thousands of wetbacks still working in Texas, Arizona, New Mexico and California. There is the border crossing system, which provides thousands of farm workers along the border states. These are combinations of the total system of the farm labor markets, and all of them have a very important effect upon the domestic worker. It keeps him as a kind of secondary factor. The domestic farm worker continues to be a reservoir rather than a prime factor because so much labor is available through these other devices.

Now as to income, the situation of a farm worker is not much better than it was in the past. The average hourly income for the entire United States for farm labor last month was 99 cents. There are farms in California that are paying today as much as $1.40, but there are farms also that are still getting away with $1.00 an hour for seasonal labor. I have seen farms in Texas and Louisiana employing Mexican-Americans that pay as little as $.50 an hour within the last two years. I am only talking about hourly earnings, I am not talking about yearly income. I have talked to families in the last year whose yearly income as a family, not as an individual worker, was less than $1500.

What about housing? The outlook of the agricultural worker (and I keep slipping back to the Mexican-American because he is such an important part of the labor force and because he particularly suffers from these conditions) with respect to housing has steadily deteriorated. Family housing for farm workers has disappeared, or almost disappeared. During the Second World War, in view of the dire need of manpower for agriculture, the federal government experimented with labor camps. These were scattered throughout the Southwest; for a time there was even the possibility that in these labor camps, these migrant labor camps, a form of farm labor community could take shape. These camps, funded by the federal government, were labor supply centers, but they were also places where farm workers could gradually take root and build their own communities. This was all right during the war, World War II, but when the war was over the employers' associations, notably in Texas and California, realized that if this system was allowed to continue, these farm labor camps could be called autonomous communities—communities where hundreds and thousands of farm labor families could reside more or less permanently and would develop a base for unionization, in other words for independent bargaining power, and this of course was not to be tolerated. So immediately after the Second World War, a very deliberate attempt was made by the employers' associations to destroy this threat, and it succeeded. Many of these camps were sold at bargain rates back to the growers' associations, and some of them proceeded to let them deteriorate and to disappear in order to discourage the permanence of an autonomous farm labor community with bargaining power of its own.

The picture which I gave previously and which I want to call attention to again is that out of 225 crop areas reporting last—two weeks ago in the state of California—only some 20 offered housing facilities to families. I want you to ponder on that figure and relate it to what I have just been saying. It has been the deliberate policy of employment, employers, management and government, state and national, to discourage facilitating family housing of a permanent nature to farm workers. This is a fact; and this being so, it shouldn't surprise us that we can still observe situations such as the one I observed in Fresno about six weeks ago. In Fresno there were 400 farm workers with whom I stayed for an evening and a day. Between 350 and 400 workers resided during the very heavy rains of this spring on the ditch banks surrounding the city, living from whatever handouts they could get from the city. The situation was so bad that even just a little protest on the part of a handful of citizens was sufficient to move the authorities in Fresno to action. These are again vestiges, samples of situations which years ago were widespread and chronic but which are still there enough to demonstrate what this system is like and how it operates.

Now I will say a word about social assistance services. When a class of our citizens—farm workers—are not able to drive its roots into a community; when they can be driven out of farm labor camps, as they were after World War II; when they can be told there are literally 200 crop areas in California where they can expect no lodging if they are traveling with their families—[this] obviously creates the atmosphere in which services—social services—are needed, including social assistance and public health. I could probably tell you, and I am not going to, stories of communities in which you live and work in which the big problem is the location of some kind of a group, some kind of basis for the distribution of public health services to these people who are constantly on the move. There is nothing which is nailed or based. The migrant farm workers are a sand dune, and the winds that blow them from place to place are deliberately crested by social and economic forces in our society. So you people, the public health workers, are constantly and necessarily up against the fact that you are trying to serve people who are psychologically and physically on the move: not because they want to, not because they prefer to, but because they have to.

We have a governor who as soon as he took office began to use the meat chopper on budgets, such as those for mental health and public health. I understand that a cutback of some 10% is in order for the public health services in the state of California. When this happens, to whom can the profession turn for political support? It cannot turn to its clients. The clients who were here yesterday are gone, and those few who remain as permanent residents and recipients of these programs are politically so ineffective, so disorganized, so inarticulate that you cannot look to them to protest these supports.

This is now becoming obvious in the field of housing, in the field of public health, and in the field of education; and so more and more we are seeing that in America, particularly in the agricultural states, we seem now to be in a period of retraction, of false economy, We see agencies and the people who work in them distressed and perplexed by the fact that they cannot, will not get political support from the people who are receiving these services. So what happens—I suppose you are all familiar—some individuals within agencies take these cutbacks in silence. Others protest quietly and in the privacy of their own offices or homes;

and they, very, very, very few take the risks of protesting this kind of mayhem on public assistance. I don't know whether the end is in sight in California or not. I have reason to feel personally that the end is not in sight. We have a man in Sacramento who, for instance in the field of conservation, takes the view that when you have seen one tree, you have seen them all. I suspect that if he were pressed, he would tell you if you have seen one human being, you have seen them all. That is why I say I don't think we are at the end of our troubles.

Furthermore, during this period, the farm worker in the Southwest, particularly the migrant, has gone through a whole cycle of experiences with respect to collective bargaining. After all, he is a worker, and the only pattern that he has before him to imitate is that of the trade union movement of the United States. The trade union movement is based on, of course, the theory and practice of collective bargaining, and the farm workers in the Southwest have been trying to adapt collective bargaining to their powers. But if we have a close look at history, we find that once more the farm worker, the migrant, has been selected and picked out for very special treatment. The special treatment consists of a concerted attack on his efforts to organize the farm worker in California and Texas. It is happening in Starr County today, it's happening in Delano and Central Valley, and the history of farm labor confirms that just as soon as a group of farm workers begin to show enough maturity, promise, skill and enough potential to really organize and force employers—corporation farmers particularly—to come to the bargaining table, at that point the forces of management, employment, and the government coalesce to destroy that bargaining power. This, at least, is what I see in the history of farm labor in the Southwest, and this in turn means, in my judgment, that we cannot foresee for the next 10 or 20 years the creation of general bargaining power by the farm worker on his own behalf.

Finally, to give you another view of another aspect of the farm worker's social and economic view, I will say just a word about political action. The farm worker I know is politically very, very sensitive, and, I think, very wise and along with these qualities, very nonparticipating. The farm worker of California and the Southwest generally is a nonentity politically because of the constant migration, [the constant] shifting of place, and because he is numerically such a small group. Keep in mind that in California, for example, out of the present labor force of 140,000 men and women employed at the moment in the fields, 140,000, let's round it out to 150,000, you must compare that figure with the total labor force of California, which is about 5,000,000. In cross political terms, this doesn't mean a thing. If we assume that 150,000 farm workers were united, had a union, had collective bargaining power, and so forth, at the very best optimum this would still be small potatoes for the politicians—150,000 out of 5,000,000 workers is—well, you can just write that off.

Now are there any general comments that would round this out to make some sense? I have a few, which I would like to offer. When you raise the issue, as indeed you have raised it in your program, of the farm laborer as a person who is hard to reach, I keep asking myself, really, who is hard to reach? Is it the farm worker or is it the profession? Is it the agencies or is it the families? Is it the man who is unemployed or on relief or is it the administrator of some program? This has become one of the clichés of social work currently, e.g., the hard-to-reach person, the hard-to-reach community, the hard-to-reach family. I am convinced that the hard to reach are not in the fields. I know this because for 40 years I have been reaching them. It takes very little by way of honesty and fair dealing to reach the minds and hearts of these people. As a matter of fact, it is so easy I have to constantly watch myself that I do not come running back into the agencies and betray some of their confidences. They are not hard to reach. What's happening is that their experience in fifty years has been so bitter, disappointing, and traumatic that a high barrier of caution, suspicion, and reticence has been raised, necessarily so, and this is what creates the impression these people are hard to reach. In my judgment, the hard-to-reach people are the federal agencies, the state agencies, the state governors, etc. You cannot reach them and when something like New Mexico happens, when something like Delano is contrived, the thing I think about day and night is how can we encourage these people. I am not a violent man myself and I don't believe in violence. I don't believe, in this society, that violence on the part of an infinitely small minority is going to get anywhere. But these are symptoms of a deep illness of our society as a whole. So it is my feeling that these hard-to-reach people who finally take up arms, protest, and march are telling us that the hard to reach are not in the fields—they are in the positions of power.

Now what has happened, therefore? I think what has happened is we have reached what I would call the crisis of the client system. I have been a client. I have never been on public assistance, not due to any particular ability on my part but to a lot of luck, but I have been a client in other respects and have worked with thousands of people who are clients—clients of public welfare programs, public health, etc. I suddenly realized after thinking back over these 35 or 40 years that we have unconsciously allowed ourselves to accept the client concept as the thing. As I travel around and observe programs in action, I am overwhelmed by the chore, money, time, skill, and talent—sometimes even genius—that goes into mounting the apparatus of the public welfare assistance program. I see only the creation there of these enormous machineries that are intended to bring better housing, [better] health, or better education to the people in the fields. Over here I see not only a lack of community but a deliberate effort on the part of some people to destroy that community when it shows possibilities of being created. This is the crisis of the client system as long as we have programs, federal or state. We do not think of the workers in the Southwest as a class of people but as people who are striving to break through and organize their own communities, to live together as groups so they can enjoy at their own economic level the advantages of collective action, mutual support, reciprocal assistance, understanding, sympathy and emotional contact. These are the valuable things in human life, and as long as our social system and the politicians who run it and those behind them who really lay out what is to be done with the resources of our society, as long as they are deliberately or unconsciously or more or less in a happenstance manner dealing with the lack of community within the farm labor group, as long as this is going on, you have no choice.

You have to deal with the individual before you have an individual client. I want to tell you that until you get down to brass tacks and change the emphasis and begin looking for communities with which you can deal; when you don't find them help create them and when they exist in miniature or potential and someone calls it to your attention that efforts are being made to dislodge this community, to deprive it of its economic base, it seems to me at this point you are called upon to stand up and lay aside your professional role whatever the risk may be and help these people organize communities. So what I am saying is that the crisis of the client system is simply the reverse of one coin.

On the other side of the coin I would say we have the crisis of community in our country. So far as Mexican-Americans are concerned, the crisis of community is present. It's terrible, and it is very significant for those of you who engage in public programs. When I point out to you again that whereas 30 years ago more than 80% of the Mexican people in California lived in rural areas and today more than 80% live in the urban areas, I don't want you to get the impression that the problems of the old order have been liquidated, that the deprivations of the farm workers do not appear in the city areas, that by bringing the farm workers to the cities and creating ghettos in the cities, we are not going through the same process. My view is that we are repeating the cycle with people who have been transplanted.

I just want to call your attention very briefly, in closing, to the fact that the difficulties which the Mexican-American has always found in agriculture—in creating communities—he is now facing in the cities. Only it has a new name, it is called urban redevelopment. Urban redevelopment in California, Texas, Colorado, New Mexico, and Arizona, as I have observed it, is a fancy word to describe a massive weapon for sweeping the Mexican-Americans and the Negroes under the rug. Now 25 or 30 years ago it was possible to find another rug—the cities that were just growing. But now we don't have another rug; we have improved our vacuum cleaners, but we don't have another rug under which to sweep these people, and they are not likely to stay under there like so much dirt.

Perhaps what I am trying to do here today is raise the whole question of whether or not there could be in the professions of public health, social work, and education another dimension—not a professional dimension but a dimension which understands that whoever or whatever it is which persistently and continuously and deliberately destroys them so that they may never reach a state of maturity of self-determination, autonomy, power, if you will, so they can become significant fellow citizens of our country, wherever you see this happening, at that point I venture to ask you to raise this question, whether you as professional public health workers do not have an obligation to add a new dimension to your profession. When you do, you will be joining hands with these people who are today pretty much lost, who need this kind of an alliance outside of themselves to make it. Otherwise, it is likely that in ten years you will be highly computerized, you in public health will be doing miraculous things with computers, but you will be just as hard to reach as the computers.

I think I have just exactly consumed my time, I am about two minutes over, but I want to thank you for listening to me on this warm morning.

STRANGERS IN OUR FIELDS

Excerpt from Ernesto Galarza, *Strangers in Our Fields: Based on a Report Regarding Compliance with the Contractual, Legal, and Civil Rights of Mexican Agricultural Contract Labor in the United States* (Washington, D.C.: United States Section, Joint United States–Mexico Trade Union Committee, 1956).

This 1956 report methodically addresses every aspect of the international labor agreement between the United States and Mexico, drawing upon official documents, visits to camps and job sites, and interviews with *braceros*. It was made possible by a grant-in-aid that the Fund for the Republic awarded to Galarza in 1955. The fund was set up by the Ford Foundation in 1952 to support efforts that sought to push back against infringements of civil liberties and constitutional rights during the years of McCarthyism. Galarza's work to expose how the Bracero Program violated many civil liberties and workers' rights, including the right to bargain collectively, fit well with the mission of the fund. This report was so widely circulated in academic and policy circles that copies quickly sold out and a second printing (now in book form) was almost immediately commissioned and put into production. This publication was part of a larger coordinated effort that helped end the official practice of labor exploitation by the agriculture industry under the Bracero Program.

Notable life events during this era:

- 1956: Galarza is named an officer in the Order of the Condor of the Andes by the Bolivian government for his service to the working people of Bolivia.
- 1956: Galarza is part of the organizational body that transitions the National Farm Labor Union (NFLU) into the National Agricultural Workers Union (NAWU). At that point, he had been part of the labor movement for eleven years and was an expert on the politics of organized labor and its relations with management and the state.

WHO THEY ARE

"In this camp," one Mexican National told me, "we have no names. We are called only by numbers." The man I was talking to had been in the United States only a few weeks, and he was referring specifically to the labor camp in which he lived. But he could almost as well have been describing the nearly complete anonymity of all the Mexican citizens who work in U. S. fields under an agreement between the two nations.

During their short stay in this country, the Mexican Nationals come close to being nameless men. Every year, thousands of them come under an agreement between the United States and Mexico which began in 1942. Since that date over one million Mexican citizens have passed through the United States as agricultural workers. The program of which they are a part involves one of the most significant population movements in the Western Hemisphere in the last twenty-five years. During recent years Mexican Nationals have worked in more than one-half the states of the United States. Yet most U.S. citizens are probably not even aware of their existence.

What follows is part of the story of the Mexican Nationals—citizens of Mexico who enter the United States legally, as opposed to the Wetbacks who cross the border on their own to bootleg their labor at cut-rate prices. This report does not pretend to be a complete account of a program almost fifteen years in operation. That story has yet to be written. But although not complete, this account presents a part of the picture most people know nothing about. And if the story is sometimes depressing, it is an important one.

Who are these strangers in our midst, these men who leave home and family in Mexico to work in the fields of the United States? What brings them here? And how does the program work? . . .

To attract, sort, reject and approve potential day laborers[,] or "*braceros*"; to transport, feed, contract and deliver those who are accepted; to keep the thousands of men (over four hundred thousand in 1955) in a state of maximum flux that will be responsive to the whims and demands of a nervous, sprawling industry; to return these men to their homes after their terms of service—these are the tasks of the agencies that manage the program. To these agencies, in the course of time, other individuals and groups have attached themselves. These make up a fringe of camp followers and extra-legal beneficiaries who profit, at the expense of the Mexican National, from the confusion, shortcomings, and often the congenital blindness of the official program itself.

A typical example of the men who work U. S. fields might be Pito Perez. Perez lives with his wife and four children in Rancho de la Mojonera, Michoacán. He has at times vaguely thought of trying to get on as a *bracero*. He is earning about 4 pesos a day as a farm laborer—approximately 32 cents United States currency. . . .

The official machinery that has brought Perez up to this point had been [in place] long before his name was called. The Mexican Bureau of Migratory Labor Affairs had set up and staffed the recruiting centers, and assigned quotas to the various states in the republic. The state governors, in turn, had rationed their respective quotas among local officials, whose runners make the first contact with the prospective *braceros*.

In the meantime, in the United States, steps had already been taken to spark the system into action. State employment departments had received requests from growers' associations and individual employers for *braceros*. These requests had been approved through a "certificate of need" issued to employers who stated that they were unable to obtain the labor they needed from the domestic supply of farm manpower. These certificates of need had been approved by the Secretary of Labor in Washington, and a schedule of requirements had been drawn up. As this schedule develops, orders are placed by the United States representative at the recruiting center with the Mexican official of corresponding rank.

The men accepted each day for processing are given a medical examination by the Mexican Department of Health. They are then cleared by police and military authorities for compliance with Mexico's military service laws. The process continues, and the *bracero* passes through the hands of U.S. medical examiners and Department of Justice security officers. Once these hurdles are behind him, the Mexican worker is given his numbered contract and identification card. However, he is not yet under contract; he has only received preliminary approval by the employer's agent.

The day's quota of *braceros* leaves the recruiting center in buses, which make one continuous run to the reception centers, located along the United States side of the border. Here the men are subjected to a second series of medical and security checks. The rejects at this stage are comparatively few. At the reception center they are again inspected by employer's agents, who make the final selection of crews. . . .

The [growers'] association labor pools [at state-funded reception centers] themselves operate on their own local schedules of manpower needs. The associated growers, who maintain the pools from their private funds, place their orders for men with the association manager. The men are taken in trucks, cars and buses to the fields directly from the central labor pools, or redistributed to smaller camps in the area, where they remain until transferred to other fields via the association's clearing system. If he has survived the system so far, Pito Perez is ready for work in the United States.

HOW IT ALL BEGAN

The process which brought Pito Perez to the United States is roughly typical of what all Mexican Nationals encounter before they arrive in this country, ready to work. To most of them, the whole experience is completely new. But the program has been going on for many years.

The first group of *braceros* contracted for employment in California arrived in September 1942. During the previous month the governments of the United States and Mexico, in an exchange of diplomatic notes, had set the legal foundations for recruitment. Before the program got under way, the Mexican government obtained guarantees that its Nationals would be exempt from military service in the armed forces of this country, that they would not be subject to discriminatory practices, and that in general Mexican labor standards would be adhered to in the employment of *braceros*.

The immediate and overriding reason for initiating the program was the acute manpower shortage in the United States, where the economy was then going into high gear for national defense. The first contingents of men were assigned to agriculture. By April 1943 the program had been extended to employment in railroad maintenance. This provision was dropped after the war. . . .

In the United States the permanence of these arrangements was recognized by the passage of Public Law 78 in July 1951 "for the purpose of assisting in such production of agricultural commodities as the Secretary of Agriculture deems necessary, by supplying agricultural workers from the Republic of Mexico." The powers and authority granted [the] Secretary of Labor for this purpose were confirmed by Public Law 319 of the 84th Congress without substantial change.

Under these powers the Secretary may: recruit workers in the Republic of Mexico; provide them with transportation and subsistence; operate reception centers; assist workers and employers in negotiating contracts of employment; guarantee performance of such contracts by employers with respect to wages and transportation; and negotiate agreements with the Republic of Mexico.

The Mexican government too, has indicated that it regards the recruitment programs as a permanent part of its international relations. In January 1952, there was created in the Department of Foreign Relations the Bureau of Migratory Labor Affairs (Dirección de Asuntos de Trabajadores Agricolas Migratorios) which has operated continuously to the present time. Its main responsibilities are to supervise the administrative machinery for the recruitment of *braceros*, to coordinate the interests of the various federal departments affected by the program, and to supervise the diplomatic representatives of Mexico in the United States in securing compliance by employers with the individual work contracts.

With the beginning of the second decade of operation, the Mexican labor recruiting program entered a third and far more active phase. The number of Nationals contracted nearly tripled over the highest total recruited in any wartime year. Over 700,000 contracts and 72,000 renewals were registered in the three year period 1952–53–54. In December 1953, there were 48,822 *braceros* at work in the United States; a year later the number had increased to 78,350. During the calendar year 1953 the contracting centers in Mexico processed over 245,000 applicants for recruitment, of whom 39,585 were rejected and over 205,000 were transported to jobs north of the Rio Grande. . . .

In the agricultural areas of California, Texas and Arizona, a marked dependence on Nationals had become a characteristic of the industry by 1953. In that year 87 per cent of the cotton pickers in Texas (Diablo-Edwards area) were Nationals and [Nationals accounted for] 74 per cent of those hired to take care of livestock. In the Yuma Valley (Arizona) cantaloupe harvest of that year nearly 50 per cent of the pickers were Mexican contract aliens. Of the Imperial Valley's total for seasonal hired labor of 17,200 persons for February 1953, slightly more than one-half of the labor force was imported from Mexico. By the harvest season of 1954, percentages of Nationals ranging in some crops between two-thirds to four-fifths were not uncommon.

By 1955, the Mexican labor program was clearly playing an important part in the farm economy of the United States. According to estimates published by the U. S. Department of Labor, there were for the period June 1–15, 1955, more than 60,000 Mexican *braceros* in farm employment in the states of Arizona, California, Colorado, Idaho, Montana, Nevada, New Mexico, Oregon, Utah, Washington and Wyoming. These figures represented 18 per cent of the hired seasonal workers in these states. For the same period, there were 110,000 Nationals in 24 States, or better than 10 per cent of a total of 996,000 hired seasonal workers. . . .

Despite misleading interpretations, the Mexican National in California has established a firm grip on the seasonal labor market, as the above figures suggest. But even these examples do not give a complete picture of the degree to which the *bracero* has taken over as the mainstay of certain agricultural operations. Percentages of manpower distribution by types of workers do not, for example, call attention to the fact that some crews, notably those supervised by farm labor contractors, are composed entirely of *braceros*. There are ranches and orchards in considerable number which are harvested entirely by crews of this type, because temporary domestic workers are not welcome. In some areas, therefore, the fact that the Nationals may represent from 25 to 50 per cent of the seasonal labor force means that for certain crops they may get up to 80 or 90 per cent of the jobs. On some corporation farm-type operations, they may represent an even higher percentage of the total labor force.

Such is the setting of the problem which this report analyzes; the degree to which the Mexican alien farm worker, recruited and contracted under the auspices of the governments of the United States and Mexico, actually enjoys the legal, contractual and civil rights to which both governments have been committed since the inception of the program in 1942.

THEIR RIGHTS

By 1942, experience had already shown what Mexican migrants who entered the United States illegally for seasonal work might expect at the hands of unscrupulous employers. Left to their own devices, the forces that had created the great demand for Mexican manpower, particularly along the border states, had proved how great the evils of unregulated mass migration could be. The protection of the contractual and civil rights of the *bracero* while residing in the United States was therefore a fundamental aim of the original executive agreement between the two countries.

When the recruitment program was originally begun, Mexico insisted, and the United States was glad to concede, that the affair should be conducted with close and scrupulous regard for the rights of the Mexicans to be transported to labor in the north. Indeed, in the minds of the Mexicans the matter went deeper than that, although never formally set down in solemn international instruments. The protection of the Mexican *bracero* was to be guided by the principles of Mexican social legislation. He was to enjoy, as far as possible, working conditions comparable, if not equal, to those guaranteed all Mexican workers in their national constitution. Discrimination against him on grounds of race or national origin was to be strictly forbidden.

It has been frankly admitted by Mexican writers and students of the program that during the early years these important commitments were very often forgotten. Non-compliance with the explicit rights of the *braceros* can be explained on a number of plausible grounds. The program was novel, and there was little recorded experience to point the way. New men had to be trained for unfamiliar tasks in a delicate and sometimes tricky area of international relations. The emphasis was on production, at least until the strain of war had passed. The mechanics of recruiting, transportation and contracting required agencies that had to be created from scratch when the program was launched.

This report is not primarily concerned with the past. The grievances of Mexican Nationals arising out of violations of their rights during the war years have been amply documented in the official records of the Mexican Consular Service and of other agencies, both public and private, that became involved in the protection of the Nationals. They form no part of the current history of the subject, but serve only to show that the basic problems of compliance with the terms of the International Executive Agreement, with the individual labor contracts, and, in a broader sense, with the fundamental concepts of individual rights and privileges of citizens of the Americas, have been reasonably clarified and defined over a period of nearly fifteen years.

"I take good care of my documents. I have the contract, passport, the blue card that gives the name of the contractor. The blue card is only in English. I don't know what's the advantage of these documents except in the case we get lost. It seems we are lost even when we are right in camp." Conditions existing in the program have been exploited by the Mexican press in both the U.S. and Mexico. [One] Los Angeles newspaper displayed a typical headline referring to the *braceros* as "modern slaves."

The pressures of war which gave rise to the government-administered recruitment program disappeared ten years ago, yet by 1955 the program had become far more significant than during the war years. Important sectors of farming in the United States are now in a position of critical dependence on an alien source of labor. The program has extended through periods of shortages and feverish production as well as through periods of surpluses and falling commodity prices. Through war and peace, scarcity and plenty, the Mexican labor program has become a fixed characteristic of the agricultural economies and the international relations of Mexico and the United States. Crisis has become a permanent condition.

In Mexico, the responsibility for administering the program is given to the Bureau of Migratory Labor Affairs of the Department of Foreign Relations. In all matters relating to the recruitment of *braceros* the Bureau maintains liaison with the Federal Departments affected by the program—Agriculture, Interior and Labor. Responsibility for compliance with the individual work contracts, as well as the terms of the International Executive Agreement, is placed on the Mexican Consuls in the United States, working under and through the Bureau of Migratory Labor Affairs.

In the United States, the agency designated by law to administer the program is the U.S. Department of Labor, through the Bureau of Employment Security. Under the Bureau, regional federal offices coordinate their activities with those of the state departments of employment. Agreements are entered into between the federal and state agencies to accomplish such coordination. In the field, the Bureau of Employment Security maintains a corps of compliance officers whose duty it is to investigate violations of the International Agreement and the individual work contracts. In 1955 there were fifteen of these officers or field representatives in California and Arizona. The Mexican consuls with jurisdiction in the same area numbered twelve.

The entire structure of the Mexican labor programs has rested on the International Executive Agreements, the latest of which was negotiated in 1952 and renewed for one year a few days before it expired on December 31, 1955. The agreements are negotiated under Congressional authority given to the Secretary of Labor, with the Departments of State, Labor and Justice represented in the negotiations. The Agreement prescribes the recruiting and contracting process, establishes the duties of employers and workers, provides for individual work contracts and defines the rights which the *bracero* is to enjoy while residing in the United States.

The individual work contract is signed at the reception center immediately before the *bracero* is turned over to his employer. The document itself contains 24 articles of close print in Spanish and English, and a copy of it is supposed to be in the possession of the worker at all times.

The Agreement between the two countries is negotiated by virtue of specific Congressional authority under its constitutional powers. The individual work contract is unusual, and perhaps peculiar, in this respect: the provisions of the Agreement between the United States and Mexico "are specifically incorporated herein by reference," reads the first Article of the contract. It is, therefore[,] no ordinary contract of employment. The signature of the United States Government is affixed to it[s] solemn obligations twice—once when the Executive Agreement is negotiated, and again when the individual work contract is closed at the reception center.

a) The International Agreement

The Migrant Labor Agreement of 1951, as amended, spells out certain fundamental rights of the Mexican National working in the U.S. Among the ones of particular interest enumerated by the International Agreement are these:

- The right of the worker to choose the type of farm work he desires is recognized (Article 13).

- The National is guaranteed wages at the prevailing rate paid domestic workers for similar work in the area of employment (Article 15).

- The wages paid the *bracero* shall be sufficient to cover his "normal living needs," and the Secretary of Labor shall take proper steps to correct any situation that does not meet this requirement (Article 15).

- The worker is guaranteed the opportunity to work not less than three-fourths of the workdays of the total period of his contract, beginning the day after his arrival at the place of employment and ending on the date of the termination of his contract (Article 16).

- The worker must be provided with a statement, in Spanish and English, at the end of each pay period, indicating the rate of pay, total earnings for the pay period, hours worked and deductions itemized (Article 18).

- When the contractee is not given the opportunity to work at least four hours a day, because of weather or other conditions beyond his control, he is to receive subsistence from the employer, which is to be noted on his pay record (Article 18).

- The workers have the right to elect their own representatives who shall be recognized by the employer "as spokesmen" . . . for the purpose of "maintaining the work contract" (Article 21).

- If the services of the Mexican worker are not required before the expiration of his contract, he is to be notified in writing by the employer (Article 25).

- The *bracero* shall enjoy impartially and expeditiously the rights which the laws of the United States grant him (Article 35).

- In the contracting of Mexican workers private employment or labor contracting agencies operating for a profit shall not be permitted to participate (Article 36).

b) The Standard Work Contract

Since the terms of the International Agreement are explicitly incorporated in the individual work contract, the foregoing rights are specifically included in the standard work contract.

In addition, the contract further specifies that the Mexican National has the following rights:

- Hygienic lodgings adequate to the climatic conditions of the area of employment shall be provided free of charge, including blankets, cots and mattresses (Article 2).
- Occupational risk insurance at no cost to the worker, shall be provided by the employer in accordance with State law or in its absence, with conditions defined in the contract (Article 3).

- If the worker is disabled as a result of a physical injury or disease, and is not hospitalized, he is to receive subsistence for each day he is unable to work for a maximum of six weeks (Article 3). This provision is subject to Article 1 of the International Agreement, which limits its application to disease or injury arising in the course of employment.
- When higher wages are paid for specialized tasks such as the operation of vehicles or machinery the worker is to be paid the wages assigned to such tasks (Article 4).
- The worker shall be furnished all tools, supplies and equipment required for the performance of his duties (Article 5).
- No deductions are to be made from the worker's wages except those provided by law, advances against wages, payment for articles of consumption purchased voluntarily by the worker, meals, overpayment of wages and losses caused by damage or destruction by the worker of property of the employer (Article 6).
- Meals are to be served at cost, and in no event shall the charge be more than $1.75 a day (Article 6).
- The worker's living quarters shall be adequately heated at no cost to him (Article 8).
- After the expiration of his contract if the worker is obliged to wait for transportation to the reception center and is not offered employment, he is to receive subsistence at the expense of the employer (Article 9).
- Transportation is to be furnished the worker by the employer where the place of employment is not within walking distance of the nearest town (Article 11).
- The worker may elect to prepare his own meals in which case he is to receive a daily subsistence allowance of 25 cents less per day than the sum charged for meals to workers who utilize the restaurant facilities of the employer (Article 12).

c) Civil Rights

The International Agreement appears to have the effect of a treaty made by Congressional authority under the Constitution of the United States. By specific definition the terms of the Agreement are incorporated in the work contract. Article 35 of the International Agreement, entitled "Protection of Rights under United States Law," states: "The Government of the United States of America agrees to exercise special vigilance and its moral influence with state and local authorities, to the end that Mexican Workers can enjoy impartially and expeditiously the rights which the laws of the United States grant them."

It can be maintained that the definition of economic rights contained in both the International Agreement and the work contract was certainly not intended to exclude or limit the fundamental civil rights recognized in the Constitutions both of Mexico and the United States. And it should be noted that in addition to freedom of speech, of the press, of peaceable assembly, of petition for the redress of grievances, the Mexican Constitution specifies other fundamental, unalienable rights, such as right of the worker to participate directly in the determination of minimum wages and arbitration through his own economic organizations.

Mexican students of the farm labor program seem to agree that the protection of the civil rights of the *bracero* is an aim that is implicit in the Agreement and the work contract. Thus, the *Revista de Economía* (February 1951) in an article by Edmundo Flores, stated: "The utilization of Mexican workers in the United States is carried out in such a way that it obtains for them all the guarantees established by our Constitution and more specifically the benefits of present labor legislation."

The director of the Bureau of Migratory Labor Affairs, Manuel G. Calderon, has written in the same vein: "The work contract is a bilateral instrument signed by the worker and the employer, officially underwritten and guaranteed by the two governments. It is an unusual example in International Law of collective bargaining between two democratic governments, in which the civil rights of the two contracting parties are recognized." His statement illustrates the importance attached by high Mexican officials to the civil rights aspect of the legal relationships created and recognized by the International Agreement and the individual work contract.

d) State Law

The International Agreement specifically extends to Mexican Nationals the impartial and expeditious enjoyment of the rights granted by the laws of the United States, and this provision is included by reference in the work contract. Article 3 of the contract provides an illustration of how this rule is to be understood.

In Article 3, certain benefits for accidental disability or death are established— only, however, in the absence of applicable state law. By implication this important principle may also extend to the *braceros* the benefits of state legislation dealing with the important matters of housing and transportation safety. In both of these areas, the provisions of the Agreement and the work contract are superficial, almost cursory, in comparison with those of state laws.

In California, for example, the statutes prohibit crowding in sleeping quarters and define such crowding specifically in a ratio of cubic footage to each occupant. The requirements for trucks used in the transportation of workers to and from the fields are precise. It seems quite clear that the Mexican National is entitled to receive the protection of these state laws, just as he is in general entitled to the protection of all the laws of the United States, where these do not explicitly exclude agricultural workers from such protection. Where such exemption is intended, it is explicitly set forth, as in Section 505 (a) of Public Law 78, which specifies that Section 210 (a) of the Social Security Act, as amended, is amended by adding at the end thereof a new subparagraph as follows: "(c) Service performed by foreign agricultural workers under contracts entered into in accordance with title V of the Agricultural Act of 1949, as amended."

e) Non-Occupational Insurance

Also under the head of contractual and legal rights to be enjoyed by Nationals are those written into insurance policies for non-job injuries, death and illness, Occupational accidents and illness are provided for in the work contract. Beyond this the Mexican Government enters into agreements with American insurance companies for the provision of medical care of *braceros* in case of illness or of accident or death not covered by state compensation laws. The cost of this insurance is borne by the worker, and the monthly premium of the policy is checked off from his wages.

Every Mexican National who entered the United States in 1955 was covered by this type of insurance. The indemnity for specific losses arising out of accidents usually provides for the payment of $1,000 in case of death, with the scale falling to $25.00 for the loss of a finger. The policies also provided for medical expenses, hospitalization, surgery, dental care, weekly indemnity, laboratory service and drugs.

The United States government does not make itself a party to these non-occupational insurance arrangements. Nevertheless, they fall within the jurisdiction of state insurance commissions, and therefore may be regarded as another instance of the extension to Mexican contract workers of the protection of the laws of the United States.

Summary

In brief, then, it can be said that the Mexican National has certain clear and unmistakable legal and civil rights while residing in the United States under contract. The sources of these rights are: the International Executive Agreement; the individual work contract; the laws of the United States; the laws of the individual states; and the insurance contracts entered into by the Mexican government with U. S. companies for non-occupational compensation.

Thus the legal situation in which the *bracero* finds himself is probably unique among agricultural workers in the Western hemisphere. In theory, the civil liberties recognized by the Constitution of the United States, the specific economic rights granted by the International Agreement and the work contract, the provisions of hard-won progressive state laws and the immediate obligations of private companies to attend him in sickness and disability form a wide and solid base for personal security and individual dignity.

If, on close inspection, it turned out that hundreds of thousands of Mexican alien contract workers were actually enjoying these rights, privileges and prerogatives as law and custom seem to intend they should, the example would be impressive. What are the facts? Do theory and practice come even reasonably close? Unfortunately, the answer has to be negative. Anyone who thinks otherwise should talk to the *braceros* themselves, as I did.

AS THEY SEE IT

"Some of us have read the contract but it cannot be mentioned to the boss," a Mexican National told me, in a typical complaint. "The contractor laughed and he said, 'The contract is a filth of a paper.' If you want to know how useless is the contract, try to see somebody about it. This is the first time we have talked with anybody who has listened to us. The sheep over there in that field are better than we are. They have a shepherd to watch the flock and dogs that protect them instead of biting them. Here in the camp it is one bite after another. They bite your wages and they bite your self-love."

Asked about working conditions, another *bracero* said: "Three days ago our crew stopped work right in the field. There were fifty men in the group. It was explained by one of the men who could express himself that it was not our desire to make a strike but we wanted to have eight hours work or to have our board without charge if we worked only one or two hours. The foreman said that assuredly there would be plenty of work and we went back to the cutting. The next day the *bracero* who had spoken for us was not in the camp. The foreman said he had been taken to the Association but he did not know the motive. In the field the boss said there are plenty more where we came from if we are disgusted. I have read my contract, but it is not worth the pain to insist on the clauses. Here the contract has no value."

A third *bracero* was a man of experience. "Eight times I have been in the United States," he said, "four times as a Wetback and four times as a *bracero*. I have had so many experiences in this country that I could be taken for an American except for the circumstances that I do not speak the idiom and that I am very brown. The new ones without any experience have the illusion of the contract, but not me. When you come as a *bracero* it passes the same as when you come as a Wetback."

Such comments by *braceros* on working conditions and the value of their contract are not untypical. To get the facts on the treatment of Mexican Nationals, a detailed study was made of actual conditions in southwestern Arizona and California in the latter part of 1955.

The areas picked for this investigation were carefully chosen. The statistics for 1954 illustrate how widely distributed Mexican Nationals are. That year, Mexican contract labor was to be found in Skagit County, [Washington,] which is a few miles from the western terminus of the Canadian-United States border; in Imperial County, [California,] where the extreme southwest corner of the United States touches Mexican territory; in Cameron County, two hundred miles below the heart of Texas; in Arenac County, [Michigan,] on the shores of Lake Huron; and even in central Georgia's Dooly County.

In 1955 more than 400,000 Mexican Nationals worked in the United States at some time during the year. But in the area covered by this study there were probably more than 60,000 *braceros*, many of them in camps away from travelled roads and out of the public eye. For the purposes of this inquiry, one hundred and fifty-six separate camps were visited, and some were revisited as many as four times.

The camps selected for observation were the larger camps, such as the Airport Camp at Stockton, California, the Gondo Camp in Watsonville, the Santa Maria Camp near Guadalupe, the El Centro Associated Farmers Camp, and others similarly important in size and strategic location. The total population of the camps visited was probably in excess of 10,000—a figure which certainly represents a statistically significant sample out of the total number of 60,000 *braceros* in the area.

Detailed interviews were carried out with hundreds of Mexican Nationals. The *braceros* who were interviewed were not handpicked. Their statements represent a cross-section of remarks made by *braceros* encountered completely at random. If their remarks show a common pattern of consistent violation of their rights, it is because this theme runs through the free interviews of all *braceros*. . . .

Before he was interviewed, each worker was first assured that his name or contract number would not be revealed to third persons, so that he would feel free to speak without fear of reprisals. He was then asked to show his identification card, his work contract or his camp card to prove that he really was a Mexican National. Any man who could not or would not show such identification was not interviewed.

Statements made by the men concerning wages, deductions and rates of pay were checked against paycheck stubs, field receipts or other documentary evidence, and with the consent of the workers some of these documents were kept. Wherever it was possible to do so, other statements by the *braceros* were also checked; if a man stated, for example, that he was not given punch cards or other records of the work done by him, his crew was observed at work the next day in order to check the accuracy of his statement.

The results of this study may seem startling. But to anyone who is familiar with the workings of the international recruitment program, there is really nothing novel about them. The author of this study has had considerable experience with the program's operation during the years it has been in existence. Year after year he has visited the camps in which Mexican Nationals have been billeted while working in the United States; he has made personal inspections of the recruiting centers in Mexico and has participated in Congressional hearings on the operation of the program; he has had thousands of interviews with Mexican Nationals in various parts of the United States and has investigated hundreds of individual grievances on their behalf. Nothing in this study contradicts what he has observed in the past.

The pattern remains the same. Although the inclination to take advantage of the situation undoubtedly varies in intensity from employer to employer and from region to region, a widespread tendency does exist toward loose enforcement of the law and toward shameful neglect of the legal rights of Mexican Nationals.

This report does not claim that the conditions described here are present everywhere and precisely to the same degree. But suppose that the hundreds of workers interviewed for this study were, for some reason or other, not representative; suppose that the camps visited were not typical; or suppose that the working conditions encountered were unmatched elsewhere—suppose all these things, mathematically improbable as such suppositions are. The fact still remains, at the very minimum, that the findings of this report are in themselves disturbing enough to warrant immediate action by the authorities involved. For in almost every area covered by the International Agreement, United States law, state law, and the provisions of the work contract, serious violations of the rights of Mexican Nationals were found to be the normal pattern rather than the exception.

THE BRACERO HIMSELF

Many observers have commented on what they take to be the remarkable patience of the *bracero*. It is true that some are patient; more are simply cautious, with a caution born of experience.

As one Mexican National put it to me: "These things have to be tolerated in silence because there is no one to defend our guarantees. In a strange country you feel timid—like a chicken in another rooster's yard."

Within any large group of Nationals, of course, there are elements of a feeling of community and collective interest. Such feelings exist between workers from the same town or province, for example, or between men who speak the same Indian dialect in addition to Spanish, or between brothers or cousins who occasionally are assigned to the same camp. From these feelings—[which are] weak because they affect so few—there occasionally arise spontaneous acts of mutual aid that momentarily give the *braceros* a reassuring feeling of solidarity. These acts are generally the collections of money to help a worker who has fallen ill or suffered a serious accident, or to pay the expenses of someone to travel to the nearest consulate to present a complaint. Grocery pools to supplement meals that are distasteful or inadequate are also frequent expressions of collective action.

But these occasional signs of community of interests are sporadic and meaningless in the face of the general isolation in which the *bracero* lives. They are certainly not strong enough to nerve the men for joint action on the problems of wages, hours, meals, housing, and decent treatment. Such action requires leadership, and leadership needs a climate of freedom, knowledge, and opportunity that does not exist in the camps. The fact that men who speak up for themselves and their fellows are removed to another camp, denied work, or repatriated is well known.

The *braceros* work in a foreign land, surrounded by strangers whose language they do not understand. They are totally unorganized—or more accurately, almost totally *dis*organized. The National may have ample grounds for complaint but he is accustomed to look around and measure the distance between him and the help he would need if his claim is denied and resented.

He does not live shut up in camp by force. He is free to walk to town or to roam about the roads when he is not working. But he also sees that no outsiders come to visit him; that camps are heavily posted against trespassing; that the quiet talk of the camp quickly gets to the cook or the foreman; that consuls and inspectors are rarely if ever seen around; that on his occasional visits to town he is welcomed only by those who want him to spend his "cents."

The distance between his camp and the surrounding community has to be measured not only in miles but in terms of vast differences in language, customs and outlook. The common respect for legal obligations, as well as for civil and human rights, found in the general American community serves as a firm foundation for the protection of the individual. The Mexican National in the United States does not have the benefit of this powerful sanction. The local press rarely publishes anything about the conditions under which he lives and works; it never prints his views. Only when a *bracero* has been killed in a crash or knifed in a brawl is the community aware of the Nationals in its midst.

There is a sub-community that partly fills this gap, composed of local residents of Mexican ancestry who speak Spanish and have kept many of the cultural traits of the *bracero*. But his contacts with this sub-community are of a special kind, limited for the most part to merchants and others who in one way or another make a small living from the needs of the National. There also are the displaced domestic Mexican farm laborers who may have feelings of hostility or pity but who in any case are themselves a minority group within the larger community.

In addition to all this, it must be stressed that the Nationals are a group apart from the organized labor movement of the United States. They play a vital part in the process of production; without their labor many trucks would not roll and countless canneries would close. Nevertheless, from an organizational point of view, the thousands of Mexican farm workers do not exist. This fact only adds to the *bracero*'s real isolation.

He works under the protection of a contract and that contract is a weighty document, printed in two languages. His signature on it may be nothing more than a fingerprint, but there is also the signature of the representative of a growers' association. Most important of all, it is signed by the representatives of two powerful governments—Mexico and the United States.

But he has heard foremen, contractors and others deride the contract and laugh at those who held it in respect and even awe. The National I met who had had his contract snatched from him and torn to pieces on the field was both impressed and bewildered when he commented: "And it had the signatures of the governments on it." A *bracero* with a more practical turn of mind said only: "The contract means nothing. It only keeps us from taking a job where we could make a better wage."

Many *braceros* cannot read. The long and sometimes involved terms of the Agreement and work contract have not been read and explained to him. He carries the document around with him, but he does not understand it.

Even the National who is literate and has studied his contract and the International Agreement does not know half his rights, for those documents are not the

whole of the law. It is provided that the two governments may issue Joint Interpretations and that these are to be incorporated in the contracts with the same
force and effect of the original provisions. A set of such Joint Interpretations was
issued by the two governments in March 1954, containing important provisions
on wages, withholdings, subsistence allowances and treatment of workers on the
job. After the Interpretations of 1954 were approved all contracts were rubber
stamped on the cover in Spanish and English: "The amendments to this Work
Contract approved . . . on March 10, 1954, are specifically incorporated herein
and made a part hereof and supersede any provisions of this Work Contract with
which they are inconsistent." The *braceros* are not provided with copies of these
Joint Interpretations; it is safe to say that . . . not one National in a thousand
understands their provisions.

All the *bracero* knows is that he must pay an insurance premium once a week
and have as much as a week's pay withheld to guarantee his transportation expenses back to the reception center. The state that protects him when he is hurt on
the job; the obligations of his employer to transport him in a safe and reasonably
comfortable vehicle; his right to a minimum of hygiene in camp—these rights are
largely unknown to him. Not knowing what ground to stand on, he is by turns
obsequious, reserved, quietly resentful, or fatalistic.

When the National is in need of counsel or advice or some immediate personal
service, he turns to those around him who speak Spanish and know the lay of
the land. The truck driver, the camp caretaker, the field foreman, the bartenders,
the small merchants and the taxi drivers are the makeshift counselors and social
workers to whom the Nationals look. Those persons are almost never known
other than by their first names. [One] *bracero* left several week's wages in the
safekeeping of a town bar but did not ask for a receipt because "it seemed ugly
to me." Typically, he knew nothing else about the transaction except that "it was
in Stockton and the bartender's name was Pete."

Somewhat more important services are offered by the fixers who play upon the
bracero's ignorance and anxieties. For a price they offer to negotiate extensions or
renewals of contracts or to locate "some small rancher who will give you steady
work." More enterprising and experienced Nationals who may decide to skip
their contracts or to remain as Wetbacks after the expiration date are sought out
by runners and contact men who provide transportation and hideouts.

Such legitimate and bootleg services sustain a shifty fringe of camp followers
who are familiar to the *bracero* at least by their first names. In contrast, most
Nationals do not know the location or address of the nearest consulate or how
to get there. They do not call on the U.S. Department of Labor compliance officers because they do not know who they are or where they can be found; if they

did the consulates and field offices would be busy places indeed, taking care of complaints for which they are not staffed, located or equipped.

The *bracero* thinks twice and perhaps oftener before he complains of a shortage in his pay check or unexplained deductions from his wages. His immediate superior may consider such a complaint the moral equivalent of a strike and the forerunner of rebellion. The worker can write to the Consul, but he fears the letter will be turned over to the boss with a request for an investigation and a report—as has happened. If he takes the bus to travel to the consulate, he may have to walk several miles to the nearest town, lose a day's pay and try to conceal the reason for his trip. Somehow the boss invariably finds out and he is in for a public dressing down, if not a transfer or repatriation. These are formidable obstacles to a man on a 45-day contract in a strange land. Almost always he decides to "leave it for the peace."

The brevity of the contract period acts as a powerful deterrent to the exercise of his rights or the assertion of his prerogatives. If the work is slack he wants a renewal to mend his bad luck; if he makes good wages during his first contract period, he would like to stay on for another period or two. In either case, to press a grievance, even to utter one, means that his chances for a renewal will drop. As the expiration date of the contract nears, the good graces of the foreman or the contractor may be an important factor in being chosen for another term. Certainly the choice will not fall on one who has been reported as a malcontent. "It is not convenient to be reported as a subject of doubtful conduct. It is best to remain quiet and wait."

If, on the other hand, the *bracero* has no prospects of renewal, the demands he feels he has a right to make will be weighed against conflicting blocks in his mind. He is "living in somebody else's house," as the National phrases it. Puzzled and uninformed, he usually concludes: "What's the use of complaining now? They will be sending me home in a few days." To remain on his own to press a claim, however important, is out of the question. He will have no place to sleep and no assurance that he will eat.

In two different camps, three hundred miles apart, and within a period of ten days, two *braceros* summarized the two points of view in a matter of grievances under short-term contracts. One of them said: "I've just arrived and I don't want them to 'fly' me back." The other asked: "What can you do in the last five days?"

If the National has already completed his contract and he is allowed to work in the fifteen day period of grace, he realizes that he is staying on sufferance. "Now we are truly in the doubt," one put it. In camp he is daily reminded of the precariousness of his condition. Even when work is slack, he sees new groups of other Nationals arriving, and he knows that he must compete with them for jobs which are already scarce. He knows what the contractor means when he says: "For every one of you complainers we can get 20 more from Mexico."

If he is transferred from stoop labor to machine tending or irrigating at the same wage, more than likely he will be grateful rather than insistent on the terms of his contract regarding wage differentials. The change means escape from monotonous work. It raises his prestige among his fellow workers. It may lead to a permanent transfer to the easier job. He has a chance to learn to drive a tractor, run water, or operate a sorter. It may even mean that he is liked by the boss, and this in turn may mean a longer contract.

If worse comes to worse, with no renewal in sight and small earnings behind, the National may decide to skip and join the thousands of his fellows who have entered the United States legally and remained as Wetbacks. If the camp is many hundreds of miles from the border, the chances are fair that some additional days or weeks of work can be obtained before the border patrol catches up with him.

In some camps contract skipping is frequent. Often it is a mode of protest against conditions that the worker feels cannot be corrected through the grievance procedure of the Agreement. In skipping out, he expresses his basic agreement with the Department of Labor official who stated that "the National cannot change jobs freely, thus seeking better conditions or higher pay." The Mexican Nationals puts it this way: "The Wetback is more free." That statement is, surely, a sad commentary.

The *bracero* who stays in this country illegally is, however, in the minority. Most return to Mexico, and there many [who] file official complaints through their government, usually for wages. Each year thousands of dollars are recovered by the Mexican Department of Foreign Relations on behalf of claimants who were not able to square their accounts before being repatriated. How many thousands of dollars which are rightfully due to Mexican Nationals go uncollected is beyond computation.

Once they are back in their own country, many Nationals regain enough self-confidence to express their discontent with what they encountered in the United States. Mexican newspapers frequently carry such protests by returning *braceros*, men who under other circumstances might have returned to Mexico as ambassadors of good will.

This, then, is the end of the story of the Mexican National. He is home again. Unless he is very lucky, he has encountered ignorance, prejudice, and discrimination; he has learned what loneliness in the midst of a crowd can mean; he has suffered exploitation, abuse, and injustice. If he is lucky, the *bracero* may have returned to Mexico a little richer; if unlucky, he may be poorer. In either case he certainly is wiser.

PART 6

LETTERS FROM
AN ACTIVIST

TO ALFRED BLACKMAN, CALIFORNIA DIVISION OF INDUSTRIAL SAFETY, JUNE 20, 1957.

This letter is illustrative of many hundreds of letters Galarza wrote to officials in state and federal agencies regarding violations of laws and regulations, particularly abuses under the Bracero Program. In 1957 nearly 500,000 *braceros* were contracted to work on various corporate farms throughout the Southwest. The California agriculture industry received nearly 200,000 workers from the *bracero* pool in this year, which is considered the height of the *bracero* era.

Mr. Alfred C. Blackman
Division of Industrial Safety
Department of Industrial Relations
965 Mission Street
San Francisco, Calif.

1031 Franquette Ave.
San Jose, Calif.

June 20, 1957

Dear Mr. Blackman:

It has been brought to my attention that a Mexican national by the name of Toribio Rodriguez was killed in a fall from a truck while employed by the De Candia Farms near Stockton, California.

The death occurred on May 26, I believe. Rodriquez, according to the testimony of fellow workers, was riding with 47 other workers on a truck which was not provided with the safeguards prescribed by law.

A month before the accident which killed this man and injured others the Nationals in the camp had asked the Mexican Consul to investigate the unsafe conditions under which the men were being transported. I understand that this request was referred by the Consul to the Employers Service Representative in the area.

There is a statement of record signed by the workers who were riding in the truck when Rodriquez was killed.

I would appreciate it if you could give me additional information on this case.

Sincerely yours,

Ernesto Galarza

TO CONGRESSMAN JAMES ROOSEVELT, DECEMBER 20, 1957

In addition to being the principal speaker, pamphleteer, researcher, and organizer for the National Agriculture Workers Union, Galarza was an indefatigable lobbyist, who kept constant pressure on elected officials and high-level bureaucrats.

When the union was denied access to public information about braceros and growers, Galarza reached out to Congressman James Roosevelt (1955–1965), the son of former president Franklin D. Roosevelt. Congressman Roosevelt was considered a liberal democrat and a staunch opponent of Senator Joseph McCarthy because of his red-baiting tactics that recklessly attacked the character and patriotism of individuals and organizations. Galarza argued that denying the union access to the data was indicative of the Bracero Program's corruption.

Hon. James Roosevelt   1031 Franquette Ave.
5308 West Adams Street   San Jose, Calif.
Los Angeles, Calif.

December 20, 1957

Dear Congressman Roosevelt:

During the past few weeks we have been sending you, to your office in Washington, copies of recent complaints of domestic farm workers who live in San Joaquin County. The complaints are based on the continuing violations of Public Law 78, specifically the provision that domestic farm workers shall be given preference in agricultural employment over Mexican contract Nationals.

Because of the peculiar investigatory procedures followed in such cases by the Department of Employment; and because of the screen of secrecy which has been drawn across public information now available only to growers, it is no longer possible for the members of our Union and other domestic farm workers to expect fair and equitable treatment, in accordance with the law, either from the state agencies involved or from the West Coast officials of the Department of Labor.

The Mexican National labor recruitment program, still sound in principle, has become a corrupt system of exploitation of the Mexican contract workers, and a device to drive domestic farm labor from the land by wage cuts and other equally drastic methods of harassment.

The Mexican farm labor recruitment program is the creature of Congress, and we do not believe that its present sorry state was intended by Congress.

If it is at all possible I should like to discuss this entire matter with you in Los Angeles on Friday, December 27, or any other date during the first week of January which you may suggest.

Sincerely yours,

Ernesto Galarza

OPEN LETTER TO MEMBERS OF THE HOUSE OF REPRESENTATIVES, CO-SIGNED BY NAWU PRESIDENT H. L. MITCHELL, FEBRUARY 17, 1958

This is another example of Galarza's lobbying. Galarza liked to be known as director of research and education, but for the purpose of this letter he was the union's secretary. The National Agricultural Workers' Union viewed Public Law 78 (1951) as the single greatest obstacle for the farm worker labor movement. This law outlined the conditions of employment and recruitment of *braceros* from Mexico. One of its provisions explicitly denied *braceros* the right to organize or act collectively to better their conditions. Grower associations used P.L. 78 to recruit *braceros* to work on farms that had organizing campaigns, then force them to act as strikebreakers.

February 17, 1958

Dear Congressman:

Will you use your influence to bring a thorough investigation of the operation of the Mexican Farm Labor Importation Program? Under Public Law 78, the Secretary of Labor is authorized to bring in Mexican Nationals to be employed as seasonal harvest hands. In 1956 and again in 1957, nearly one-half million Mexican contract Nationals were employed on 68,000 of the largest farms in this country.

We believe that a full scale investigation by Congress will reveal that the administration of this Mexican Farm Labor Importation Program has broken down and that it now approaches a state of corruption. In a memorandum attached to this letter we cite specific cases which we are confident are not isolated incidents, but symptoms of mal-administration by the Secretary of Labor who has apparently abdicated his public responsibility to private interest.

We are enclosing a copy of a recent letter from Robert C. Goodwin, Director of the Bureau of Employment Security, addressed to "All Employers of Mexican

Nationals" which substantiates our contention that this program involving nearly 500,000 foreign workers is fraught with corruption and illegal activities on the part of large farm operators and their associations.

We also call your attention to the introduction of a series of bills in the House of Representatives on January 29th which are designed to make the Mexican Farm Labor Importation Program a permanent feature of American agriculture. HR 10360 by Mr. E. C. Gathings of Arkansas and identical bills by four other members would strike out Section 509 of Public Law 78 which is as follows: "No worker shall be available under this title for employment after June 30, 1959."

In view of the existing situation affecting this program, we urge that no action be taken on these bills and that requests for appropriations made by the Department of Labor for operation of the Mexican Program be delayed until a thorough and complete investigation can be undertaken by Congress to determine the extent of corruption in this program.

Sincerely yours,

H. L. Mitchell, President
Ernesto Galarza, Secretary

TO HENRY P. ANDERSON, APRIL 2, 1958

Anderson was a graduate student at the School of Public health at UC Berkeley, where he was studying the Bracero Program under a grant from the National Institutes of Health. The result of this research was *The Bracero Program in California, with Particular Reference to Health Status, Attitudes, and Practices* (Berkeley: School of Public Health, University of California, 1961), which exposed a world of cruelty, corruption, and exploitation under the guise of the bracero system. Grower associations eventually pressured the university to terminate Anderson's research. Galarza then recruited Anderson to the farm worker labor movement and mentored him in action research.

April 2, 1958

Dear friend,

Renner is changing homes just now, also considering the possibility of going into business in Mexico. I expect to see him in the next two weeks in Stockton and will ask him to get in touch with you.

I did receive the 100 pages you sent and thought I had promptly acknowledged it. Sorry. It is a very useful job. I hope it will be properly released sometime.

It is true that the growers have been considering an about face on PL 78 and a plan to use the immigration law on a large scale. In fact they have been experimenting with it recently. There is a division of opinion on this policy among the associations. I have a hunch one of the reasons they want to scuttle the law is that they hope thus to avoid a searching investigation of past practices.

On your questions:

- I don't know of any democratic organization that has taken a forthright stand on the foreign contract labor issue other than the Contra Costa central committee, I believe. No one of any state standing has spoken out. I would be interested in your friend[']s decision on this point. He might want to see the last of our "knight letters". I believe I sent you the previous two.

- Every print of the DiGirogio film that I know of has been destroyed. There may be one in Washington. I'll inquire and let you know it may take a little time. There are no prints that I know of in California.
- I have had no reliable information on PL 78 hearings. I get the impression that Congressman Saund is in a stalemate in the House Agricultural Committee and that the House Labor Committee is still marking time over protocol. If the hearings are called in connection with the Saund bill I would be little interested. We are demanding an investigation rather than a hearing.

If in your travels you happen to pick up any recent individual work contracts— (the wage sheet rather than the printed text) I would appreciate the loan of them for photocopying. We are pursuing a wage analysis for which we need the wage data from the contracts.

The situation of the bracero asparagus cutters on the "islands" would interest you from a health standpoint. Yesterday I saw crews of them cutting grass in flooded fields without rain gear, pants legs rolled up.

Best wishes,

E Galarza

TO HENRY P. ANDERSON, APRIL 30, 1958

"Knight letters" is a reference to occasional broadsides Galarza sent to Goodwin J. Knight, Republican governor of California. He also sent copies to the press and other interested parties.

April 30, 1958

Dear friend:

The "knight letters" will continue for another number or two. I trust their substance will continue to square with the facts as you know them.

We have already collected evidence that the $4.00 per month deduction for insurance is not enough. Some men are being charged at the rate of $6.00 per month.

I did not know that the consular staff in LA receives free medical services from Pan American. This does interest me. Can you suggest a follow up that would enable me to report this first hand? It is much too "delicado" a subject to permit second hand reference.

Undoubtedly the details of the operation of the medical service program will prove as fascinating as any other phase of The [Bracero]Program. We can only snatch glimpses of three defects you note. I'm afraid we will have to depend finally on the Public Health Service report for the complete story. We are going to push what we do know already to the limit.

Your previous question as to the hearings in Washington I still can't answer. It appears that the associations are ducking all publicity and have decided to soft pedal such hearings.

We have documented also the lay-over of Nationals in San Joaquin and Fresno counties. They have remained through the winter on a sort of extremely extended grace period.

If you can pick up contracts of men returning it would be best of all. We want them for Santa Clara, San Joaquin, Sutter, Monterey, Imperial and Stanislaus. Next to the original, we can use an abstract showing (a) the name and counties covered (b) contract number (c) date of opening and closing of the contract (d) employing association (e) certification number and (f) text of work and wage provisions. Two or three such abstracts of originals for each of the indicated areas would be enough.

I met Luisa Moreno only once and very briefly. She was not with our Union. That was more than five years ago. I haven't the foggiest idea where she would be now.

Can your observer at the Center tell us whether there are heating units in the barracks now?

If you are up this way let me know. I might be in the area and we could talk over these angles and others.

Cordially,

E Galarza

P.s. I have not seen a copy of Goodwin's March 28 letter

LETTER TO
HENRY P. ANDERSON,
JUNE 24, 1958

This letter is a reply to a long letter Anderson had written about his first trip to Washington, D.C., during which he found that members of the "Eastern liberal establishment" lacked any real passion about the *bracero* system or farm labor in general. The attempt by Anderson and Galarza to shake them up soon led to the termination of Anderson's research project at UC Berkeley.

June 24, 1958

Dear friend Hank:

Your very interesting letter rushed me back ten years to the time I fled Washington, for much the same reasons, but with this difference: I had felt a growing entombment under a mass of filed information, administrative hypocrisy, empty ritual and ineffectual good will. It had taken me another ten years to realize fully—and document perversely by reason of ingrained academic compulsion to prove all things—what you discovered in the bare ten days that shook Hank Anderson.

Your appraisals are not unjust. There are extenuations in one or two cases, the evolution of which I know too intimately. And your conclusions are good logic driven by deep feeling—the best combination I know of to live by.

Personally, the situation is neither hopeful nor hopeless. Reality never seems to be as drastic as the decisions one must make to face it. I am making mine, one at a time and with a concluding date on or about election time in November. Much as my best friends would like for me to grow stale in the present pattern of things, the gentleman is not for burning, as Mr. Fry would say. It is not a question of putting a quietus on failure, but, again as Mr. Fry would say, of terminating a progress. For I have learned a great deal since 1948, a rehash of which requires a long evening over good wine.

And for this purpose, among others, I'm coming to Los Angeles the weekend of July 11, hoping to find you at home and agreeable to dinner with me. I expect to arrive late in the day and will as usual hole in at the Stillwell Hotel.

In the meantime I am mailing you extra copies of some of our releases presuming on your good inclinations to help us by mailing them to people you know. I have sent copies to your home, but perhaps you missed them.

Mitch has sent me instructions to track down one Mamer John at U.C. in Berkeley, but I am demurring pending my talk with you. It seems to me unwise for three people to be bailing for a single leak. The tempest that Mitchell unloosened has become an undertow, and I'm a good swimmer only in familiar waters.

Speaking as one egg-head to another, I look forward to discussing with you our descent to the grass roots, where apparently the noodle-spines dare not follow us.

Cordially,

Eg

TO JACK LIVINGSTON, AFL-CIO DEPARTMENT OF ORGANIZATION, AND NORMAN SMITH, AFL-CIO ORGANIZER, MAY 5, 1959

When Galarza wrote this letter, he had just been put on the AFL-CIO payroll as assistant director of the Agricultural Workers Organizing Committee (AWOC). Livingston was head of the national AFL-CIO Department of Organization. This was the first time Galarza had had to deal directly with the bureaucratized labor movement. During most of his years with the National Farm Labor Union (later the National Agricultural Workers Union), he basically had to make do with his salary (much of the time $125 a month), sometimes getting money for gasoline and other expenses if and when H. L. Mitchell could pry some loose from the National Sharecroppers Fund.

Jack Livingston was one of the founders of the United Autoworkers (1933) and served in high-ranking leadership positions in the UAW until 1955. He then moved on to become the first director of organization for the newly formed AFL-CIO. Norman Smith was a rank-and-file union organizer in the auto industry from 1936 to 1942. He was recruited by Livingston and sent on behalf of the AFL-CIO to assist Galarza's farmworker organizer efforts. Smith was eventually appointed as the first director of AWOC.

May 5, 1959

To: Jack Livingston
Norman Smith

To clarify a number of questions on reports and expenses:

1. Is there a special voucher or form to report public transportation (buses and trains don't extend receipts)?
2. Some of my mileage will have to be reported as use of my 1953 Ford. A 1959 Chevy is unhandy for driving in and out to camps and ranches at odd hours to make contacts. The official car is fine for city trips or non-farm calls. Is this agreeable?

3. Because of the peculiarities of our work some interesting information and useful contacts can best be obtained on Saturday nights and Sundays. These activities do not represent a full day's work so I will report them simply for your information but not for the purpose of expenses. Only in case of full time required activity will expenses be noted.

4. Telephone and telegrams: I have all union costs of this kind charged to my home phone in order to have a record of transactions. These are billed to me once a month. Will run about $20.00 a month or so. Is the monthly statement to be submitted to Washington? Is it covered by per diem? Do I send it to Norman Smith?

5. Postage: I average about 40 letters a week on union business and an additional average of ten pieces of other mail (usually requests for Union literature, releases, etc.) My postage expenses will run around $3.00 a week. Do I send PO receipts to Washington or Norman Smith?

6. I make out three report sheets—white, green and blue. The green and the blue were returned to me with corrections on my first report. What do I send to Washington? What do I keep?

E. Galarza

TO NORMAN SMITH,
DECEMBER 5, 1959

By this point, Galarza had come to a parting of the ways with AWOC because it was not assigning its members to the NAWU, as he had understood it would. However, he was still on good personal terms with Smith, the AWOC director, and thus asked for a modest contribution to meet NAWU's legal needs. But Smith was answerable to Livingston, Livingston was answerable to Meany, and Meany was one of the labor leaders who heartily disliked Galarza, Mitchell, and the NAWU.

Dec. 5, 1959

To: Norman Smith

Copy to John Livingston

We are ready to bring legal pressure to bear on Driscoll Associates, Anderson Estates and Ferry-Morse Seed Company. Driscoll is the largest grower and processor of strawberries in the United States. Anderson is agricultural supervisor to President Eisenhower. Ferry-Morse has a 1000 acre operation in Hollister, with national and international connections.

We have been carefully preparing cases involving all three and are now ready to call in legal counsel. The cases are so prepared as to lead into the matter of the hiring of Mexican Nationals and discrimination against domestic workers.

At some stage of the cases we will involve the growers associations to which all three of the above employers belong.

The services of an attorney for these matters are required right away. I have already spoken in this connection of James E. Murray, who has given a great deal of volunteer, unpaid legal advice to the union in the past.

We ought to get the proceedings indicated above under way before the end of December. We are not at present in a position of asking for Mr. Murray's professional services because we pay him no fees.

Can Mr. Murray be retained as of January 1 for a period of six months? Can an additional amount for his legal service be earmarked from the AWOC budget for court and other expenses? I would suggest a monthly retainer of $100.00 and an additional $1500 reserve against which Mr. Murray can draw for litigation actually carried out.

—*E.G.*

TO "LIBERAL FRIENDS WHO LIVE IN THE EAST," MARCH 18, 1960

This is vintage Ernesto Galarza, complete with a quote from an elegiac ode by Catullus. The context of this memo was a controversy over the extension of Public Law 78. Galarza was an "impossibilist" who believed the opponents of the bracero system should hold out for no extension at all. A good Eastern liberal, George McGovern of South Dakota (later Democratic nominee for president), proposed a phase-out over five years. Some of Galarza's eastern friends evidently thought that was an acceptable idea, and in a good liberal compromise, Public Law 78 was extended in 1960 for two years, then extended twice more before finally being eliminated.

San Jose, Calif.

March 18, 1960

Memorandum written in Despair to my Liberal Friends who live in the East . . .

A year ago I tried to warn you that the appointment of an Advisory Committee by Secretary of Labor Mitchell was a white-tie hearing intended to confuse and divide the groups that have been opposing Public Law 78.

I have just read H.F.11211 (Mr. McGovern), the fruit of the Advisory Report. Here is, therefore, the political situation on the eve of the hearings:

1. The National Agricultural Workers Union, the only organization that has fought with the growers toe to toe for a decade[,] is left isolated. You may be sure that the NAWU will be dismissed with sophisticated scorn by the powers that rule the committee. NAWU has been the lifeline to reality in the fields for you, my friends, and that line has been broken.

2. My liberal friends, perhaps charmed by the duplicitous politics of the Secretary of Labor, have given him and the corporation growers 5 years when the growers only asked for two.

3. In the remote event that Congress should pass this bill, the liberals will have accepted an obligation to silence, for they have agreed to a phasing

out plan in which the vices of administration and the knavery of management will be theoretically diminished by 20 per cent each year.

4. Between now and 1966 the growers associations will have time to perfect other "systems" which they have already been experimenting with in California. Do my liberal friends have any idea who is going to keep water in the fields?

5. The diminution by 20 per cent each year actually betrays the purpose of the Bill ("protection against unfair competition from corporate agriculture to the American family farm"). Here is the reason: The growers' associations control the Mexican program. The associations are in turn controlled by the corporate or large family operators whose income and profits seem high. It will be very easy to squeeze out the small farmers from who[se] quota I believe the 20 per cent reduction can be culled for at least two years.

6. No such formula as the one in this Bill can be a substitute for courageous political action in Washington and militant vigilance in the fields. In the winter of 1957–1958 the NAWU single-handed, without staff or money, reduced the quota of Mexican contract pruners in Northern California by nearly 100 per cent.

7. Finally, the Bill gives the liberal and administrative blessing to the outrageous principle that "domestic workers must be offered terms and conditions comparable to those offered foreign workers."

Please don't advise me that politics is the art of the possible. The NAWU in California has proved that it is the art of the impossible.

Ave atque vale: I wish that I could go and see
The friends whose love is strangling me,

—*Galarza*

PART 7

APPENDIX

VALE MÁS LA REVOLUCIÓN QUE VIENE

Speech by Mae Galarza at the Eighth Annual Ernesto Galarza Symposium, San Jose State University, April 3, 1992.

I have two comments ending this 8th symposium to commemorate the life and work of Ernesto Galarza.

This evening has meant much extra work for the Association of Chicano/Latina faculty and staff of this university. As we all know, it takes many extra hours and cooperation to organize this type of gathering. But now, I wish particularly to express my appreciation and I know that the community representatives do also.

As for Ernesto Galarza, that modest and self-effacing man would drop his head in thought and smiling would consent with a warm glow of appreciation.

The university and students are appropriately pleased that the total number of scholarships with this evening has risen to 35 donated by 10 organizations, several of which have contributed each year.

My second comment has to do with a word in a sentence that Ernesto Galarza wrote in a book that he had written and given to a friend. But first let me tell you of an experience that I had in Mexico in 1940, the first time that I had visited a foreign country. We traveled by automobile over quite a little area east and west of the capital city, rolling hills, beautifully unspoiled, sparsely populated, with hamlets and churches. There were many signs painted on roadsides, walls, bridges and markets. Every sign carried this word, "Revolución," even those near the religious saints tucked in the crevices of the rock embankments along the roadway, reviving the spirits of the weary peasants as they walked to and from the country markets. Every sign became dramatic with this word "Revolución." It seemed to be a most honorable word. It was most perplexing to me. I had thought of it as an underground word. It wasn't in my vocabulary. People would think that you were a communist, and no patriot would want to be in that class.

Now, I want to skip up to the present. Mrs. Clare Villa, an artist for several years, made this creative silk screen to be given at the 1991 symposium. Her husband, Professor Jose Villa, brought me one. I was impressed. It was excellently and thoughtfully composed and then the statement across the heading. Here was

Ernesto and Mae Galarza. Courtesy of the Seaver Center for Western History Research, Los Angeles County Museum of Natural History.

"revolución" again 50 years later. Although more dramatic—still not used by our press. For the journalists would use civil war or rebellion or various other terms. "*Vale más la revolución que viene que la que se fue*" [the revolution to come is worth more than the one that has passed] was the brief greeting written in the frontispiece of Ernesto Galarza's latest book, *Farm Workers and Agribusiness in California,* that he was presenting to Professor Jose Villa. This "vale mas" statement was the very essence of Ernesto Galarza's philosophy. This gave him the energy to continue learning and acting through research, associations, encouragement, writing, lecturing, persuasion—endless interesting hours.

Galarza had no thought of bringing out the guns, bombers, and tanks. No! It was knowledge that would bring about change in culture, change in our sensitivity to our fellow man. A justice through education in school and out that would naturally provoke and propel us into a new local and worldly environment. So in this statement revolution means, change, advance, progression in a way the less advantaged earn a living in an environment of much hostility. Ernesto Galarza became an associate of these workers in the fields, personally meeting them in small groups, listening to their problems, making suggestions, encouraging them as a friend. The learning was poignant and practical, touching immediately the living conditions of these hardworking people which had to be reported to the citizenry everywhere, carried in the press to the legislature, and particularly to the halls of Congress. Galarza was a charmer with the journalists, and they were important allies. Committees in Congress were working on the laws and said they needed truthful information about living and working in agriculture. These lawmakers were hearing of no housing, accidents, sickness of children, poor food, and lack of payment in wages.

So Ernesto Galarza talked to the workers in Spanish and the lawmakers in English. He gave lectures to many groups and began writing books for students in school and government agencies. He flew across the country from California to Washington, writing outlines along the way, and so tied information among many sensitive and powerful people. It was slow revamping their thinking and action, and so it continues. More justice and fairness will prevail when more of our citizens declare that it must.

This effort was Ernesto Galarza's revolution.

Leaders are necessary, and young people, students in school today, will do their part we feel sure.

Vale más la Revolución que viene.

Thank you and good night.

SELECTED BIBLIOGRAPHY

1928   *The Catholic Church in Mexico.* Sacramento: The Capital Press.
            188 pp.

1934   *What Is Progressive Education: An Outline for Parents.* Jamaica
            Estates, Long Island: The Yearlong School. 20 pp.

1935   *Thirty Poems.* Jamaica Estates, Long Island: The Yearlong School.
            30 pp.

1935–1930   Six untitled articles on Latin America for The Foreign Policy As-
            sociation; one article for *The Nation*; one article for the *New York
            Times.*

1941   *La Industria Eléctrica en México.* Mexico City: Fondo de Cultura
            Económica. 232 pp.

1942   *Labor in Latin America.* Washington, D.C.: The American Council
            of Public Affairs. 23 pp.

1942   Edits the Pan-American Union's series for young readers.

            Various authors contribute ten short stories about historic characters
            and peoples and places that serve as an introduction to the study
            of Latin America, including *The Pan American Union, The Panama
            Canal, The Snake Farm at Butantan, Francisco Pizarro, Cabeza de
            Vaca's Great Journey, The Guano Islands of Peru, The Incas, Jose de
            San Martin, The Pan American Highway,* and *The Araucanians.*

1947   *Labor Trends and Social Welfare in Latin America.* Washington,
            D.C.: Pan American Union, Office of Labor and Social Informa-
            tion. 60 pp.

1949   *The Case of Bolivia.* Inter-American Reports no. 6. 32 pp.

1955   *Plantation Workers in Louisiana.* Washington, D.C.: Inter-Ameri-
            can Education Association. 160 pp.

1956   *Strangers in Our Fields.* Washington, D.C.: Joint United States-
            Mexico Trade Union Committee. 80 pp.

1964   *Merchants of Labor.* Santa Barbara, Calif.: McNally & Loftin. 284 pp.

1969   *Economic Development by Mexican-American, Oakland, California: An Analysis and a Proposal.* Berkeley, Calif.: Social Science Research & Development Corporation. 36 pp.

1969   *Mexican-Americans in the Southwest* (with Herman Gallegos and Julian Samora). Santa Barbara, Calif.: McNally and Loftin. 94 pp.

1970   *Spiders in the House and Workers in the Fields.* Notre Dame, Ind.: University of Notre Dame Press. 306 pp.

1971   *Barrio Boy.* Notre Dame, Ind.: University of Notre Dame Press. 275 pp. Translated in 1977 as *Traspasando Fronteras.* Serie Frontera, Secretaría de Educación Pública. Reprinted in a 40th anniversary edition by University of Notre Dame Press in 2011.

    Excerpts published in various school texts for junior high through college students:

       1972   *Basic Reading Code Book.* McCracken & Walcutt, Lippencott & Co.

       1973   *Outlooks through Literature.* Scott, Foresman and Co.

       1974   *Readings to Enjoy.* Literary Heritage Series. Macmillan Publishing Co.

       1975   *Chicano Voices.* Houghton Mifflin Co.

       1979   *Types of Literature.* Ginn and Company.

1973   *Alviso: The Crisis of a Barrio.* San Jose, Calif.: Mexican American Community Service Agency. 46 pp.

1976   Publishes eight poems in Theodore Clymer, *Where Do Stories Come From?* (Lexington, Mass.: Ginn and Company), a fourth-grade reader. 96 pp.

1977   *Farm Workers and Agri-Business in California, 1947–1960.* Notre Dame, Ind.: University of Notre Dame Press. 405 pp.

1977   *The Tragedy at Chualar.* Santa Barbara, Calif.: McNally and Loftin. 106 pp.

1982   *Kodachromes in Rhyme: Poems.* Notre Dame, Ind.: University of Notre Dame Press. 60 pp.

SELECTED CHRONOLOGY

1905   Born August 15 in Jalcocotán, Nayarit, Mexico.

1910   Mexican Revolution begins.

1911   Immigrates to the United States.

1913   Participates in his first labor action.

1917   Mother dies of influenza in Sacramento.

1921   Mexican Revolution ends.

1923–27   Attends Occidental College; graduates with a B.A.

1928   Marries Mae Taylor.

1929   Earns M.A. in history and political science from Stanford.

            Publishes "Life in the United States for Mexican People: Out of the Experience of a Mexican," in *Proceedings of the National Conference of Social Work [Formerly National Conference of Charities and Correction] at the Fifty-Sixth Annual Session Held In San Francisco, California June 26–July 3, 1929* (Chicago: University of Chicago Press), 399–404.

1932–36   With Mae, establishes the Year-Long School, an experimental elementary school, in Jamaica, New York.

1936   Begins to serve as education specialist for the Pan-American Union; publishes analyses of labor and education in Latin America.

1939   Becomes a naturalized U.S. citizen.

1940   Heads the new Division of Labor and Social Information for the Pan-American Union.

1942   Bracero Program begins.

1946   Earns Ph.D. in history and public law from Columbia University.

1947   Resigns as head of the Division of Labor and Social Information of the Pan-American Union.

            Joins the Southern Tenant Farmers Union (later the National Agricultural Workers Union).

Helps lead organizing drive and strike against the DiGiorgio Corporation; strike lasts for thirty months.

1948   Writes "Poverty in the Valley of Plenty: A Report on the Di Giorgio Strike, May 14, 1948" (unpublished report).

1950   Writes "Mexican–United States Labor Relations and Problems," presented at the Southwest Council on Education of Spanish-Speaking People, Albuquerque, New Mexico (unpublished essay), Department of Special Collections and University Archives, Stanford University Libraries.

Leads a strike of tomato pickers in Tracy, California.

1951   Leads a strike of cantaloupe pickers in Imperial Valley, California.

1953   With H. L. Mitchell, co-founder of the Southern Tenant Farmers' Union, organizes strikes of sugar-cane workers and strawberry pickers in Louisiana.

1955   Receives grant from the Fund for the Republic, a branch of the Ford Foundation, to study the Bracero Program.

1956   National Farm Labor Union merges with the National Agricultural Workers Union (NAWU).

Publishes *Strangers in Our Fields* (Washington, D.C.: Joint United States–Mexican Trade Union Committee).

Bolivian government awards Galarza the Order of the Condor of the Andes.

1959–60   AFL-CIO passes Galarza over for leadership of the newly chartered Agricultural Workers Organizing Committee. Galarza leaves organized labor.

Serves as advisor to the House Committee on Education and Labor.

1964   Bracero Program ends.

1965   Serves as Urban Affairs Consultant to the Ford Foundation.

Gives the speech "How the Anglo Manipulates the Mexican-American" at the Mexican-American Leadership Conference, Camp Max Strauss, Los Angeles.

Writes "Community and the Child" (unpublished essay), Department of Special Collections and University Archives, Stanford University Libraries.

1966   Begins community organizing in Alviso, California.

Publishes *Economic Development by Mexican-Americans in Oakland, California: An Analysis and a Proposal* (Berkeley, Calif.: Social Science Research and Development Corporation).

1967   Boycotts the conference of the Inter-Agency Committee on Mexican American Affairs; is elected chair of the Raza Unida Unity Conference in El Paso, Texas.

Gives a speech entitled "The Farm Laborer: His Economic and Social Outlook" to the Western Region Migrant Health Conference, UCLA, June 26–28.

1968   With Julian Samora, co-founds the Southwest Council of La Raza (later the National Council of La Raza).

1969   Testifies before the Subcommittee on Migratory Labor of the Senate Committee on Labor and Public Welfare.

Gives a speech entitled "Minorities: The Mirror of Society" to the California Council for the Social Studies annual conference. Later published in *Ghosts in the Barrio: Issues in Bilingual-Bicultural Education,* ed. Ralph Pablano (San Rafael, Calif.: Leswing Publishing, 1973).

1970   Publishes "Chicano Studies: Research and Scholarly Activity" in *Civil Rights Digest* 3 (Fall 1970): 40–42.

1971   Receives honorary doctorate in human letters from Occidental College.

Founds the Studio Laboratory for Bilingual Education, a resource center for the students and faculty of the San Jose Unified School District.

Publishes *Barrio Boy* (Durham, N.C.: Duke University Press).

1973   Receives a grant from the John Hay Whitney Foundation to study bilingual education.

Publishes *Alviso: The Crisis of a Barrio* (San Jose, Calif.: Mexican American Community Service Agency).

1974   Writes "A Cautionary Memorandum for Bilingual Educators" (unpublished essay)

Publishes *Action Research: In Defense of the Barrio. Interviews with Ernesto Galarza, Guillermo Flores, and Rosa Muñoz* (Los Angeles: Aztlán Publications).

1977   With San Jose community members, develops the Community
        Organization to Monitor Education (COME) to increase commu-
        nity input in bilingual education.

        Gives the speech "Hispanic Americans: Reclaiming a Heritage" at
        the National Catholic Education Association 74th Annual Con-
        vention in San Francisco, California.

1978   Publishes "The Reasons Why: Lessons in Cartography" in *Rural
        America* (September).

1979   Nominated for the Nobel Prize in Literature.

1980   Receives Friends of VISTA Award for exceptional service and
        work to end poverty.

1982   *The Burning Light: Action and Organizing in the Mexican Commu-
        nity in California* is published, a series of interviews with Galarza
        conducted by Gabrielle Morris and Timothy Beard in 1977, 1978,
        and 1981 (Regional Oral History Office, The Bancroft Libraries,
        University of California).

1983   Occidental College Alumni Association gives him the Alumni
        Seal Award.

        Publishes *Kodachromes in Rhyme: Poems* (University of Notre
        Dame Press).

1984   Dies June 22 in San Jose, California.

INDEX

bilingualism, 154
Blackman, Alfred, 259
Border Belt, 136
Border Protection, Anti-Terrorism, and Illegal Immigration Control Act (2006), xx, xxi
bracero program, xv, 203; abuses and violations, 259–260, 261–262, 265–266; accidents causing injury or death, 259–260; corruption and illegal actions, 263–264; "Eastern Liberal Establishment," 269–270; history, 238–240; individual *bracero* interviews, 251–254; individual work contract, 243; Mexican Nationals vs. Mexican immigrants, 261–262; Migrant Labor Agreement of 1951, 243–250; union organization impact, 180–181; U.S.-Mexican relations, 181–183; wetback relationship, 180–181; workers' opinions, 248–250; workers' rights, 241–248. *See also* U.S.-Mexico international labor agreement
Brotherhood of Sleeping Car Porters, xvii
Brown, Edmund G. "Pat," 188
Bureau of Employment Security, 242
Butchers' Union, 185

California American Federation of Labor, 202
California Central Valley. *See* Central Valley of California
California Department of Employment, 57, 173, 188
California Federation of Labor, 184
California geography and history: Central Valley, 47–50; farm labor history, 56–61; immigrant labor history, 55–60; land ownership, 48; Mexico-U.S. border, 50; Spanish exploration and settlement, 46–48. *See also* Central Valley of California
California Packing Corporation, 48

canteloupe pickers' strike, Imperial Valley, 33
Central Valley of California, xxi, 47; land ownership history, 48–49; migrant farm laborers, 227–228, 229; seasonal farm labor, 49–50. *See also bracero* program; *colonias; specific organizations; specific strikes and boycotts*
Chambers, Pat, 190–191
Chapultepec Conference, 35
Chavez, Cesar E., xviii, 187
Chicano students' call to action, 66–68
Chualar accident, 173
civil liberties: deprivation, 39; violations prevention, 42–43
civil rights movement, Galarza and, xx
Cleland, Robert Glass, 59
colonias, 38, 54, 144; as labor pools, 78–79, 104, 150; locations, 34, 38, 199; Oakland, 89; urbanization, 94, 96, 151–152, 158; wetback traffic, 52. *See also barrios*
Columbia University, xv, 192
Common Ground article, 32–45
community development and educational reform, Galarza's, xviii, xxiiin5
community organizing, Galarza's, xxii
Congressmen, 263–264
Congress of Industrial Organizations (C.I.O.), 223. *See also* AFL-CIO
Consortium, 67
contractors, proposed regulation of, 43
cotton pickers' strikes, 169, 188
cultural anthropology terminology, 132–135
cultural maintenance considerations, 135
culture traits, 133

Decker, Caroline, 191
Delano union, 178
Department of Employment, 57, 173, 188
Department of Labor, 242

Di Giorgio, Joseph, 48, 179

Di Giorgio Fruit Corporation strike, xvii, xxii, 177, 183, 188, 192; community prejudice, 200–201; Congressional investigation, 200; corporate responses, 194; documentary film, 202; Galarza interview, 178–181; Galarza report, 192–202; housing, 199–200; illegal workers, 197; Kern County agriculture, 193–194; mechanization, 199; Mexican workers, 198–199; participants, 193, 200; positive results, 202; public assistance for striking workers, 196–197; race tensions, 201; segregation, 201; strike breakers, 194, 195, 201–202; unemployment and poverty, 196; unions, 202; violence, 195–196

discrimination, 37–38; wage, 34–35

East Bay Spanish-Speaking Foundation proposal, 77–78

"Eastern Liberal Establishment," 269–270, 275–276

Economic Opportunities Act, 172, 174

education, 67–70, 154, 156–157; limitations for Mexican immigrant laborers, 38–39; reform, xviii, xxiiin5, 42–43. *See also* bilingual education

El Solyo Ranch, 48

emigration, Mexican, history and statistics, 50–55

Fair Employment Practices Commission (FEPC), 42

family in Mexican Southwest culture, 143–144, 165

Farm Placement Service of the California Department of Employment, 57, 188

farm workers. See *bracero* program; Mexican immigrant laborer problems; Mexican Nationals; migrant farm laborers; wetbacks

Farm Workers and Agribusiness in California (Galarza), 280–281

Federal Advisory Council on Human and Civil Rights, 44

Ford Foundation, 167, 224, 236

Friends of the Volunteers in Service to America, 65

Fund for the Republic, 203, 236

Galarza, Ernesto, *66, 73*; childhood after immigration, 15–21; childhood in rural Mexican village, 3–24, 6; early education, 16–17, 19–20; as elementary school teacher, xviii; on ethnic labels, xix; as farm laborer, 21–24, 161–162; and Ford Foundation, 167, 224, 236; and Fund for the Republic, 203, 236; higher education, xv, xxii–xxiiin1; individual limitations, 66–67; *La Raza Unida* conference and party, 77; letters, 259–276; marriage, 27, *280*; neglect, xiii–xiv; Nobel Prize for Literature nomination, xxii, 65; as nonviolent revolutionary, 279–281; Occidental College, xv, 3, 27, 177; Order of the Condor of the Andes, 236; Sacramento years, 15–24; scholarship, xv–xvi; Stanford University, xv, 27; Studio Lab, 3; union activism overview, xvi–xviii; VISTA, 65

Galarza, Mae Taylor, 27, 177, 279–281, *280*

Gallegos, Herman, 167, 224

Giannini Foundation, 190

Goldschmidt, Walter, 56–60

Gonzalez, Gilbert G., xviii

"Good Neighbor" policy, 35

Gorman, Pat, 185

Grand Central Market, 97–98

growers' associations, 57–58, 191

Hayes, Ed, 188

history, 67–70

Hoffa, Jimmy, 185–186

housing: and Di Giorgio Fruit Corporation, 199–200; housing agency control
eligibility, 43; and migrant farm laborers, 230–232; substandard, 38
human geography vs. political maps,
72–73

immigrant laborers. *See* Mexican immigrant laborer problems; Mexican
immigrant laborer solution recommendations
imperialism critique, xviii–xxi
Inter-Agency Committee on Mexican
American Affairs, xx, 77
Inter-American Association, 203
Inter-American Conference of Bogotá,
35, 35–36
Inter-American economic system, 34. See
also *bracero* program; Mexican Nationals; U.S.-Mexico international labor
agreement

Jalcocotán, Nayarit, Mexico, 3–24
John Hay Whitney Foundation research
grant (1973), 100, 101

Kern County cotton pickers' strike (1954),
169, 188
Kern County Land Company, 48
Knight, Goodwin J., 265
"knight letters," 265–266
Kodachromes in Rhyme: Poems (Galarza),
177

Labor Management Relations Act,
219–220
labor movement in Mexico, 183
labor organizing strategies, 177; *bracero*
program, 180–183; DiGiorgio Fruit
Corporation strike, 178–181; organized
labor power structure, 183–186; United
Farm Workers of America, 186–189;
U.S.-Mexican relations, 181–183;

wetbacks, 180–181. *See also specific
organizations*
labor pool, concept and practice, 56–60
labor unions. *See* unions; *specific unions*
land ownership, 48–49; failure, 147–150
La Opinion, 87
La Raza Unida, xx, 137, 152, 157–160; Unity
Conference and political party formation (1967), 76
La Voz, 87
Livingston, Jack, 271–272
locales, 54, 164, 165
Los Angeles' Grand Central Market,
97–98
Louisiana plantation workers' strikes,
203, 223; Galarza participation, 33;
growers' associations efforts to import
alien labor, 207–208; legal actions and
decisions, 219–222; multiple facilities, 210–212; planters' actions against
striking workers, 212–222; union efforts
on members' behalf, 204–208; union
research project, 212

manipulation. *See* Anglo manipulation of
Mexican-Americans
McWilliams, Carey, xiii
Meany, George, xvii, 185–186, 187, 203, 273
mechanization of agricultural equipment,
228–229
mercados (markets), 96–98, 157
Merchants of Labor (Galarza), xx
Mexicali, California, 228
Mexican American civil rights movement
overview, xxii
Mexican American Legal Defense Fund
(MALDEF), xxii, 224
Mexican-Americans, Anglo manipula-
tion of. *See* Anglo manipulation of
Mexican-Americans
Mexican Bureau of Migratory Labor Af-
fairs, 236–237, 239
Mexican Department of Health, 238

"specials," 52
Spicer, Edward H., 131, 134–135
Spiders in the House and Workers in the Field (Galarza), xiii
Stanford University, xv, 27
Strangers in Our Fields (Galarzo), xxii, 203
strategies. *See* labor organizing strategies
strikes and boycotts, 33, 77, 169, 188, 203–223. *See also* Di Giorgio Fruit Corporation strike
students, message to Chicano, 66–68
Studio Laboratory for Bilingual Education, 3, 67, 70, 100
Sugar Act, 204
sugar cane workers' strikes. *See* Louisiana plantation workers' strikes
sweetheart contracts, 185–186

Taylor, Paul, 34
Teamsters Union, 185–186
Teatro Campesino, 157
Teatro del Barrio, 157
Texas, 227–228
Tobin, Dan, 185–186

unions: AFL-CIO, xvii, 187–188, 271–274; Agricultural Workers Organizing Committee (AWOC), xvii, 203, 270; Amalgamated Meat Cutters, xvii, 270; American Federation of Labor, 202, 223; Brotherhood of Sleeping Car Porters, xvii; California American Federation of Labor, 202; California Federation of Labor, 184; National Agricultural Workers Union (NAWU), 236; National Farm Labor Union (NFLU), 192, 236; Southern Tenant Farmers Union (STFU), xvii, xxiiin3, 192, 203; United Farm Workers of

America, xviii, 186–189; United Packinghouse Workers of America, xvii
United Farm Workers of America, xviii, 186–189
United Packinghouse Workers of America, xvii
universities and Mexican-Americans, 88, 156–157
urban *mercados* (markets), 96–98, 157
urban shift, 78–79, 82–83
U.S. Department of Labor, 242
U.S.-Mexico borderlands, 50, 72–74, 228. *See also* Mexican Southwest culture
U.S.-Mexico international labor agreement, 238–248. See also *bracero* program; Mexican Nationals; U.S.-Mexico borderlands

Valley Fruit Growers Association of Fresno, 57–58
village life in rural Mexico, 3–24, 6
Volunteers in Service to America (VISTA), 65
Voz, La, 87

wages: discrimination, 34–35; minimum wage law reform, 43; of wetbacks, 237
Western Grower and Shipper, 57
Western Regional Migrant Health Conference (1967), 224–235
wetbacks: in Alviso, 102; Anglo vision, 146; *bracero* program, 180–181; civil liberties, 39; employers and contractors, 58–59; entry, 237; explained, 36–37; immigration law, 42; locations, 36, 52–53, 162, 229; numbers, 59; powerlessness, 53–54, 60; variations, 163, 253, 255; victimization, 53–54; wages, 237

ARMANDO IBARRA is an assistant professor in the School for Workers at the University of Wisconson–Extension and a faculty member in Chicano/Latino studies at the University of Wisconsin-Madison. RODOLFO D. TORRES is a professor of urban planning, political science, and Chicano/Latino studies at the University of California, Irvine. His other books include *Race Defaced: Paradigms of Pessimism, Politics of Possibility*.

THE WORKING CLASS IN AMERICAN HISTORY

*The University of Illinois Press
is a founding member of the
Association of American University Presses.*

Designed by Kelly Gray
Composed in 9.75/13.25 Minion
with Avenir and Marat display
by Jim Proefrock
at the University of Illinois Press
Manufactured by Sheridan Books, Inc.

University of Illinois Press
1325 South Oak Street
Champaign, IL 61820-6903
www.press.uillinois.edu